ISSUES
and Physical Science

SECOND EDITION

SEPUP
Issue-Oriented Science

ISSUES
and Physical Science

SECOND EDITION

THE LAWRENCE
HALL OF SCIENCE
UNIVERSITY OF CALIFORNIA, BERKELEY

LaB-aiDS®
Experiencing Science

This book is part of SEPUP's middle school science course sequence:

ISSUES AND EARTH SCIENCE, 2nd Edition

Studying Soil Scientifically
Rocks and Minerals
Erosion and Deposition
Plate Tectonics
Weather and Atmosphere
The Earth in Space
Exploring Space

ISSUES AND LIFE SCIENCE, 2nd Edition

Experimental Design: Studying People Scientifically
Body Works
Cell Biology and Disease
Genetics
Ecology
Evolution
Bioengineering

ISSUES AND PHYSICAL SCIENCE, 2nd Edition

Studying Materials Scientifically
The Chemistry of Materials
Water
Energy
Force and Motion
Waves

Additional SEPUP instructional materials include:
SEPUP Modules: Grades 7–12
Science and Sustainability: Course for Grades 9–12
Science and Global Issues: Biology: Course for High School Biology

This material is based upon work supported by the National Science Foundation under Grants No. 9252906 and No. 0099265. Any opinions, findings, and conclusions or recommendations expressed in this material are those of the authors and do not necessarily reflect the views of the National Science Foundation.

For photo and illustration credits, see pages I-17 through I-19, which constitute an extension of this copyright page.

The preferred citation format for this book is SEPUP. (2012). *Issues and Physical Science*. Lawrence Hall of Science, University of California at Berkeley. Published by Lab-Aids®, Inc., Ronkonkoma, NY

ISBN: 978-1-60301-502-8
ISBN: 1-60301-502-7

SEPUP
Lawrence Hall of Science
University of California at Berkeley
Berkeley CA 94720-5200

e-mail: sepup@berkeley.edu
Website: www.sepuplhs.org

Published by:

17 Colt Court
Ronkonkoma NY 11779
Website: www.lab-aids.com

A Letter to *Issues and Physical Science* Students

As you examine the activities in this book, you may wonder, "Why does this book look so different from other science books I've seen?" The reason is simple: it is a different kind of science program, and only some of what you will learn can be seen by leafing through this book!

Issues and Physical Science uses several kinds of activities to teach science. For example, you will observe and test the properties of elements and compounds. You will model the atoms and molecules that make up these substances. You will design and conduct investigations to explore energy transfer. You will investigate the motion of a cart on a ramp, and apply what you learn to the physics of automobile accidents and safety features. A combination of laboratories, investigations, readings, models, debates, role plays, and projects will help you uncover the nature of science and the relevance of physical science to your interests.

You will find that important scientific ideas come up again and again in different activities throughout the book. You will be expected to do more than just memorize these concepts: you will be asked to explain and apply them. In particular, you will improve your decision-making skills by using evidence to weigh outcomes and to decide what you think should be done about the scientific issues facing our society.

How do we know that this is a good way for you to learn? In general, research on science education supports it. In particular, the activities in this book were tested by hundreds of students and their teachers, and then modified on the basis of their feedback. In a sense, this entire book is the result of an investigation: we had people test our ideas, we interpreted the results, and we then revised our ideas! We believe the result will show you that learning more about science is important, enjoyable, and relevant to your life.

SEPUP Staff

ISSUES & PHYSICAL SCIENCE PROJECT

Director (2003–2012): Barbara Nagle

Director (2001–2002): Herbert D. Thier

Coordinator: Janet Bellantoni

AUTHORS

Unit A: Manisha Hariani, Sara Wilmes, Daniel Seaver

Unit B: Sara Wilmes, Barbara Nagle, Donna Markey

Unit C: Barbara Nagle, Laura Lenz, Asher Davison

Unit D: Janet Bellantoni, John Howarth, Lee Trampleasure, Donna Markey, Daniel Seaver

Unit E: Janet Bellantoni, Daniel Seaver

Unit F: Janet Bellantoni, John Howarth, Christopher Keller

OTHER CONTRIBUTORS

Kathy Burke, Kate Haber, Vana James, Mike Reeske

We would also like to thank everyone who contributed to *Issues, Evidence, and You,* especially Robert Horvat, Mark Koker, Mike Reeske, Stephen Rutherford, Herbert D. Thier, and Mark Wilson and staff from the Berkeley Evaluation and Research (BEAR) Center, Graduate School of Education, University of California at Berkeley.

CONTENT AND SCIENTIFIC REVIEW

Dr. Stephanie Chasteen, University of Colorado, Boulder, (*Energy* and *Waves*)

Dr. Tim Erickson, Epistemological Engineering, Oakland California (*Force and Motion*)

Dr. Tanya Faltens, Lawrence Hall of Science, University of California, Berkeley (*Studying Materials Scientifically* and *The Chemistry of Materials*)

Dr. Betsy Kean, Professor Emerita, Department of Teacher Education, California State University, Sacramento (*Studying Materials Scientifically, The Chemistry of Materials,* and *Water*)

Dr. Chinh Nguyen, Lick-Wilmerding High School, San Francisco (*Energy*)

Dr. Marion O'Leary, Dean Emeritus, College of Natural Sciences and Mathematics, California State University, Sacramento (*Studying Materials Scientifically, The Chemistry of Materials,* and *Water*)

Dr. Scott Randol, Lawrence Hall of Science, University of California, Berkeley (*Force and Motion*)

PRODUCTION

Coordination, Design, Photo Research, Composition: Seventeenth Street Studios

Editing: Trish Beall

Administrative Assistance: Roberta Smith

FIELD TEST CENTERS

Issues and Physical Science is a revision of *Issues, Evidence, and You* (IEY). We are extremely grateful to the center directors and teachers who taught the original and revised program. These teachers and their students contributed significantly to improving the course. Since then, *Issues and Physical Science* has been used in many classrooms across the United States. This second edition is based on what we have learned from teachers and students in those classrooms. It also includes new data and information, so the issues included in the course remain fresh and up-to-date.

IEY CENTERS

Alaska: Donna York (Director), Kim Bunselmeyer, Linda Churchill, James Cunningham, Patty Dietderich, Lori Gilliam, Gina Ireland-Kelly, Mary Klopfer, Jim Petrash, Amy Spargo

California-San Bernardino County: Dr. Herbert Brunkhorst (Director), William Cross, Alan Jolliff, Kimberly Michael, Chuck Schindler

California-San Diego County: Mike Reeske and Marilyn Stevens (Co-Directors), Pete Brehm, Donna Markey, Susan Mills, Barney Preston, Samantha Swann

California-San Francisco Area: Stephen Rutherford (Director), Michael Delnista, Cindy Donley, Judith Donovan, Roger Hansen, Judi Hazen, Catherine Heck, Mary Beth Hodge, Mary Hoglund, Mary Pat Horn, Paul Hynds, Margaret Kennedy, Carol Mortensen, Bob Rosenfeld, Jan Vespi

Colorado: John E. Sepich (Director), Mary Ann Hart, Lisa Joss, Geree Pepping-Dremel, Tracy Schuster, Dan Stebbins, Terry Strahm

Connecticut: Dave Lopath (Director), Harald Bender, Laura Boehm, Antonella Bona-Gallo, Joseph Bosco, Timothy Dillon, Victoria Duers, Valerie Hoye, Bob Segal, Stephen Weinberg

Kentucky-Lexington Area: Dr. Stephen Henderson and Susie Nally (Co-Directors), Stephen Dilly, Ralph McKee II, Barry Welty, Laura Wright

Kentucky-Louisville Area: Ken Rosenbaum (Director), Ella Barrickman, Pamela T. Boykin, Bernis Crawford, Cynthia Detwiler, Denise Finley, Ellen Skomsky

Louisiana: Dr. Shiela Pirkle (Director), Kathy McWaters, Lori Ann Otts, Robert Pfrimmer, Eileen Shieber, Mary Ann Smith, Allen (Bob) Toups, Dorothy Trusclair

Michigan: Phillip Larsen, Dawn Pickard and Peter Vunovich (Co-Directors), Ann Aho, Carolyn Delia, Connie Duncan, Kathy Grosso, Stanley Guzy, Kevin Kruger, Tommy Ragonese

New York City: Arthur Camins (Director), Eddie Bennett, Steve Chambers, Sheila Cooper, Sally Dyson

North Carolina: Dr. Stan Hill and Dick Shaw (Co-Directors), Kevin Barnard, Ellen Dorsett, Cameron Holbrook, Anne M. Little

Oklahoma: Shelley Fisher (Director), Jill Anderson, Nancy Bauman, Larry Joe Bradford, Mike Bynum, James Granger, Brian Lomenick, Belva Nichols, Linda Sherrill, Keith Symcox, David Watson

Pennsylvania: Dr. John Agar (Director), Charles Brendley, Gregory France, John Frederick, Alana Gazetski, Gill Godwin

Washington, D.C.: Frances Brock and Alma Miller (Co-Directors), Vasanti Alsi, Yvonne Brannum, Walter Bryant, Shirley DeLaney, Sandra Jenkins, Joe Price, John Spearman

Western New York: Dr. Robert Horvat and Dr. Joyce Swartney (Co-Directors), Rich Bleyle, Kathaleen Burke, Al Crato, Richard Duquin, Lillian Gondree, Ray Greene, Richard Leggio, David McClatchey, James Morgan, Susan Wade

Contents

UNIT B The Chemistry of Materials

UNIT C Water

UNIT D Energy

UNIT E Force and Motion

UNIT F Waves

Studying Materials
Scientifically

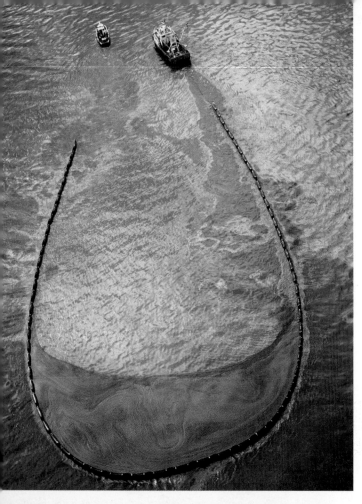

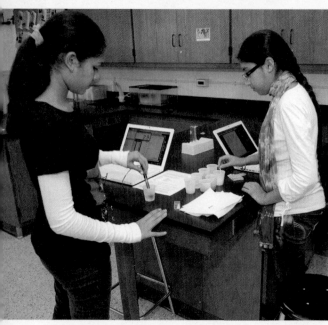

Studying Materials Scientifically

Kai, did you hear about those barrels they found by the baseball field yesterday?"

"No, what happened?" Kai stopped. She had been hurrying to get ready for the baseball game.

"They found barrels full of chemicals near the field, so they cancelled the game," Gabriela grumbled.

"What? I gave up going to the movies so I could play today."

"The town started digging into that empty lot next to the baseball field to build the new playground. When they cleared out the brush and garbage, they found at least ten old corroded barrels full of stuff."

"Do they know what is in them?" asked Kai.

"Nope, so they have to call in a hazardous materials team to open the barrels. I heard my uncle talking about it last night with my dad. My uncle works for the company that will come in and do the testing," Gabriela continued. "The testing will be done today and thus, the game is cancelled."

"Really, well that's kind of scary," Kai responded. "We have been playing there since we were little. What if the stuff in the barrels is hazardous? How are they going to figure out what it is?"

"I think they'll take samples, and do some tests," said Gabriela.

• • •

Our world is filled with substances. The liquids we drink, air we breathe, and the roads we walk on are all made from different combinations of substances. The substances people use to make products are called materials. Each material has unique properties. For example, we can identify gold by its shiny characteristic metallic color. But how can these properties help to identify unknown samples? In this unit you will look at how substances can be identified based on their chemical and physical properties. You will learn how to handle potentially hazardous substances with care as you study materials scientifically.

You are cleaning out a cabinet at home and you find an old jar filled with what appears to be a mixture of rusty pieces of metal and a thick oily liquid. What should you do? Is it safe to dump it out? How could you figure out what to do with it if you're not sure what it is?

In this unit you will work with an unlabeled jar filled with a mixture of substances. When you don't know the contents of a container, it is best to assume they are hazardous. **Hazardous materials** (HAZ-ur-dus ma-TEER-ee-uls) are substances that pose a danger to the health and safety of living organisms. They can cause injury or even death. People who are trained to clean up or dispose of hazardous materials are often members of a hazardous materials, or "hazmat," team. Before working with potentially hazardous chemicals in this unit, you will learn how to handle and identify them.

CHALLENGE

How should unidentified materials be handled?

PROCEDURE

1. Watch a segment about hazardous materials on the SEPUP DVD, "Hazardous Materials."

2. In your science notebook, make a list titled "Handling an Unknown Substance." As you watch the DVD, list the steps the hazmat team takes when approaching and handling the unidentified barrel.

3. Watch the DVD again. Record any additional precautions the hazmat team took that you did not list in your notebook in Step 2.

4. Compare your list with the lists of the other members of your group. As you do this:

   • Listen to and consider the precautions listed by others.

   • If you disagree about a precaution, explain to the rest of the group why you disagree.

5. Add to the list in your notebook any new ideas that your group members proposed.

ANALYSIS

 1. Based on what you observed on the DVD, make a list of safety precautions you would take if you found a jar of unidentified substances at home.

2. If you found a jar filled with unidentified substances at school, would you handle it differently than you would at home? Add to your list from Question 1 any additional safety precautions you would take.

 3. How could you identify the contents of an unlabeled jar? Explain ways to identify the jar's contents.

4. Could you determine the contents of the unlabeled jar through observation alone? Explain.

Key to Analysis Icons

= Answer the question by yourself.

= Discuss with your partner.

= Discuss with your group.

= Discuss the question in class.

If you found an unlabeled container in your home, how would you know whether its contents were hazardous? A hazmat team assumes the contents are hazardous until it identifies the properties of each substance, and you should do the same. Since substances can be hazardous in many different ways, it is important to be prepared for the dangers they pose.

Hazardous materials, like those in the barrel in the last activity, are transported daily throughout the United States. Whenever they are shipped in large volumes, they must be labeled according to their class of hazard, as the U.S. Department of Transportation (D.O.T.) requires.

In science classes you will encounter a variety of potentially hazardous substances. Some are more hazardous than others. To prepare to work with them, you will learn how to choose and use safe methods.

CHALLENGE → **What types of hazards do certain substances pose?**

DOT labels posted on vehicles and containers alert people to the dangers of the substances inside.

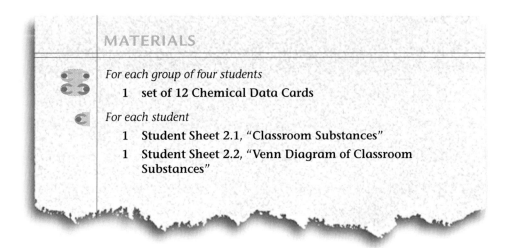

MATERIALS

For each group of four students
1   set of 12 Chemical Data Cards

For each student
1   Student Sheet 2.1, "Classroom Substances"
1   Student Sheet 2.2, "Venn Diagram of Classroom Substances"

PROCEDURE

1. Look at the table on the next page that shows the labels that the D.O.T. requires on hazardous materials. You may have seen some of these labels on large trucks or on storage containers. Discuss what each label reveals about the material.

2. Divide the set of Chemical Data Cards in half. You and your partner will work with six of the cards.

3. With your partner, read the six cards. Consider places where you might have encountered the substances on each card.

4. Familiarize yourself with each of the substances the cards describe as you fill out Student Sheet 2.1, "Classroom Substances." For each substance, list:

   • The hazard class(es) it belongs to.

   • The safety precautions people should take when using this substance.

5. When you have finished the six cards, switch sets with the other pair in your group and repeat Steps 3 and 4.

6. Work with your group to sort all 12 substances according to the hazard class(es) you assigned to each in Step 4.

7. Record the results of your sorting on Student Sheet 2.2, "Venn Diagram of Classroom Substances."

Labeling Hazardous Materials

Class	Label	Description of Class	Examples
Biohazard		Can cause infection or disease in living organisms.	Tools used for medical treatment and procedures, disease-causing microorganisms and viruses
Corrosive		Liquids that chemically wear away at solid materials.	Sulfuric acid, bleach, oven cleaners
Explosive		Materials that cause sudden release of pressure, gas, or heat when exposed to a change in pressure or temperature.	Nitroglycerin, TNT, gases stored under pressure
Flammable		Liquids that catch on fire when exposed to a spark, flame, or heat source.	Gasoline, paint thinner, paints, acetone, ethanol, kerosene
Flammable Solid		Materials that ignite in the presence of oxygen or when exposed to water or humidity.	Magnesium metal, sulfur, naphthalene (ingredient in moth balls)
Gas		Gases stored under pressure that are flammable, toxic, or explosive.	Propane, butane
Oxidizer (reactive)		Materials that react chemically to cause other materials to burn.	Hair bleach and laundry bleach products, certain pool chemicals
Radioactive		Materials that release nuclear energy that causes damage to living organisms.	Used or unused nuclear fuel, uranium ore, radon
Toxic		Materials that are poisonous if inhaled, ingested, or absorbed through skin.	Insecticides, brake and transmission fluids, household cleaners

ANALYSIS

1. Which substances from Student Sheet 2.1, "Classroom Substances," fall into more than one hazard class?

2. Explain in detail the safety guidelines you would follow when working with potassium hydroxide.

3. Of the substances listed on Student Sheet 2.1, which do you think poses the greatest hazard to the health of humans and animals? Explain.

4. If a shipment of sodium borate were sent to your classroom, which hazard label(s) do you think would be on the box?

PROBLEM SOLVING

When a hazmat team works with an unknown substance, the team first tries to identify it, after taking care of any immediate hazards. The substance could be a **mixture**—a combination of two or more pure substances that can be physically separated. It is essential for the team to know what is in the mixture so that they can determine how to store and dispose of its different substances.

The first step in identifying an unknown substance is to take a sample of each part of the mixture. In this activity, you will design a three-part plan to:

- separate the liquid and solid substances.
- separate the different liquids.
- separate and clean the different solids.

CHALLENGE   **How can you separate the substances in a mixture?**

MATERIALS

For each group of four students

1   plastic cup with lid, containing unidentified mixture
2   pairs of plastic forceps
2   droppers
1   funnel
2   pieces of filter paper
1   metal screen
1   piece of steel wool
1   SEPUP tray
3   small plastic cups with lids
1   cup of water
    paper towels

For each student

1   pair of safety goggles

⚠ SAFETY

Wear safety goggles while working with chemicals. Do not touch the mixture or bring it into contact with your eyes or mouth. Keep the lid on the cup. Wash your hands after completing the activity.

PROCEDURE

1. Your teacher will provide you with a sealed sample of an unidentified mixture. With your group, carefully examine the sample.

2. Record in your science notebook your observations about the mixture and each substance it contains. Be as descriptive as possible.

3. With your group, discuss ways to separate the different substances and the safety precautions you will need to take. Be sure to consider the tools available to you in the materials list.

4. Work with your group to create a procedure for safely separating the substances. In your plan, be sure to:

   • List materials or tools you will use.

   • Explain each step in detail.

   • Describe safety precautions you will take.

5. Record the procedure in your science notebook.

6. Because the solids and liquids were mixed together, the solids may still have some liquid on them. Discuss with your group how you can remove the liquid.

7. Record these additional steps in your science notebook.

8. Obtain your teacher's approval of your plan.

ANALYSIS

1. Based on your observations, how many substances do you think there are in the unidentified mixture? Explain.

2. Compare your plan with the plans of others in your class. What ideas do they have for separating the substances that you did not think to include in your plan?

3. What safety precautions will you take when separating the mixture?

4. What is the purpose of separating the different substances in the mixture?

5. You are walking down the sidewalk and see a puddle of green, oily liquid on the ground. Could you identify the contents of the puddle through observation alone?

ROLE PLAY

One way to reduce the risk of household hazardous chemicals is to dispose of them when they are no longer needed. But how can you handle and get rid of them without harming yourself, others, or the environment? In this activity you will read about Hassan, who must decide how to dispose of the contents of an unlabeled jar he found when cleaning at home.

CHALLENGE

How should unwanted household hazardous materials be handled?

MATERIALS

For each student
1   **Student Sheet 4.1, "Intra-act Discussion: Household Hazardous Materials"**

PROCEDURE

1. Assign one of the following roles to each person in your group. Note that there are two roles that change from Act 1 to Act 2. Two people should be ready to change to new roles for Act 2.

   Act 1
   - *Hassan, a middle school student*
   - *Mother, head of purchasing for Community Hospital*
   - *Maya, his 12-year-old sister*
   - *Grandfather*

   Act 2
   - *Hassan*
   - *Mother*
   - *Mark Chu, Director of Waste Collection Center*
   - *Karen Greenbach, Environmental Engineer*

2. In your group, read the role-play aloud. As you read, think about what each character is saying.

3. With your group, discuss the types of products you might find at home that could pose a hazard.

4. Mark whether you agree or disagree with the statements on Student Sheet 4.1, "Intra-act Discussion: Household Hazardous Materials." Then predict what you think other members of your group will say.

5. Discuss the statements with your group. Have each person share and explain his or her opinion about each statement.

HAZARDOUS MATERIALS AT HOME

Act 1: At Hassan's Home

Mother: Hassan, did you finish cleaning out the cabinet? I want to put the new cleaning supplies there when you're done.

Hassan: Almost. I found this jar filled with oily stuff. I have no idea what it is.

Grandfather: The people who lived here before sure left a lot behind. You'd think they were running a chemical factory. What is it?

Hassan: I really can't tell. Most of the jars don't have labels, or the labels are so faded I can't read them. This jar is filled with an oily mess with pieces of metal and something else in it.

Maya: Can I see?

Hassan: Be careful! It might be dangerous. How do you think I should get rid of it?

Grandfather: Why don't you just dump it down the drain?

Maya: But what if it's hazardous? We learned at school that a lot of the things we buy to clean our homes and take care of our gardens contain chemicals that are bad for us and the environment.

Mother: Some household products can be very reactive, toxic, or flammable. At the hospital, I work with other department heads to be sure we make good decisions about the hazardous products we use.

Hassan: Why would a store sell cleaning products if they're harmful? They're being diluted with water when you put them down the drain. Doesn't that take away any hazard?

Grandfather: That's what I think. I always wash everything down the sink, or throw it in the garbage. They treat wastewater don't they? And the garbage is taken to a dump, so what's the harm in that?

Mother: All those chemicals dumped down the drain build up. Imagine all the homes around the world over 20 years—that's a lot of cleaning supplies in the water systems. These chemicals can do long-term harm to animals, organisms, and habitats.

Grandfather: I've been dumping cleaners down the drain for years.

Mother: But now we are more aware of how chemicals can affect us and other organisms. I read an article in last week's newspaper that said it is no longer legal to throw out batteries in the garbage. Batteries have to be recycled by dropping them off at a recycling center.

Grandfather: But batteries are made to be disposable. I don't see why they need to be recycled.

It is estimated that in most homes in the United States there are 10 to 40 liters (3 to 10 gallons) of hazardous materials in household products.

Maya: We learned about recycling batteries at school. They contain heavy metals that can leak into the ground if they sit in landfills.

Mother: *(looking at Grandfather)* That reminds me. Remember how Mama used to take our temperature with a mercury thermometer? It was filled with silvery metal. Once, when the thermometer broke, we played with the little metal beads of mercury liquid. Now liquid mercury is known to be hazardous and is not used in thermometers.

Grandfather: Who would have thought that it was harmful? Mercury was used in so many different products like batteries, light switches, and thermometers.

Mother: Not anymore. Research has shown that it is toxic. If you're exposed to it for long periods of time, it can affect your nervous system.

Hassan: But what should I do with the jar?

Mother: We need to figure out what it is. A postcard came in the mail last week announcing a "Household Hazardous Waste Drop-off Day" at the Waste Collection Center. Let's take it there and see if they can help us. We'll drive over after we drop your sister off at soccer practice.

Act 2: At the Waste Collection Center

Director Chu: How can I help you?

Hassan: We'd like to know if we can dump this down the drain to get rid of it.

Director Chu: Do you know what it is?

Hassan: No, it wasn't labeled.

Mother: Hassan found it while he was cleaning out one of our cupboards at home. It l ooks like it has been there for a long time.

Director Chu: It will take some testing, but we will identify what is in it. Then we will know how to dispose of it. This is Karen Greenbach, our environmental engineer, who is an expert on testing methods. *(Turning to Karen)* Karen, we have an unlabeled jar here. Can you help these people?

In 2005, regulations in more than 30 states prohibited throwing batteries in the trash. They can leak toxic chemicals that can harm organisms.

Household hazardous waste collection days are a way to safely dispose of latex paint, batteries, and other hazardous substances.

Karen Greenbach:	I'd be happy to. We will send it to a lab where it will be separated. Then they will run tests to identify each of the parts.
Hassan:	If it was bought in a store, wouldn't it be safe to just throw it out?
Director Chu:	Sometimes the chemicals that are toxic, flammable, or corrosive are what make a product work. There aren't strict regulations about what is put in household products, so it is important to consider what hazards they pose when you are buying, using, and throwing them out.
Mother:	When people buy products for their homes they usually choose what is most affordable and the best at doing the job. They don't often take into account the health or environmental hazards they might cause.
Director Chu:	There have been many cases of people mixing and storing products incorrectly and getting hurt. It's important to know what you're working with and to consider their hazards.
Karen:	The next step with your jar will be for us to send it to a lab to determine what is in it. It looks like a mixture of several liquids and some solids.
Hassan:	Then what will you do with it once the parts have been identified?
Karen:	If it is not hazardous, we will dilute it and pour it down the drain. But if it is hazardous, we will package it and put it in a special hazardous waste landfill. These sites are made so that hazardous material contained in them will not leak into the ground and groundwater.
Mother:	Thank you for helping us.
Hassan:	We have to tell Grandpa: No more dumping everything down the drain!

ANALYSIS

 1. In what ways can household products be harmful?

2. Give an example of a product that can no longer be discarded in the garbage. Explain why this is no longer allowed.

3. Where in people's homes do you think they are likely to have the greatest number of potentially hazardous products?

4. **Reflection:** Why do you think there are now more regulations about the use and disposal of hazardous substances than there were 20 to 40 years ago?

EXTENSION

When is your community holding a hazardous waste drop-off day? See if you can locate information in your area about when and where to take potentially hazardous materials.

5 Separating the Mixture

LABORATORY

To properly dispose of the unidentified mixture found in the jar, you need to identify the substances it contains. In this activity, you will follow the separation procedure that you developed in Activity 3, "Developing a Separation Plan." Once the substances are separated, you will be able to perform tests to determine the identity of the liquids. Since you do not yet know what the substances are, treat them as if they are hazardous.

CHALLENGE ⟹ **How can the substances in the mixture be separated?**

MATERIALS

For each group of four students

1 **plastic cup with lid, containing unidentified mixture**
2 **pairs of plastic forceps**
2 **droppers**
1 **funnel**
2 **pieces of filter paper**
1 **metal screen**
1 **piece of steel wool**
1 **SEPUP tray**
3 **small plastic cups with lids**
1 **cup of water**
  paper towels
  access to hot soapy water

For each student

1 **pair of safety goggles**
1 **copy of separation plan from Activity 3**
  Student Sheet 5.1, "Chemical Safety Data Sheet"

Identifying an unknown substance in the field often takes several steps to first isolate a sample and identify its contents.

A-19

SAFETY

Wear safety goggles while working with chemicals. Clean up any spills immediately. Do not touch the mixture or bring it into contact with your eyes or mouth. Wash your hands after completing the activity.

PROCEDURE

1. Your teacher will return to you the cup that contains a sample of the unidentified mixture.

2. Review with your group your written procedure for safely separating the parts of the mixture. Be sure you have included all essential safety procedures.

3. Work with your group to follow your procedure to separate the solids from the liquids, and then clean the solids. If you need to change any steps as you work, be sure to record the new steps in your procedure.

4. Place the cleaned, separated solids in a small plastic cup with a lid. You will test them in Activity 7, "Identifying Solids."

5. Separate the liquids, placing them into two separate small plastic cups. You will perform tests in Activity 6, "Identifying Liquids," to find out what the liquids are.

6. For each substance you isolated from the mixture, start an entry on Student Sheet 5.1, "Chemical Safety Data Sheet." You will fill in more information about each substance in future activities.

ANALYSIS

1. What changes did you have to make to your separation procedure while you were performing the procedure? Why?

2. What safety precautions did you take while working with the unidentified mixture?

3. How would you separate:

   a. oil and vinegar?

   b. salt and iron shavings?

   c. salt and sand?

LABORATORY

Now you will investigate the liquids' physical and chemical properties. **Physical properties** are characteristics that can be observed or measured about a substance without changing it into something else in the process. Color, texture, and appearance are some of the physical properties you will determine in this activity. **Chemical properties** are traits of a substance that you find by seeing if it reacts in certain ways with other chemicals. You will do tests for the chemical properties of corrosiveness and toxicity. Assume the liquids are hazardous until you identify them.

CHALLENGE

What are the liquids in the mixture?

After an oil tanker accident, the crude oil floats on top of seawater because it is less dense. An inflatable barrier can then be used to separate the oil, which has different properties than the seawater.

MATERIALS

For each group of four students
1   small cup of Liquid A
1   small cup of Liquid B
1   dropper bottle of ethanol
1   dropper bottle of potassium thiocyanate
2   plastic vials with lids
1   pH color scale

For each pair of students
1   pair of plastic forceps
1   dropper
1   SEPUP tray
2   cobalt chloride paper strips
2   pieces of pH paper
    paper towels
    access to hot soapy water

For each student
1   pair of safety goggles
    Student Sheet 5.1, "Chemical Safety Data Sheet"

SAFETY

Wear safety goggles while working with chemicals. Clean up any spills immediately. Do not touch the mixture or any part of it, and do not bring it into contact with your eyes or mouth. Wash your hands after completing the activity.

PROCEDURE

1. Review the information contained in Table 1, "Tests to Identify Liquids" on the next page. It lists the tests that you will use to gather evidence about the liquids you separated from the mixture. Listen carefully as your teacher demonstrates the procedure for each test.

Table 1: Tests to Identify Liquids		
Test	**Procedure**	**Interpreting Test Results**
Appearance	Examine the liquid. Observe its color, transparency, and thickness.	Describe your observations in detail.
Miscible in water	1. Add 50 drops of water to a vial. 2. Add 10 drops of the liquid being tested. 3. Secure the top on the vial. 4. Observe.	If the liquid beads up or forms a separate layer on the top or bottom of the water, it is NOT MISCIBLE in water. If the liquid mixes, it is MISCIBLE in water.
Miscible in ethanol	1. Add 50 drops of ethanol to a vial. 2. Add 10 drops of the liquid being tested. 3. Secure the top on the vial. 4. Observe.	If the liquid beads up or forms a separate layer on the top or bottom of the water, it is NOT MISCIBLE in water. If the liquid mixes, it is MISCIBLE in water.
Contains water	1. Place a dropperful of the liquid to be tested in a clean cup in the SEPUP tray. 2. Dip a piece of cobalt chloride paper into the liquid. 3. Remove it, and place it on a paper towel. 4. Observe.	If the paper remains blue, water is NOT PRESENT in the liquid. If the paper turns pink, water is PRESENT in the liquid.
Corrosive	1. Place a dropperful of the liquid to be tested in a clean cup in the SEPUP tray. 2. Dip a strip of pH paper into the liquid. 3. Remove and place it on a paper towel. 4. Match the color of the moistened strip to the pH color scale.	If the pH is 3–11, the solution is NOT CORROSIVE. If the pH is less than 3 or greater than 11, the solution is CORROSIVE.
Toxic	1. Place a dropperful of the liquid to be tested in a clean cup in the SEPUP tray. 2. Dip 1 drop of potassium thiocyanate solution. 3. Observe.	If the solution does not turn red, the liquid is NOT TOXIC. If the solution turns red, the liquid is TOXIC.

2. In your notebook, create a table similar to the one shown below, "Properties of Separated Liquids," to record the results of your work.

Properties of Separated Liquids

Test	Liquid A	Liquid B
Appearance		
Miscible in water		
Miscible in ethanol		
Contains water		
Corrosive		
Toxic		

3. Work with your partner to test the liquids. Record the results of each test in your table.

4. Follow your teacher's directions for cleanup.

ANALYSIS

1. Look at Table 2, "Information on Selected Liquids," on the next page.

   a. Compare the information from this activity with the information in the table. Look for similarities.

   b. Based on their properties, what are the identities of Liquid A and Liquid B?

   c. Support your answers with at least three pieces of evidence for each liquid.

2. Based on the information in Table 2, would you label Liquid A or Liquid B from the mixture as hazardous?

3. Using evidence from this activity, add the following to Student Sheet 5.1 for Liquid A and Liquid B:

   a. The name of the liquid you identified.

   b. Under "Hazards," write yes or no for those categories that apply.

Table 2: Information on Selected Liquids

Type of Liquid	Appearance	Miscible in Water	Miscible in Ethanol	Contains Water	Corrosive	Flammable	Toxic
Iodine solution (used in disinfectants)	Transparent, yellow to brown liquid	Yes	Yes	Yes	Not corrosive	Not flammable	Toxic
Iron nitrate solution (used in garden fertilizers, vitamins)	Transparent, orange liquid	Yes	Yes	Yes	Corrosive	Not flammable	Toxic
Isooctane (used in fuels)	Transparent, colorless liquid	No	No	No	Not corrosive	Flammable	Toxic
Lauric acid solution (used in soaps and shampoo)	Transparent, colorless liquid	No	Yes	No	Not corrosive	Flammable	Slightly toxic
Mineral oil (used in furniture oils, baby oils, cleaning products)	Transparent, colorless to pale yellow liquid	No	No	No	Not corrosive	Flammable	Not toxic
Citric acid solution (used in foods, household cleaners)	Transparent, colorless or pale yellow liquid	Yes	Yes	Yes	Slightly corrosive at very high concentrations	Not flammable	Not toxic

LABORATORY

N ow you will test and identify the solid substances. The solids appear to be metal and plastic, but you need more information to determine what they are made of. The tests that you used for identifying the liquids do not help to identify solids. So in this activity, you will perform a set of different tests to determine the physical and chemical properties of the solids. This information will help you identify the solids. Assume the solids are hazardous until you identify them.

CHALLENGE ⟹ **What are the solids in the mixture?**

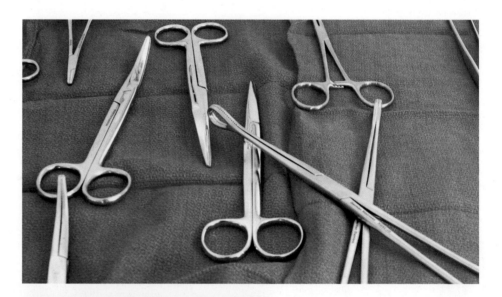

Easy-to-rip candy wrappers and durable surgical scissors are both made of silver-colored metal. However, the unique physical properties of the metals are quite different and, as a result, the scissors are much stronger than the wrapper.

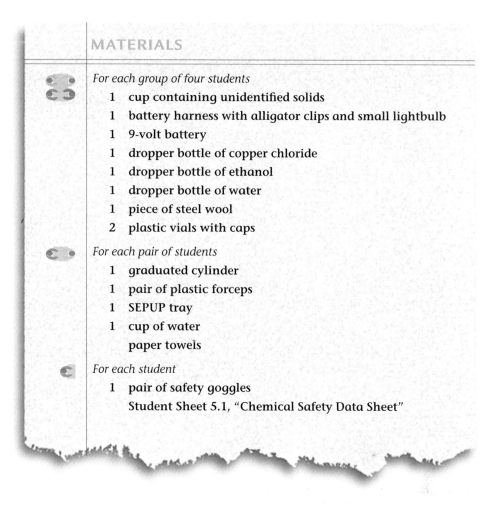

MATERIALS

For each group of four students

1   cup containing unidentified solids
1   battery harness with alligator clips and small lightbulb
1   9-volt battery
1   dropper bottle of copper chloride
1   dropper bottle of ethanol
1   dropper bottle of water
1   piece of steel wool
2   plastic vials with caps

For each pair of students

1   graduated cylinder
1   pair of plastic forceps
1   SEPUP tray
1   cup of water
    paper towels

For each student

1   pair of safety goggles
    Student Sheet 5.1, "Chemical Safety Data Sheet"

Scientists can identify types of rock from the moon, based on their chemical and physical properties.

SAFETY

Wear safety goggles while working with chemicals. Clean up any spills immediately. Do not touch the mixture or any parts of the mixture, and do not bring them into contact with your eyes or mouth. Wash your hands after completing the activity.

PROCEDURE

1. Review the information contained in Table 1, "Tests to Identify Solids." It describes tests that you will use to gather evidence about the solids you separated from the mixture. Listen carefully as your teacher demonstrates the procedure for each test.

2. In your notebook, create a table similar to "Properties of Separated Solids," shown below. Decide with your class what you will call each type of solid. Record these names in the top row of your table.

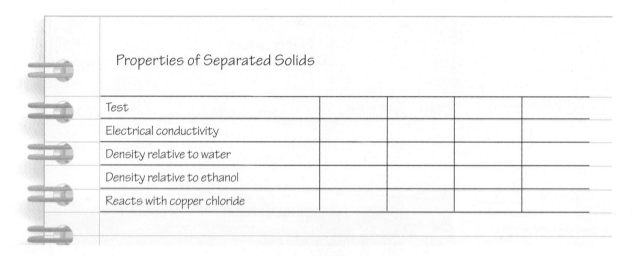

Properties of Separated Solids

Test				
Electrical conductivity				
Density relative to water				
Density relative to ethanol				
Reacts with copper chloride				

3. Be sure each solid is prepared for testing. If a solid has a coating, gently clean the surface with steel wool, rinse it, and dry it well.

4. Work with your partner to test one of the solids. Record the results of each test in your table.

5. Rinse and dry each solid, and place it back in its container.

6. Work with your partner to repeat Steps 4 and 5 for each type of solid from the mixture.

7. Follow your teacher's directions for cleanup.

Table 1: Tests to Identify Solids

Test	Procedure	Interpreting Test Results
Electrical conductivity	1. Snap the battery into the battery harness with lightbulb. 2. Attach the clips on opposite ends of the solid being tested. 3. Observe the bulb.	If the bulb does not light, the material does NOT CONDUCT electricity. If the bulb lights, the material CONDUCTS electricity.
Density relative to water	1. Put 5 mL of water into a vial. 2. Gently place the solid being tested in the vial. 3. Secure the cap on the vial and gently shake. 4. Observe.	If the solid floats, it is LESS DENSE than water. If the solid sinks, it is MORE DENSE than water.
Density relative to ethanol	1. Put 5 mL of ethanol into a vial. 2. Gently place the solid being tested in the vial. 3. Secure the cap on the vial and gently shake. 4. Observe.	If the solid floats, it is LESS DENSE than ethanol. If the solid sinks, it is MORE DENSE than ethanol.
Reacts with copper chloride	1. Place the solid being tested in a cup of the SEPUP tray. 2. Place 5 drops of copper chloride on the solid. 3. Observe for signs of chemical reaction. Signs of a reaction may include a color change, bubbling, temperature change, or precipitate forming. Note: If a reaction does occur, use the forceps to dip the solid in water to stop the reaction.	If no signs of a reaction are visible, the solid does NOT REACT with copper chloride. If one or more signs of a reaction are visible, the solid REACTS with copper chloride.

ANALYSIS

1. Look at Table 2, "Information on Selected Solids," on the next page.

    a. Compare your data with the information in the table. Look for similarities.

    b. Based on their properties, what are the solids?

    c. Support your answer with at least three pieces of evidence for each solid.

2. Were you able to identify what material each solid was made of? Explain.

3. In this activity you performed four tests on each solid. List which test(s) identified:

    a. physical properties of the solids?

    b. chemical properties of the solids?

4. Using evidence from this activity, add the following to Student Sheet 5.1 for each type of solid:

    a. The name of the solid material you identified.

    b. Under "Hazards," write yes or no for those categories that apply.

5. You have been asked to submit a report to your state's Hazmat Training Center explaining the safety procedures you followed while identifying the solids. Write a letter to the hazmat director that explains:

    a. all safety steps taken during this activity.

    b. why each was necessary.

This equipment, including a meter, is being used to test the conductivity of a sample. Which materials from Table 2 would you predict conduct electricity?

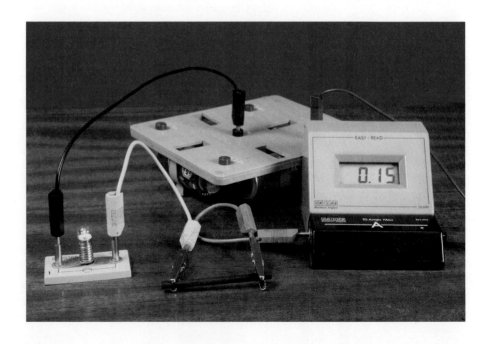

Table 2: Information on Selected Solids

Type of Solid	Physical Description	Conducts Electricity	Density Relative to Water	Density Relative to Ethanol	Reacts with Copper Chloride	Hazards
Plastics						
High-density polyethylene (HDPE)	Plastic, produced in different colors, shapes, and sizes	No	Floats	Sinks	No	None
Polystyrene (PS)	Plastic, produced in different colors, shapes, and sizes	No	Sinks	Sinks	No	None
Polyvinyl chloride (PVC)	Plastic, produced in different colors, shapes, and sizes	No	Sinks	Sinks	No	None
Metals						
Aluminum	Silver gray metal	Yes	Sinks	Sinks	Yes	None
Beryllium	Silver gray metal	Yes	Sinks	Sinks	Yes	Toxic
Iron	Silver gray metal	Yes	Sinks	Sinks	Yes	None
Magnesium	Silver gray metal	Yes	Sinks	Sinks	Yes	Flammable
Zinc	Silver gray metal	Yes	Sinks	Sinks	Yes	Flammable, toxic

LABORATORY

In the last activity, you compared the density of several solids to water. In the next three activities, you will learn how to determine density and use it to identify a substance. You will begin by learning how to measure the volume of an object. **Volume** is the amount of space a material takes up. The material can be a solid, liquid, or a gas. You use volume measurements in your daily life to describe amounts of things such as one gallon of gas, two liters of soda, or one quart of milk. The metric system units scientists use to measure volume are the liter (L) and the cubic meter (m³). Smaller volumes are often measured in milliliters (mL) or cubic centimeters (cm³). The table on the next page shows metric units used to measure mass, length, and volume that you will use in this unit along with the English units commonly used in the United States.

In this activity, you will focus on measuring the volume of solid objects using two different methods—measurement and calculation and water displacement. This will prepare you to determine the volume of the metallic solids from the mixture.

CHALLENGE ⟹ **How do you measure the volume of a solid object?**

What volume of liquid is currently in the measuring cup? This glass measuring cup, commonly found in home kitchens, measures volume in both English and metric units.

Units of Measurement		
	Common Metric Units	**Common English Units**
Length	Centimeter (cm) Meter (m) Kilometer (km)	Inch (in) Foot (ft) Yard (yd) Mile (Mi)
Mass	Gram (g) Kilogram (kg)	Ounce (oz) Pound (lb)
Volume	Milliliter (ml) Liter (l) Cubic centimeter (cm³) Cubic meter (m³)	Cup (c) Quart (qt) Gallon (g)

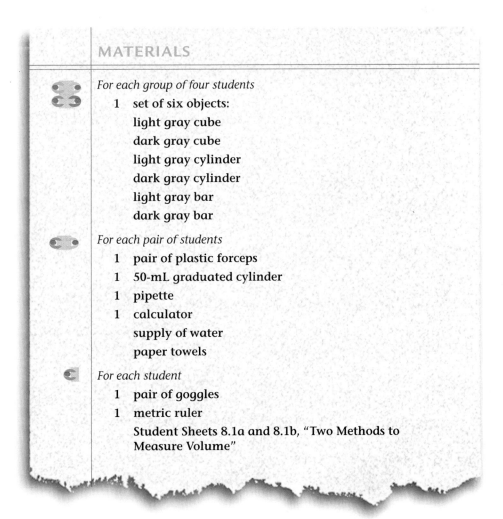

MATERIALS

For each group of four students

1 set of six objects:
light gray cube
dark gray cube
light gray cylinder
dark gray cylinder
light gray bar
dark gray bar

For each pair of students

1 pair of plastic forceps
1 50-mL graduated cylinder
1 pipette
1 calculator
supply of water
paper towels

For each student

1 pair of goggles
1 metric ruler
Student Sheets 8.1a and 8.1b, "Two Methods to Measure Volume"

SAFETY

Review the procedure and decide on appropriate safety measures for working with the unknown solids. If you do not know what material an object is made from, assume it is hazardous until you prove otherwise.

PROCEDURE

1. Record on Student Sheet 8.1a, "Two Methods to Measure Volume," the letter on your group's cup of objects.

2. Remove the six objects from the cup so that you can observe each one.

3. Predict the order of the six objects from least to greatest volume. Record your predicted order in your notebook.

4. Watch your teacher demonstrate how to measure the volume of an object using two methods:
   - measurement and calculation
   - water displacement

5. Divide the six objects into two sets so that each pair in your group gets either the light gray set or the dark gray set. Each pair will begin by measuring the volumes of the three objects in one set.

6. Decide which method listed in Step 4 above is best for determining the volume of each object.

7. Determine the volume of each object. Record your data and calculations on Student Sheet 8.1b.

8. Exchange objects with the other pair of students in your group, and repeat Steps 6 and 7.

9. Compare your data for each object with the results found by the other pair of students in your group. If you think any of your results are inaccurate, repeat your measurements and calculations.

10. Based on your data, list the six objects from least to greatest volume. Record the measured volume of each of the six objects in your notebook.

ANALYSIS

1. Choose one of the objects from Student Sheet 8.1b. Which method— water displacement or measurement and calculation—did you use to determine its volume? Explain why you chose that method.

2. Look at the way you ordered the objects by volume in Step 3. Compare this with the measured volumes you recorded in your notebook in Step 10. Were they the same? Explain.

3. Copy the three lists of measurements shown below. Pay close attention to the units that follow each number.

List 1	List 2	List 3
150 mL	2 mL	1 L
11 mL	801 mL	999 mL
200 mL	27 cm^3	998 cm^3

   a. Cross out the smallest volume in each list.

   b. Circle the largest volume in each list.

4. How would you measure the volume of:

   a. a cardboard shoebox?

   b. a plastic pen?

   c. an irregularly shaped stone?

   d. a child's wooden block?

   e. some orange juice?

   f. the two metallic solids from your mixture?

5. In this activity, you were working with unidentified materials. Explain the safety steps you took when working with the solids.

6. How would you explain volume to a 10-year-old?

   • Include at least two examples that would be familiar to a child and that would clarify your explanation.

   • Include a diagram to help you explain your ideas.

LABORATORY

Density is a physical property that describes the mass of a substance per unit of volume. It is one of many physical properties of a substance that can be useful when trying to identify what a substance is made from. In previous activities you determined whether substances were more or less dense than water, alcohol, and saltwater. This was comparison of one substance to another. But to calculate the exact density of a material, it is necessary to make measurements of a substance's mass and volume. Then you can calculate density by using the following formula:

$$\text{Density} = \frac{\text{mass}}{\text{volume}}$$

You now know how to measure volume. Once you have also measured an object's mass, you can calculate its density. The **mass** of an object describes how much matter is in the object. An object with greater mass has more matter than an object with less mass. Mass is measured in the metric unit grams (g), or related units such as kilograms (kg).

In this activity you will measure mass so that you can calculate the density of different materials. This is determining **quantitatively** (kwan-ta-TAY-tive-lee)—with numbers. Because pure substances have characteristic densities, you can use the calculated density to identify the type of material an object is made from.

CHALLENGE

How can you use the mass and volume of an object to calculate its density?

The objects on the balance have the same volume, but different masses.

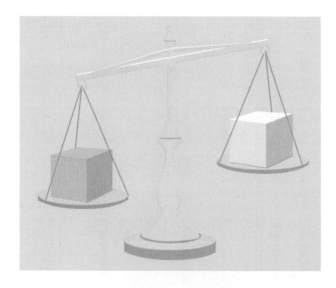

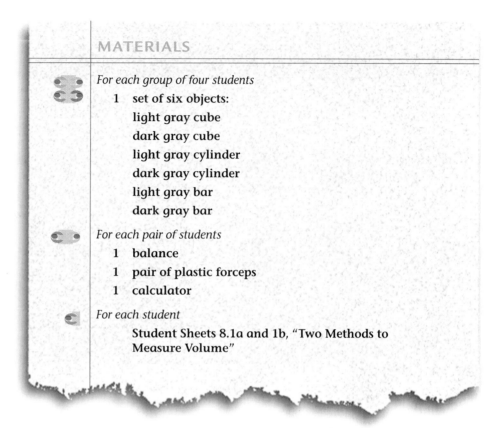

MATERIALS

For each group of four students

1   set of six objects:
    light gray cube
    dark gray cube
    light gray cylinder
    dark gray cylinder
    light gray bar
    dark gray bar

For each pair of students

1   balance
1   pair of plastic forceps
1   calculator

For each student

Student Sheets 8.1a and 1b, "Two Methods to
Measure Volume"

SAFETY

Review the procedure, and decide on appropriate safety measures for
working with the unknown solids. If you do not know what material an
object is made from, assume it is hazardous until you prove otherwise.

PROCEDURE

Part A: Measuring Mass

1. Obtain the same set of objects you used in Activity 8, "Measuring
    Volume."

2. In your science notebook, create a data table similar to Table 1, "Mass,
    Volume, and Density of Six Objects," on the next page. You will use it
    to record your data and calculations.

3. Divide the six objects into two sets so that each pair in your group has
    either the light gray set or the dark gray set. Each pair will begin by
    determining the masses of the three objects in one set.

4. Use a balance to find the mass of each object to the nearest 0.1 gram
    (g). Record your data in your table.

5. Exchange objects with the other half of your group, and repeat Step 4.

Part B: Calculating Density

6. In Table 1, record the volume of each object from Student Sheet 8.1b, "Two Methods to Measure Volume."

7. Work with your partner to calculate the density of each object, dividing its mass by its volume. Record this data in your table.

$$\text{Density} = \frac{\text{mass}}{\text{volume}}$$

8. Compare your results with the results of the other pair of students in your group. If you think any of your results are inaccurate, repeat your measurements and your calculations.

Table 1: Mass, Volume, and Density of Six Objects

Object	Mass (g)	Volume (cm^3 or mL)	Density Calculation	Density (g/c m^3 or g/mL)
Light gray bar				
Dark gray bar				
Light gray cube				
Dark gray cube				
Light gray cylinder				
Dark gray cylinder				

Part C: Using Density to Identify Materials

9. Now that you have calculated the density of several objects, you will use this to identify the material each of the objects is made from. In your science notebook, make a table similar to Table 2, "Identifying Objects' Material Using Density."

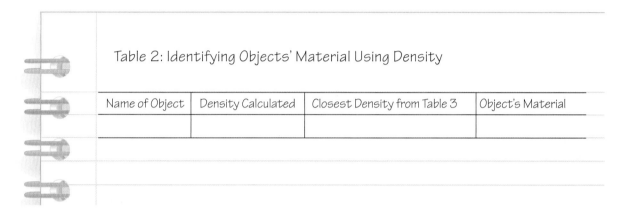

Table 2: Identifying Objects' Material Using Density

Name of Object	Density Calculated	Closest Density from Table 3	Object's Material

10. In your new table, fill in the name and density calculated for each object from Table 1, "Mass, Volume, and Density of Six Objects."

11. Compare the densities you calculated in Table 2 with the densities shown in Table 3, "Densities of Selected Solids," on the next page. Find the density closest to the density of each object, and enter that in Table 2.

12. Identify the material that might make up each of the six objects.

    Hint: Look for the material that has a density closest to the density that you determined for each object. Write the density and the material of this object in Table 2.

This bowling ball and balloon have very similar volumes, but because the bowling ball has more mass per volume, it is more dense.

ANALYSIS

1. What material is each metallic solid made of? Use data from this activity to support your explanation.

2. Now that you have identified what each solid is made of, look at the hazards for each in Table 2, "Information on Selected Solids," in Activity 7. What safety precautions must you take when working with these materials?

3. A block of wood is 4 cm wide, 5 cm long, and 10 cm high. It weighs 100 grams.

   a. Calculate its volume.

   b. Calculate its density.

   c. Will the block sink or float in water? Explain. (Remember, the density of water is 1.0 g/cm³.)

   d. Imagine cutting the block into two exactly equal halves. Calculate the volume, mass, and density of each piece.

   e. How do the densities of the new pieces compare with the density of the original block? Use your answer to Question 3d and a diagram to illustrate your answer.

Table 3: Densities of Selected Solids	
Type of solid material	**Density (g/cm³)**
Plastics	
High-density polyethylene (HDPE)	0.95
Polystyrene (PS)	1.1
Polyvinyl chloride (PVC)	1.3
Metals	
Magnesium	1.7
Beryllium	1.9
Aluminum	2.7
Titanium	4.5
Zinc	7.1
Iron	7.9
Tungsten	19.4

INVESTIGATION

In Activity 9, "Measuring Mass, Calculating Density," you saw that determining the density of an object can help determine the material it is made from. In this activity, you will use density to identify the remaining two unknown metallic solids you separated from the unidentified mixture. Once you have identified the parts of the mixture, you will use the information you collected to create a hazard label for it.

CHALLENGE

How can you use density to identify solids?

Density is one of the many properties of materials that can be found in reference tables.

MATERIALS

For each group of four students

1   cup containing metallic solids separated from the mixture in Activity 5, "Separating the Mixture"

For each pair of students

1   50-mL graduated cylinder
1   metric ruler
1   cup of water
1   pair of plastic forceps
1   pipette
1   calculator
1   balance
    paper towels
1   Material Safety Data Sheet (MSDS) booklet

For each student

1   pair of safety goggles
    Student Sheet 10.1, "More Density Data"
    Student Sheet 5.1, "Chemical Safety Data Sheet"
    Table 3, "Densities of Selected Solids" from Activity 9

SAFETY

Review the procedure, and decide on appropriate safety measures for working with the unknown solids.

PROCEDURE

Part A: Identify Solids Using Density

1. Look at the two metallic solids you separated from the unlabeled mixture. Discuss with your partner how to best calculate the density of the metal solids. Be sure to consider the tools included in the materials list.

2. Work with your partner to create a procedure for determining the density of each solid. In your plan, be sure to:

    • List the materials or tools you will use.

    • Explain each step in detail.

    • Describe safety precautions you will take.

3. Record the procedure in your science notebook.

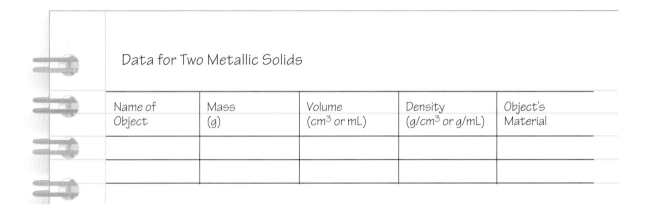

Data for Two Metallic Solids

Name of Object	Mass (g)	Volume (cm³ or mL)	Density (g/cm³ or g/mL)	Object's Material

4. Make a data table similar to the one above. You will use it to record your data during your investigation.

5. Obtain your teacher's approval of your plan.

6. With your group, decide which pair will work with which object first.

7. Conduct your investigation for that object, and record your results in your data table. Be sure to include units of measurement for each measurement you record.

8. Switch objects with the other pair in your group. Repeat Step 7.

9. Compare your density calculations with those of the other pair in your group. Are your measurements the same? If not, perform additional calculations to verify the density of each solid.

10. Use the densities you calculated to determine the material each object is made of. To do this:

   a. Look at the information in Table 3, "Densities of Selected Solids," on page A-40 in Activity 9.

   b. Find the density in the table that is closest to the density you calculated for each solid.

   c. Record the name of the material in the column, "Object's material."

Part B: More Density Data

11. Look at Student Sheet 10.1, "More Density Data." The data shown was measured by a lab that made additional measurements of the two metallic pieces from the mixture. The lab took several mass and volume measurements using instruments with more precision.

12. Using the mass and volume measurements on Student Sheet 10.1, calculate the density for each set of data. Record your answers on Student Sheet 10.1.

13. Compare the densities determined by the lab with your measurements from "Data for Two Metallic Solids." With your group, determine the amount of variation, and discuss the reasons for the variations.

14. Using both the data on Student Sheet 10.1, and your measurements, identify the material each metallic piece is made from. To do this, look once again at the density values, "Densities of Selected Solids," on page A–40 in Activity 9. Use this information to determine the type of materials the objects are made from.

Part C: Constructing a Label for the Unlabeled Mixture

15. With your partner, make a label for the unlabeled mixture.

16. As you design a label, consider:

    a. What information from your Chemical Data Sheets will you include?

    b. What directions about handling, storage, and disposal of the mixture will you include?

    Note: If you wish to include storage and disposal guidelines on your label, refer to the Material Safety Data Sheet booklet for information about each substance.

ANALYSIS

1. Based on your density calculations and the data on Student Sheet 10.1, what are the two metallic solids from the unlabeled mixture? Provide evidence from the activity to support your answer.

   Hint: Compare values with those listed in "Densities of Selected Solids" on page A-40 of Activity 9.

 2. How many substances were in the unlabeled mixture? What were they?

3. Review your answer to Analysis Question 1 in Activity 3, "Plan to Separate the Mixture." How close was your prediction about the number of substances in the unlabeled mixture?

4. Reflection: What are the three most important things you learned in this unit about identifying and studying materials scientifically?

11 Choosing a Cleaner

TALKING IT OVER

You are the Safety Officer for Sunnyvale Hospital. Your job responsibilities include monitoring procedures and products used for cleaning the hospital. When you choose cleaning products to be used by the hospital, you must know how they are stored and disposed of, and be aware of any hazards they pose to the cleaning staff who use them daily.

You have been asked to evaluate information about four window-cleaning products. You will analyze the trade-offs of selecting one product rather than another. This means you will consider the benefits and drawbacks of each and choose one to purchase for the hospital.

As you evaluate the products, keep the following in mind:

- The glass cleaner you choose will be stored in a locked room that is located next to the hospital's boiler room. This makes the room very warm in winter months.

- The cleaner will be kept in a large cabinet that also contains other cleaning products including bleach used to disinfect laundry and hospital surfaces.

- The hospital recently started a recycling program. All containers used by the hospital are recycled if possible.

CHALLENGE ⟹ **Which glass cleaner will you select for the hospital?**

Cleaning products are used in homes every day. But when used in different settings, like hospitals, potential hazards may change.

← Emergency

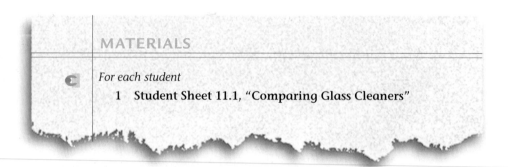

MATERIALS

For each student

1   Student Sheet 11.1, "Comparing Glass Cleaners"

PROCEDURE

1. On the next page are descriptions of possible ingredients in glass cleaners. Review this information to familiarize yourself with these ingredients.

2. With your group, read the product information provided for each of the four glass cleaners on pages A-48 and A-49. Use this information to help decide which cleaner to select for the hospital. As you read, make a list of the categories of information in the labels.

3. Compare your list with the factors shown in the left-hand column of Student Sheet 11.1, "Comparing Glass Cleaners." If there are factors in your list that are not listed on the student sheet, add them to the left-hand column.

4. Record information about each cleaner on the student sheet. You will use this information to compare the glass cleaners.

5. Decide which of the four glass cleaners you will select for the hospital. Begin by re-reading the introduction to this activity. Based on how the cleaner will be used, stored, and disposed of, decide which three factors are the most important in making your decision. Draw a star to the left of the three factors you selected on the student sheet.

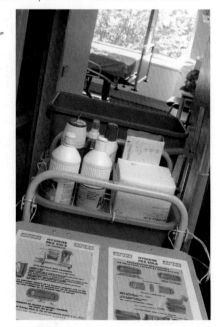

6. With your group discuss which product you will purchase. Consider the evidence and trade-offs for selecting each product. Remember to listen to and consider the ideas of the other members of your group. If you disagree with the other members of your group, explain why you disagree.

What's in a Cleaner? Possible Ingredients in Glass Cleaners

Ammonia *(ah-MOAN-ya)* is good at dissolving grease. Because it kills microorganisms it is a disin-fectant. If mixed with bleach it releases toxic vapors.

2-Butoxyethanol *(2 bew-tox-ee-ETH-an-all)* is a transparent, colorless liquid that has a fruit-like odor. It is a solvent, which dissolves dirt. It is also a disinfectant. It can be listed under several names, including butyl cellusolve, butyl glycol, and butyl oxitol.

Coloring is added to make a cleaning product pleasing to the eye. Coloring does not add to the cleaning ability of the product.

Fragrances, such as pine, lemon, or floral, are sometimes added so the cleaning solution does not have an unpleasant chemical smell, or to help get rid of bad odors in a house or other building. They do not add to the cleaning power of the product.

Isobutane *(eye-so-BEW-tane)* is added in aerosol spray cans, not because it helps to rid surfaces of dirt, but because it helps force the cleaning solution out of the spray nozzle. It is very flammable.

Isopropanol *(eye-so-PRO-pa-nol)* is a solvent that is good at dissolving grease and disinfecting surfaces. It is the main ingredient in rubbing alcohol.

Surfactants *(sur-FAK-tants)* break up the surface tension of water. They are added to cleaners to prevent streaking or spotting as the cleaned surface dries.

Water is the main ingredient of most cleaners. It provides a liquid base for the other ingredients.

HW

ANALYSIS

1. Which cleaner have you selected?

   a. State your decision.

   b. Support your decision with as many pieces of evidence from the activity as you can. *Negatives*

   c. Discuss the trade-offs of your decision.

2. Did the physical characteristics of each product affect your decision? Explain.

3. Which factors were the most important in making your decision? Explain.

INGREDIENTS:
ISOPROPANOL   12%
SURFACTANT   10%
WATER   78%

CLEANING ABILITY: 80%*
*Based on customer satisfaction surveys.

COST: $6.25 FOR 1 GALLON

ENVIRONMENTAL IMPACT: MEDIUM

PRODUCT A: MATERIAL SAFETY DATA SHEET

Physical Characteristics	Transparent red liquid Floral scent Miscible in water Density 0.99 g/mL		
Toxicity	1	Scale:	3 – high risk 2 – moderate risk 1 – slight risk 0 – no risk
Flammability	0		
Warning Label	Keep out of reach of children. Avoid eye and skin contact.		
Health Effects	May cause eye and skin irritation.		
First Aid	Eye contact: Flush eyes with water immediately. Skin contact: Wash contaminated area thoroughly with soap and water. Ingestion: Drink lots of water. If pain or discomfort persists, call a doctor immediately.		
Handling	It is always good to wear gloves and goggles when handing chemicals.		
Storage	Keep out reach of children.		
Disposal	Pour down the drain with plenty of water. Recycle container.		

PRODUCT B: MATERIAL SAFETY DATA SHEET

Physical Characteristics	Transparent colorless liquid in aerosol spray can. Ammonia scent Miscible in water Density 0.99 g/mL		
Toxicity	1	Scale:	3 – high risk 2 – moderate risk 1 – slight risk 0 – no risk
Flammability	3		
Warning Label	**DANGER:** Reacts with chlorine bleach to form toxic gas. **WARNING:** Extremely flammable. Do not use near flames or sparks. Avoid contact with eyes. Breathing of vapors can be toxic.		
Health Effects	Breathing in vapors can cause irritation of nose and lungs.		
First Aid	**Eye contact:** Flush eyes with water immediately. **Inhalation:** Move to fresh air. If pain or discomfort persists, call a doctor immediately.		
Handling	Keep away from eyes. Use in a well-ventilated area.		
Storage	Store in a cool, well-ventilated area in closed containers away from heat, and open flames.		
Disposal	Place in trash ONLY if can is empty.		

INGREDIENTS:
AMMONIA   5%
2-BUTOXYETHANOL   5%
ISOBUTANE
(PROPELLANT)   5%
WATER   85%

CLEANING ABILITY: 95%*
*Based on customer satisfaction surveys.

COST: $10.25 FOR 6 12-OZ CANS

ENVIRONMENTAL IMPACT: HIGH

PRODUCT C: MATERIAL SAFETY DATA SHEET

Physical Characteristics	Transparent colorless liquid Citrus scent Miscible in water Density 0.99 g/mL		
Toxicity	1	**Scale:**	**3** – high risk **2** – moderate risk **1** – slight risk **0** – no risk
Flammability	1		
Warning Label	**CAUTION:** Slightly flammable. Store away from heat, flame, and sources of sparks.		
Health Effects	Slightly toxic. If ingested, drink lots of water and contact a physician.		
First Aid	**Eye contact:** Flush eyes with water immediately. Ingestion: Drink lots of water. If pain or discomfort persists, call a doctor immediately.		
Handling	Keep away from eyes.		
Storage	Store in a cool, well-ventilated area in closed containers away from heat, and open flames.		
Disposal	Pour do wn the drain with plenty of water. Recycle container.		

INGREDIENTS:

ISOPROPANOL	6%
2-BUTOXYETHANOL	4%
SURFACTANT	10%
WATER	80%

CLEANING ABILITY: 90%*
*Based on customer satisfaction surveys.

COST: $6.65 FOR 1 GALLON

ENVIRONMENTAL IMPACT: HIGH

PRODUCT D: MATERIAL SAFETY DATA SHEET

Physical Characteristics	White, cloudy liquid Ammonia scent Miscible in water Density 0.90 g/mL		
Toxicity	1	**Scale:**	**3** – high risk **2** – moderate risk **1** – slight risk **0** – no risk
Flammability	1		
Warning Label	**DANGER:** Reacts with chlorine bleach to form toxic gas.		
Health Effects	Slightly toxic. If ingested, drink lots of water, and contact a physician. Inhaling vapors can damage mouth, nose, throat, and lungs.		
First Aid	**Eye contact:** Flush eyes with water immediately. **Inhalation:** Move to fresh air. **Ingestion:** Drink lots of water. If pain or discomfort persists, call a doctor immediately.		
Handling	Avoid contact with eyes. Work with in a well ventilated area.		
Storage	Store in a cool, well ventilated area in closed containers away from heat and open flames.		
Disposal	Pour down drain with plenty of water. Recycle container.		

INGREDIENTS:

AMMONIA	10%
WATER	90%

CLEANING ABILITY: 85%*
*Based on customer satisfaction surveys.

COST: $6.95 A GALLON

ENVIRONMENTAL IMPACT: LOW

The Chemistry of Materials

B

The Chemistry of Materials

Janice and her father walked into the cell phone store. It was time to buy new phones. As they headed for the long row of the latest models, she noticed a sign: "Go green! Turn in your old phone and get 15% off a new phone!"

"Wow!" She thought, "I have my old phone, so I can turn it in for recycling. That's an easy 15% discount!"

They continued along the row of phones. The signs for one group displayed a logo with three green arrows in a triangle. It reminded Janice of the recycling symbol on the bottoms of plastic bottles. She noticed that the three phones with this symbol were cheaper than other phones with similar features. "I wonder why these are cheaper?" she asked. Just then the salesperson came by. Janice asked, "Excuse me, could you please tell me what this green symbol means?"

"If a phone carries a green label, it fits green criteria." the salesperson said. "That means that its materials or the way it was manufactured are less harmful to the environment than a standard phone."

"The green phones are so much cheaper than the others!" Janice said in amazement.

"Yes, isn't it great? The government offers lower taxes to electronics companies that meet green standards. They can sell their products for less."

"Yow," thought Janice, "not only do I need to choose a phone, but I have to think about the environment too."

• • •

The scenario you just read about does not exist—yet. When we buy a cell phone, there is no label that describes how much waste, some of it toxic, was created in manufacturing the phone. But should there be? When you buy a new product, do you think about what materials it is made of? How it was manufactured? What will happen to it when you no longer have a use for it? In this unit you will consider these questions as you investigate the chemistry of materials. With this information, you will be able to analyze the environmental impact of a product and decide which products to purchase.

Consider the world around you. The book in your hands, the floor underneath your feet—each is made from a type of material. The word "material" can have several meanings. To a scientist, a **material** is a type of solid matter used to make things. For example, clothing, homes, and computers are all made from different materials. **Materials scientists** and **materials engineers** study materials and design new ones. When they design these materials, some of the things they think about are:

- How will they be used?
- What resources are needed to make them?
- What will happen to them when they are no longer useful?

For example, think about the materials that can be used to make containers for drinks. Until 1947, almost all drink containers in the United States were made of glass. Consumers could return glass milk and soft drink bottles and have their deposits paid back, and the drink bottling companies would clean and refill the bottles to sell again. Today, most drink containers are made mainly of aluminum, plastic, or glass. Each material has particular characteristics, or properties, that make it useful for holding drinks. Each material is made from specific resources and has a set of effects on the environment when it is discarded or recycled.

You are a materials scientist working for a bottling company. The president of the company has asked you which type of material to use to make containers for a new drink brand. You decide to look for a material that will both work well and have the fewest bad effects on the environment. Should it be aluminum, glass, or plastic? How will you decide? What evidence will you use?

CHALLENGE ⟹ **Which is the best material for making a drink container?**

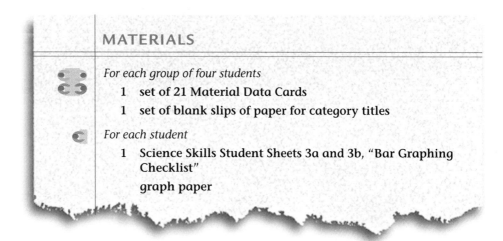

MATERIALS

For each group of four students

1 set of 21 Material Data Cards

1 set of blank slips of paper for category titles

For each student

1 Science Skills Student Sheets 3a and 3b, "Bar Graphing Checklist"

graph paper

PROCEDURE

1. Prepare a data table for recording the advantages and disadvantages of each of the three materials—aluminum, glass, and plastic. Your table should fill an entire page in your science notebook. Give the table a title.

2. With your group:

   a. List the properties of each of the three materials—aluminum, glass, and plastic.

   b. Decide whether each property is an advantage or disadvantage if you are using the material to make a drink container.

   c. Record in your data table your decision from Step 2b.

3. Spread the Material Data Cards out on a table and read the information on each card.

4. Sort the cards into categories for comparing the three materials.

   • Listen to and consider the explanations and ideas of other members of your group.

   • If you disagree with other members of your group, explain why you disagree.

5. Create a title that describes each category of sorted cards. Write the title of each category on a slip of paper and place it above that group of cards.

6. Compare your categories with those of another group in the class. Discuss any differences in the way they sorted their cards.

7. If necessary, adjust your categories and titles based on your conversation with the other group.

8. Decide if the information on each card is an advantage or a disadvantage of the material it describes. Record these advantages and disadvantages in your data table.

9. Your teacher will assign you one of the categories. Prepare a bar graph comparing the three materials in that assigned category. Be sure to label the axes and title your graph.

ANALYSIS

1. What two types of information do you think are the most important in deciding which material to use to make drink containers? Explain.

2. What additional information would you like to have about these materials? Explain.

3. Based on the information in your data table, which material is the best for making a drink container, from the viewpoint of each person listed below? Explain your answer for each of these people and support it with evidence from the activity.

   a. a consumer concerned with cost and convenience

   b. an environmentalist concerned with energy usage, litter, and problems with a bottle's impact on the environment

   c. a recycling-center owner who must handle all of the containers turned in for recycling

4. Did the graphs of the data help you make a decision about the advantages and disadvantages of each material? Explain.

5. What do you think is the best material to use to make drink containers? Write a letter or prepare a presentation to the president of the drink company describing your recommendation. Support your answer with evidence and identify the trade-offs of your decision.

When deciding what material will be used to make a drink container, it can be helpful to think about what is needed to make the container, how it will be made, and what will happen to it when it is no longer being used. All of these stages together are called the **life cycle** of a product. One way of illustrating each stage in the cycle is a **life-cycle diagram.** Materials engineers use life-cycle diagrams when making decisions about a product. These diagrams show how the inputs and outputs from one stage relate to the inputs and outputs of other stages. Life-cycle diagrams can be used to make decisions that reduce the harm that manufacturing and disposing of a product might cause to the environment.

In this activity, you will read about the life cycle of a drink container. Then your group will construct a life-cycle diagram for that type of container. You will then be able to use the life-cycle diagram to determine ways to reduce the harm the container might cause to the environment.

CHALLENGE ⟹ **How can a life-cycle diagram be used to make a decision about a product?**

Products like water bottles are a part of our everyday lives. It takes many steps to manufacture the material and produce the bottle.

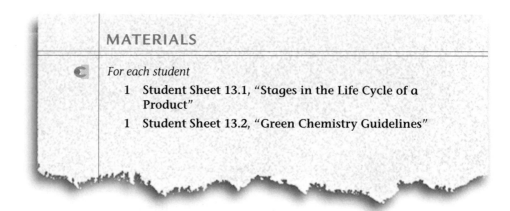

MATERIALS

For each student

1. Student Sheet 13.1, "Stages in the Life Cycle of a Product"
1. Student Sheet 13.2, "Green Chemistry Guidelines"

PROCEDURE

1. The stages in the life cycle of a glass bottle are described below. With your partner, read the description of the stages.

The Life Cycle of a Glass Bottle

RAW MATERIALS: Raw materials come from the earth. They are substances that are used to manufacture a product. It takes energy of both humans and machinery to gather or mine raw materials for products. This may include cutting down trees to make paper or mining sand to make glass for a glass bottle.

Glass is a mixture of three main raw materials: silica sand, soda ash, and limestone. Energy to mine, gather, or collect the raw materials are inputs of this stage. These materials are mined from earth's surface. Recycling a product is one way to reduce the amount of new raw materials taken from the earth to produce new products.

MANUFACTURING: In the manufacturing stage a product or material is created. Raw materials and energy are inputs. To manufacture glass for a glass bottle the three main raw materials, silica sand, soda ash, and limestone, are heated to approximately 1500°C (2700°F) to make a liquid mixture. The molten mixture is then poured into a mold where it cools and becomes solid. Once cooled, the bottle is prepared for use. It is cleaned and, if necessary, a label is printed on it. Then it can be filled and used to hold a drink. The main product of this step is the glass bottle. Other products include the wastewater used to cool the glass, and other wastes that are a result of the manufacturing process.

Raw materials of glass: sand, soda ash (sodium carbonate), limestone (calcium carbonate), yellow barium carbonate and brown iron oxide. The last two ingredients are added for color.

2. Your teacher will show and explain a life-cycle diagram that summarizes the stages below.

3. Your teacher will assign you one of the remaining types of drink containers. With your partner, read about the life cycle for the type of container you are assigned. As you read, record information about the life cycle on Student Sheet 13.1, "Stages in the Life Cycle of a Product."

4. Compare the information you have collected on your student sheet with that of the other pair in your group. If there are any differences in the information you have listed, consider adding new information to your sheet.

USEFUL LIFE: During its useful life, the product is used for its intended purpose, or, perhaps, an unintended purpose. Products that are designed from more durable materials will have a longer useful life, reducing the overall energy and resources needed to replace them.

END OF LIFE: When a product is no longer useful, it is in its end-of-life stage. This is when it is thrown away. There are several end-of-life options for glass bottles. One is to sort discarded glass by color and clean and crush each color of glass separately since each is made by adding slightly different material when the glass is made. The different pieces of glass can then be melted and reused to manufacture other glass products of the same color, such as brown jars or green bottles. An advantage of recycling glass is that manufactured glass melts at a lower temperature than the raw

A pile of broken glass sitting by the smoke-stack of a recycling plant.

materials. This can save energy in the next round of manufacturing.

Finding ways to reuse a product extends its life and can reduce the need to make more products.

5. With your group, create a diagram of the life cycle for the drink container you were assigned. The purpose of your diagram is to show the connection between the stages of the life cycle. Decide the best way to illustrate this, and then make the life-cycle diagram on a piece of chart paper. Be sure to include the information you collected on Student Sheet 13.1, "Stages in the Life Cycle of a Product," on your life-cycle diagram.

The Life Cycle of an Aluminum Can

RAW MATERIALS: Pure aluminum metal does not occur on the earth's surface. However, compounds that include aluminum are abundant. Aluminum-containing compounds are most easily mined from the earth's surface in a type of rock called bauxite.

Bauxite is ground up and mixed with a hot solution of sodium phosphate. This reaction changes the minerals chemically. Next they are exposed to an electrical current, which chemically changes the compounds into liquid aluminum metal. When the liquid is cooled it is molded into bars of solid aluminum. The process to this point is expensive and uses a large amount of energy. By the early 1900s, manufacturers realized that it is much cheaper to use recycled aluminum than to extract and process aluminum from bauxite.

MANUFACTURING: To produce aluminum cans, aluminum bars are transported to factories. There they are flattened and rolled into thin sheets. The sheets are pressed into cans.

USEFUL LIFE: The useful life of an aluminum can starts when it is labeled, filled and sealed, and shipped to a store.

END OF LIFE: Once it is empty, the can is no longer useful, and the end-of-life stage begins. It might be recycled or tossed into a trash can to end up in a landfill. If recycled, the metal is crushed and melted to produce sheets of aluminum that can be used for new cans.

(Right) Aluminum is isolated from bauxite, an ore shown in this photograph.
(Far right) An aluminum can factory where sheets of metal are cut and formed into cans.

The Life Cycle of a Plastic Bottle

RAW MATERIALS: Plastics are commonly made of hydrogen and carbon compounds called hydrocarbons. Petroleum and crude oil are the raw materials most frequently used to produce them. Oil or gas is pumped from the ground and transported to a processing factory.

Before oil can be used it is heated to temperatures greater than 980°C (1800°F). This heating causes large molecules in the oil to break apart chemically or "crack" into smaller molecules. Specific types of these smaller molecules are combined with other chemicals, including some for color. At this stage the plastic is a hot liquid. The liquid is cooled to form pellets of plastic, each smaller than a marble.

Materials engineers are inventing ways to make plastics out of non-petroleum-based materials such as plant-derived materials. Drink containers may someday be made out of plant-based plastics.

MANUFACTURING: Next, machinery physically changes the pellets as it melts them and shapes them into plastic rods. The rods are placed into a mold and formed into bottles.

Once the bottles are filled, labeled, and packaged, they are shipped to stores to enter the useful-life portion of the life cycle.

END OF LIFE: When a plastic bottle has reached the end-of-life stage, one of several things occurs. The plastic may be put into a landfill where it will last for hundreds of years. Or, the plastic bottles can be recycled. If they are to be recycled, the bottles will be sorted (the number in the recycling symbol on the bottom of a bottle indicates its type of plastic). The sorted bottles are cleaned and shredded. The shreds can be reused, but only to make other products. For example, the plastic from water bottles can be recycled to make polar fleece materials for vests and jackets. It cannot be melted at a temperature that will allow it to be formed into new bottles. Other recycled plastics can be used to make detergent bottles, storm drains, paintbrushes, and even carpet fibers. Another end-of-life option is to reuse containers to hold things such as coins, or cooking supplies like flour and sugar. Reusing containers reduces the need for new plastic materials.

(Right) Pellets can be made in any color. (Far right) The bottle on the right was molded from one of the rods shown in the pile.

ANALYSIS

1. For the drink container you were assigned:

   a. What are its raw materials?

   b. Does the product have more than one end-of-life option? Explain.

2. Use your life-cycle diagram to explain what would happen to all of the other stages in the life cycle of the drink container if:

   a. the demand for the drink container increases.

   b. the raw materials used to make the product run out.

   c. materials engineers design a way to manufacture the container with less waste produced.

3. Explain why or why not a life-cycle diagram would be a useful tool for:

   a. the director of a drink company who wants to choose a container for a new drink.

   b. a materials scientist working to reduce the negative impact a drink container has on the environment.

   c. a person buying a bottle of sports drink in a store.

4. Look at the life cycle of a product shown on Student Sheet 13.1, "Stages in the Life Cycle of a Product." Using the "Green Chemistry Guidelines" on Student Sheet 13.2, make a list of ways to reduce the negative environmental impact of this product.

5. Reflection: Based on what you've learned in this activity, do you think that the life cycle of a product should be included on the label? Explain.

Compacted bottles are ready for shredding, the next step in the plastic recycling process.

EXTENSION

Where do the raw materials come from to make products used in everyday life, such as CDs and plastic bags? What are the life cycles of these products? How many life-cycle stages does a cell phone have? Go to the *Issues and Physical Science* page of SEPUP website for links to the life cycles of different products. Use these and other Internet resources and books to find out about the life cycle of products. Then make a list of the ways to reduce the environmental harm that these products might cause.

LABORATORY

In the last activity, you compared glass, plastic, and aluminum—three materials that can be used to make drink containers. When designing a product, materials engineers consider the properties of materials to determine which is best to use. These properties can be grouped into two categories—physical and chemical. A **physical property** is one that you can identify without seeing if the material reacts with another substance. Examples of physical properties are color, hardness, and density. A **chemical property** describes how a material **reacts** with another substance, such as an acid or oxygen.

In this activity, you will test the physical and chemical properties of a variety of materials. You will then use this information to consider how those materials could best be used to make products.

CHALLENGE   **How do the properties of materials determine their uses?**

Steel can be formed into many shapes, and is very durable. This makes it ideal for external building supports and stainless steel medical equipment.

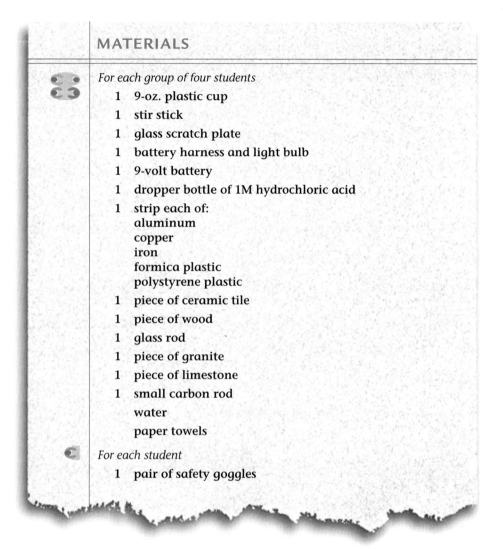

MATERIALS

For each group of four students

1	9-oz. plastic cup
1	stir stick
1	glass scratch plate
1	battery harness and light bulb
1	9-volt battery
1	dropper bottle of 1M hydrochloric acid
1	strip each of:

    aluminum
    copper
    iron
    formica plastic
    polystyrene plastic

1	piece of ceramic tile
1	piece of wood
1	glass rod
1	piece of granite
1	piece of limestone
1	small carbon rod
	water
	paper towels

For each student

1	pair of safety goggles

SAFETY

Wear safety eyewear. If a material does not bend easily, do not use more force because you could break or tear it. Watch out for sharp edges.

PROCEDURE

1. Review how to test the properties of materials by examining the table, "Testing Physical and Chemical Properties," on the next page.

2. You will test the properties of 11 materials. Make a data table in your science notebook to record your observations.

3. Put the materials you have tested into groups based on their properties. Each group must have one, two, or more properties in common. Record your groupings in your science notebook.

Testing Physical and Chemical Properties		
PHYSICAL PROPERTIES		
Properties	**Procedure**	**Interpreting Test Results**
Color	1. Observe the object material. 2. Record its color.	Describe your observations in detail.
Light transmission	1. Hold the material above some printed material, such as the facing page. 2. Observe and record whether you can: • see print clearly through the material. • see the print, but it is blurry. • not see the print.	It is TRANSPARENT if you can see through it clearly. It is TRANSLUCENT if the print is blurry. It is OPAQUE if you cannot see through it at all.
Luster	1. Hold the material near a good source of light. 2. Observe how well light reflects off your material. 3. Record whether it is very shiny, somewhat shiny, or not shiny.	It is BRILLIANT if it reflects a lot of light and is very shiny. It is GLASSY if it reflects some light and is somewhat shiny. It is DULL if it does not reflect any light and is not shiny.
Texture	1. Feel the material. 2. Record how it feels.	Describe your observations in detail. Words like *smooth, rough, grainy,* and others can be used to describe the texture of a material.
Flexibility	1. Try to bend the material gently. 2. Record how easily it bends.	If it does not bend, it is NOT FLEXIBLE. If it bends slightly, it is SOMEWHAT FLEXIBLE. If it bends easily, it is VERY FLEXIBLE.
Hardness relative to glass	1. Gently press the material across the surface of a glass scratch plate. 2. If a mark appears, see if you can rub it away. 3. Record your observations.	If a scratch appears that is not easily rubbed away, the material is HARDER THAN GLASS. If no scratch appears, or if the scratch is easily rubbed away, the material is SOFTER THAN GLASS.

PHYSICAL PROPERTIES *(continued)*

Properties	Procedure	Interpreting Test Results
Electrical conductivity	1. Attach the bulb and battery assembly to opposite ends of the object. 2. Record whether the lightbulb lights. 3. Immediately disconnect the battery harness.	If the bulb does not light, the material does NOT CONDUCT electricity. If the bulb lights, the material CONDUCTS electricity.
Density relative to water	1. Fill the plastic cup half full of water, and place the material in the cup. 2. Check to see if the material sinks or floats. With your stir stick, push underwater any material that floats, and see if it returns to the surface. 3. As soon as you have recorded results, remove and dry the material.	If it floats, it is LESS DENSE than water. If it sinks, it is MORE DENSE than water.

CHEMICAL PROPERTY

Properties	Procedure	Interpreting Test Results
Reaction to hydrochloric acid	1. Place 2–3 drops of 1 M hydrochloric acid (HCl) on each material. 2. Observe and record the results. 3. As soon as you have recorded results, rinse the material in water and dry it.	If the material does not bubble or change in any way, it DOES NOT REACT with hydrochloric acid. If the material bubbles or changes in any way, it REACTS with the hydrochloric acid.

ANALYSIS

1. Were your groupings the same as those of the other students? If they were different, explain how.

 2. Should the shape of an object be considered a property of the material? Explain.

 3. In this activity, you recorded the color of each material. Think of and explain two cases in which color does not help identify a material.

4. In your science notebook, make a copy of the table, "Selecting Materials for Products," shown below. For each product listed in the first column, complete the table by listing one material you tested that would work well and one that would *not* work well. Explain your reasons for each choice in the appropriate column.

Selecting Materials for Products

Use of Material	Materials that would work well	Reasons	Materials that would NOT work well	Reasons
Electrical wire				
Garden statue				
Toy boat				
Tabletop				
Inexpensive container for an acid, such as vinegar				

In the last activity, you grouped selected materials based on their properties. Some of those materials were elements, while others were made of combinations of elements. An **element** is a substance that cannot be broken down into simpler substances by heating it or causing it to react with other chemicals.

Did you know that there are only 90 naturally occurring elements in our world, and scientists have made about 25 more elements in laboratories? That may seem like a lot, but think of it this way: everything—yes, every-thing—around you is made from one or more of these elements. In this activity you will investigate 14 of the 90 naturally occurring elements and think of ways to group them based on their chemical and physical properties.

CHALLENGE

How can elements be grouped based on their physical and chemical properties?

Samples of elements. Clockwise from upper center, they are chlorine (Cl), sulfur (S), mercury (Hg), copper (Cu), and silicon (Si).

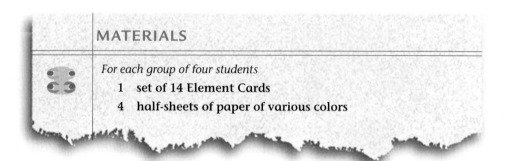

MATERIALS

For each group of four students
1   set of 14 Element Cards
4   half-sheets of paper of various colors

PROCEDURE

1. With your group, spread the Element Cards out on a table. Each card provides the following information about an element:

   - Element symbol

   - Element name

   - Whether the element is a metal or nonmetal

   - Whether the element is solid, liquid, or gas at room temperature

   - Color

   - Atomic mass: the mass of the smallest particle (an atom) of the element

   - Reactivity: how likely the element is to react chemically with other elements

   - Number of bonds to hydrogen: the number of hydrogen atoms that usually combine chemically with this element when they react

2. Examine the information on each card carefully, noting similarities and differences among the elements.

3. Working together, sort the elements into at least three groups. Each group should have at least two similar properties. Agree on a classification system. As you work remember to:

   - Listen to and consider the explanations and ideas of your group.

   - If you disagree with other members of your group, explain why you disagree.

4. In your science notebook, list the groups you made and the common features of each. Be sure to record all the elements in each group.

5. Present your classification system to the class. As you look at other students' systems, observe similarities and differences between theirs and yours. Discuss your observations with your group.

6. Your group will receive four Element Family Cards. Each card describes a group of elements called a **family**. Based on the information on the Family Cards, place each element under a card.

7. Arrange the elements in each family in order from lowest atomic mass at the top to highest atomic mass at the bottom. Place the column on a half-sheet of paper.

8. Line up the four columns of elements to form a table, so that the elements are in columns and rows. Use the atomic masses of the elements to decide on an order for the holders.

9. In your notebook, record your new classification system, complete with:

   • family names

   • similar properties within each family

   • elements in each family in order of increasing atomic mass

ANALYSIS

1. Which of the properties listed on the Element Cards are:

   a. physical properties?

   b. chemical properties?

 2. How did your first classification system compare to the second classification with the Element Family Cards?

 3. In what ways could grouping elements help scientists understand their properties?

4. Use the table of elements you constructed to find the family or families of elements that are:

   a. not usually reactive.

   b. highly reactive.

   c. all metals.

   d. all solids.

   e. all gases.

 5. The element strontium (Sr) is below calcium (Ca) in Column 2 on the periodic table. Design an Element Card that shows the properties you predict for strontium.

EXTENSION

Visit the *Issues and Physical Science* page of the SEPUP website for:

   • links to different versions of the periodic table.

   • the latest update on the number of elements.

Materials—both natural and human made—have unique properties. Some are made of one type of element, and some are made of combinations of elements. But what are elements made of, and how do they differ from each other?

Each element is made of tiny particles called **atoms.** A pure sample of an element contains many atoms of the same type. For example, the millions of iron atoms that make up a piece of iron metal are of the same type and have the characteristics of iron. Iron atoms, however, are very different from atoms of other elements, such as gold or oxygen. The properties of each element depend on its atoms.

Some elements are rarely found in a pure form. They tend to combine chemically, or **react,** with other elements. Scientists say that these elements are **reactive.** When elements react, they can form substances called **compounds.**

CHALLENGE ⟹ **What are elements, and how do they relate to compounds?**

Think of the world around you. Everything—from the air you breathe to the shoes you walk in—is made from elements or combinations of elements.

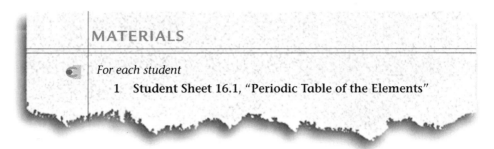

MATERIALS

For each student
1   Student Sheet 16.1, "Periodic Table of the Elements"

READING

Discovering Elements

When reading, answer the Stopping to Think questions in your mind. They can help you find out whether you understand the main ideas.

The idea that everything on the earth is made of a basic set of elements began with the ancient Greeks more than 2,000 years ago. Greek philosophers thought that fire, earth, air, and water combined to make everything in the world.

Starting in the 1600s, early chemists realized that fire, earth, air, and water were not the basic building blocks of matter. They looked instead for substances that they could not break down into simpler substances. These substances are known today as the elements.

Some of the earliest known elements were carbon, gold, silver, copper, sulfur, tin, lead, mercury, and iron—all of them elements that occur in nature. Until the 1700s, very few new elements were discovered. But in the mid 1700s through the 1800s, chemists learned how to create chemical reactions and physical ways to separate pure elements. With these new techniques, they found dozens more elements. By 1869, approximately 63 elements were known. These included hydrogen, nitrogen, oxygen, sodium, and aluminum.

Laboratory investigations in the 1700s similar to those shown in this illustration led to discoveries about the properties of elements.

STOPPING TO THINK 1

In what way were the ancient Greek philosophers right about elements?

In what way were the ancient Greek philosophers wrong?

Mendeleev and the Periodic Table of the Elements

In 1869 the Russian scientist Dmitri Mendeleev (men-deh-LAY-eff) developed the ideas that led to the modern periodic table. Other scientists had some similar ideas, but Mendeleev made the most progress and published the first version of a table of the 63 elements known at the time.

Mendeleev collected information on the properties of those 63 elements and grouped them in a way similar to what you did in Activity 15, "Families

THE PERIODICITY OF THE ELEMENTS

Photo (left) of Russian chemist Dmitri Ivanovich Mendeleev (1834–1907) and a table (right) he developed based on the properties of elements. This reference was translated into English in 1891.

of Elements." He used data that many other scientists had collected about the properties of each of the elements. When he arranged the elements according to their atomic masses and their physical and chemical properties, he noticed that there was a repeating—or periodic—pattern. For example, as the atomic mass increased from lithium to fluorine, the elements in between changed from metals to nonmetals and from solids to gases. He saw a similar pattern repeated from sodium to chlorine and again from potassium to bromine. Mendeleev predicted that there were more elements that would fit into gaps in his chart, the first version of what came to be known as a periodic table. He even used the patterns in the table to predict the properties of new elements.

Other scientists used Mendeleev's ideas and built on them to identify the elements he predicted. Later scientists found many more elements that follow the patterns he found. The modern version of the table is called the **Periodic Table of the Elements.** Based on new data about the elements, scientists around the world have agreed on some changes to the arrangement of the table.

STOPPING TO THINK 2

How did Mendeleev build on other scientists' work?

How did other scientists build on Mendeleev's work?

The Modern Periodic Table

Atomic number

6
C
carbon
12.01

Atomic mass

Today, there are more than 115 identified elements, and everything on earth is made of these elements. Look at the current periodic table shown below. Each element is represented by a symbol that includes either one uppercase letter, such as C for carbon, or an uppercase and a lowercase letter, such as Ca for calcium or Cu for copper. Each element shows an **atomic number** that corresponds to its order in the periodic table and an atomic mass, as shown in the example of the element carbon to the left.

Periodic Table of the Elements

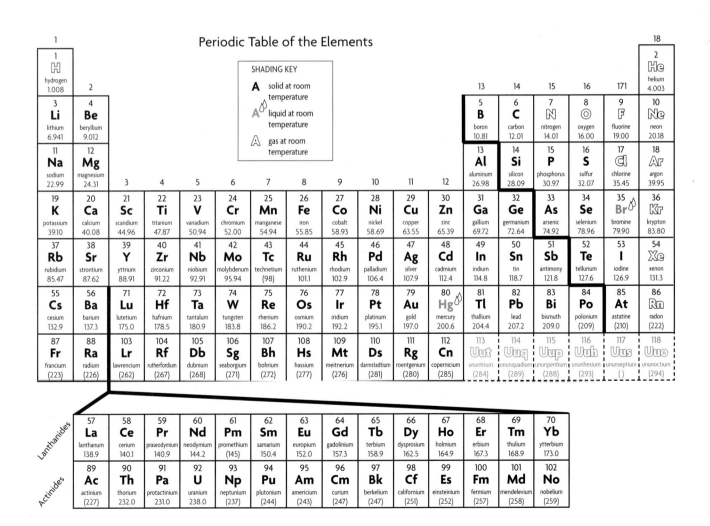

From the periodic table you can find out a lot about an element. For example, if you look at the element cesium (atomic number 55) on the periodic table shown on the next page, you will see that it is in the alkali metal column. From this you can assume that cesium is a highly reactive, soft metal. On this periodic table, you can also tell if an element is a metal or nonmetal, because a dark "stepped line" divides the table into metals to the left of the stepped line and nonmetals to its right.

Most of the elements that border the stepped line between metals and nonmetals are called metalloids. Metalloids have chemical and physical properties intermediate between those of metals and nonmetals. Aluminum is not classified as a metalloid because it has metallic properties. Metalloids are often called semiconductors because they conduct electricity better than nonmetals but not as well as metals. Semiconductors, especially silicon, are essential components of electronic products.

STOPPING TO THINK 3

Use the Periodic Table of the Elements on the next page to decide whether each of the following is a metal or a nonmetal: lithium (Li), carbon (C), sulfur (S), calcium (Ca), titanium (Ti), and bromine (Br).

Most elements are solid at room temperature. The 11 elements that are gases tend to appear on the right and near the top of the periodic table. Their symbols are white. There are two elements that are liquid at room temperature—mercury and bromine. Their symbols are shaded in gray. You might also notice that one of the newer synthesized elements, 112, is a liquid. This is interesting to note because it falls below the element mercury (atomic number 80), which is a liquid at room temperature.

You can also predict the chemical reactivity of an element based on its position in the periodic table. The **reactivity** of an element describes how likely it is to **react**, or combine, with other elements. An element that is very likely to react with other elements is described as highly **reactive**. This means that they will react with many other substances. The least reactive elements are the noble gases to the right. The most reactive metals are in the two columns to the far left of the periodic table. The most reactive nonmetals are in the halogen family in column 17.

Periodic Table of the Elements

1	2	3	4	5	6	7	8	9	10	11	12	13	14	15	16	171	18
1 **H** hydrogen 1.008																	2 **He** helium 4.003
3 **Li** lithium 6.941	4 **Be** beryllium 9.012											5 **B** boron 10.81	6 **C** carbon 12.01	7 **N** nitrogen 14.01	8 **O** oxygen 16.00	9 **F** fluorine 19.00	10 **Ne** neon 20.18
11 **Na** sodium 22.99	12 **Mg** magnesium 24.31											13 **Al** aluminum 26.98	14 **Si** silicon 28.09	15 **P** phosphorus 30.97	16 **S** sulfur 32.07	17 **Cl** chlorine 35.45	18 **Ar** argon 39.95
19 **K** potassium 39.10	20 **Ca** calcium 40.08	21 **Sc** scandium 44.96	22 **Ti** titanium 47.87	23 **V** vanadium 50.94	24 **Cr** chromium 52.00	25 **Mn** manganese 54.94	26 **Fe** iron 55.85	27 **Co** cobalt 58.93	28 **Ni** nickel 58.69	29 **Cu** copper 63.55	30 **Zn** zinc 65.39	31 **Ga** gallium 69.72	32 **Ge** germanium 72.64	33 **As** arsenic 74.92	34 **Se** selenium 78.96	35 **Br** bromine 79.90	36 **Kr** krypton 83.80
37 **Rb** rubidium 85.47	38 **Sr** strontium 87.62	39 **Y** yttrium 88.91	40 **Zr** zirconium 91.22	41 **Nb** niobium 92.91	42 **Mo** molybdenum 95.94	43 **Tc** technetium (98)	44 **Ru** ruthenium 101.1	45 **Rh** rhodium 102.9	46 **Pd** palladium 106.4	47 **Ag** silver 107.9	48 **Cd** cadmium 112.4	49 **In** indium 114.8	50 **Sn** tin 118.7	51 **Sb** antimony 121.8	52 **Te** tellurium 127.6	53 **I** iodine 126.9	54 **Xe** xenon 131.3
55 **Cs** cesium 132.9	56 **Ba** barium 137.3	71 **Lu** luterium 175.0	72 **Hf** hafnium 178.5	73 **Ta** tantalum 180.9	74 **W** tungsten 183.8	75 **Re** rhenium 186.2	76 **Os** osmium 190.2	77 **Ir** iridium 192.2	78 **Pt** platinum 195.1	79 **Au** gold 197.0	80 **Hg** mercury 200.6	81 **Tl** thallium 204.4	82 **Pb** lead 207.2	83 **Bi** bismuth 209.0	84 **Po** polonium (209)	85 **At** astatine (210)	86 **Rn** radon (222)
87 **Fr** francium (223)	88 **Ra** radium (226)	103 **Lr** lawrencium (262)	104 **Rf** rutherfordium (267)	105 **Db** dubnium (268)	106 **Sg** seaborgium (271)	107 **Bh** bohrium (272)	108 **Hs** hassium (277)	109 **Mt** meitnerium (276)	110 **Ds** darmstadtium (281)	111 **Rg** roentgenium (280)	112 **Cn** copernicium (285)	113 **Uut** ununtrium (284)	114 **Uuq** ununquadium (289)	115 **Uup** ununpentium (288)	116 **Uuh** ununhexium (293)	117 **Uus** ununseptium ()	118 **Uuo** ununoctium (294)

Lanthanides

57 **La** lanthanum 138.9	58 **Ce** cerium 140.1	59 **Pr** praseodymium 140.9	60 **Nd** neodymium 144.2	61 **Pm** promethium (145)	62 **Sm** samarium 150.4	63 **Eu** europium 152.0	64 **Gd** gadolinium 157.3	65 **Tb** terbium 158.9	66 **Dy** dysprosium 162.5	67 **Ho** holmium 164.9	68 **Er** erbium 167.3	69 **Tm** thulium 168.9	70 **Yb** ytterbium 173.0

Actinides

89 **Ac** actinium (227)	90 **Th** thorium 232.0	91 **Pa** protactinium 231.0	92 **U** uranium 238.0	93 **Np** neptunium (237)	94 **Pu** plutonium (244)	95 **Am** americium (243)	96 **Cm** curium (247)	97 **Bk** berkelium (247)	98 **Cf** californium (251)	99 **Es** einsteinium (252)	100 **Fm** fermium (257)	101 **Md** mendelevium (258)	102 **No** nobelium (259)

STOPPING TO THINK 4

Find magnesium on the periodic table.

- What is magnesium's chemical symbol?
- What family does magnesium belong to?
- Is magnesium a solid, a liquid, or a gas?

Based on its family, would you expect magnesium to be very reactive, somewhat reactive, or not reactive at all?

Forming Compounds

Elements contain only one kind of atom. Other substances contain two or more types of atoms held together by chemical bonds. Bonds form when the atoms of one element are attracted to the atoms of one or more other elements. Substances with two or more types of atoms held together by bonds are called compounds. For example, the compound water forms when the elements hydrogen and oxygen react together. Sugars are chemical combinations of the elements carbon, hydrogen, and oxygen. Groups of differing atoms that are held together by chemical attraction are called **molecules.** The diagram below shows a water molecule, made of two hydrogen atoms and one oxygen atom.

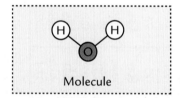

Water molecule

There are more than 115 elements, and these elements can combine to form millions of compounds. To get an idea of how many, just look at a dictionary of the English language and think about how many words are formed from just 26 letters!

Compounds have different properties than the elements that form them. For example, the compound we call water is a liquid formed from two gases—hydrogen and oxygen. Table sugar is an edible white solid formed from a black solid (carbon) and the gases hydrogen and oxygen.

STOPPING TO THINK 5

What are two ways that compounds are different from the elements that form them?

Commonly referred to as salt, this naturally-occurring compound is sodium chloride, NaCl.

Chemical Names and Formulas

Scientists have created a system for naming compounds. These names often identify the elements that make up the compound. For example, the full chemical name for table salt is "sodium chloride." This name tells you table salt contains sodium and chlorine. This is information about the compound that you would not have if you called it "table salt." Notice that the ending of "chlorine" is changed to "–ide" in the name of the compound. A **chemical formula** is a shorthand way to identify the kind and number of atoms that make up a compound. For example, the symbol for sodium is **Na**, and the symbol for chlorine is **Cl**. So you can write the formula for the compound sodium chloride like this: **NaCl**. This tells you that there is one chlorine atom for every sodium atom in sodium chloride.

Not all chemical formulas are as simple as **NaCl**. For instance, water is made up of the elements hydrogen (H) and oxygen (O), and its chemical formula is **H_2O**. (You say this "H-two-O.") That is because each water molecule is made up of two hydrogen atoms bonded to one oxygen atom. The number "2" below and to the right of the "H" shows that there are two hydrogen atoms in a water molecule. When there is no number written below and to the right of the element symbol, then there is only one of that type of atom.

....

STOPPING TO THINK 6

The chemical formula for baking soda is **$NaHCO_3$**. What elements are in baking soda? How many of each kind of atom is represented by the formula for baking soda?

....

Ocean water is a mixture of compounds, including water (H_2O), salt (NaCl), and others.

Classifying Matter: Elements, Compounds, and Mixtures

Everything around you is an element, a compound, or a mixture of both. The oxygen in the air you breathe and the copper in pennies are examples of elements. The water you drink and the salt and sugars in the foods you eat are examples of compounds. So are the proteins, fats, and carbohydrates that make up the cells in your body. Everything that is not a pure element or compound is a mixture of elements, compounds, or both. Even air is a mixture of several elements and compounds, including the elements nitrogen and oxygen and the compounds carbon dioxide and water.

ANALYSIS

1. Make a copy of the table below in your science notebook. Use the Periodic Table of Elements to find out which atoms make up a molecule for each of the substances listed. The first row has been completed for you.

Chemical Formulas of Common Substances

Substance	Chemical Formula	Atoms that make up the molecule
Water	H_2O	2 hydrogen atoms, 1 oxygen atom
Hydrogen peroxide	H_2O_2	
Carbon dioxide	CO_2	
Sucrose (table sugar)	$C_{12}H_{22}O_{11}$	
Alanine (an amino acid)	$C_3H_7O_2N$	
Oleic acid (a fat)	$C_{12}H_{24}O_2$	

2. Sodium is a metallic solid, and chlorine is a poisonous yellow-green gas. Sodium and chlorine react to form sodium chloride, which is common table salt.

   a. Is table salt an element or a compound? Explain.

   b. Describe the physical properties of table salt.

   c. How do the properties of table salt compare with those of sodium and chlorine?

3. Is seawater an element, compound, or mixture? Explain your answer.

4. Explain the relationship between an atom and a molecule.

EXTENSION

Visit the *Issues and Physical Science* page of the SEPUP website for links to learn more about Dmitri Mendeleev's work and the work of other chemists.

MODELING

Most substances on earth are not pure elements made up of a single type of atom. "Energy connections" called **chemical bonds** can hold atoms together to form molecules. Molecules are composed of two or more atoms held together with chemical bonds. Atoms can combine with atoms of the same element, with atoms of another element, or even with atoms of several elements through chemical bonds. When the atoms of more than one element bond in specific, regular proportions they form a substance called a compound. Water, for example, is a compound because its molecules are made from atoms of hydrogen and oxygen in exact proportions. These proportions (2:1) are shown in its chemical formula, H_2O.

Compounds can be found everywhere. Many everyday materials—from wood to gasoline to aspirin—are made of compounds. In this activity, you will build molecules of several compounds.

CHALLENGE

How do atoms combine to form molecules?

The Atomium, a building modeled after the crystal structure of metal, was built in Brussels, Belgium for the 1958 World's Fair.

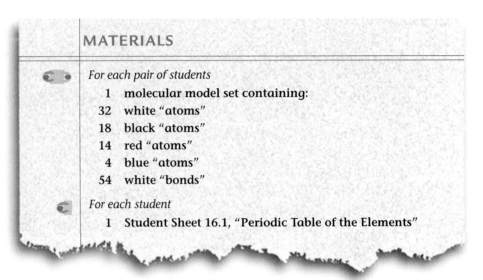

MATERIALS

For each pair of students

  1 molecular model set containing:

  32 white "atoms"

  18 black "atoms"

  14 red "atoms"

   4 blue "atoms"

  54 white "bonds"

For each student

  1 Student Sheet 16.1, "Periodic Table of the Elements"

PROCEDURE

Part A: Making Simple Molecules

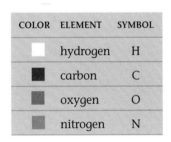

COLOR	ELEMENT	SYMBOL
	hydrogen	H
	carbon	C
	oxygen	O
	nitrogen	N

1. Build a model of a molecule of water with two hydrogen (white) atoms and one oxygen (red) atom. Use the white bonds (tubes) to make the connections that represent chemical bonds.

2. Follow your teacher's directions to draw a diagram of this molecule in your science notebook.

3. What do you think is the name and chemical formula of this molecule? Record these on your diagram.

4. Pull the model apart.

5. Every time you make a molecule, all of the bonding sites (the "sticks" on the atom models) must be connected to the sites on another atom.

    a. Using this rule, make two models: a molecule of hydrogen and carbon and a molecule of hydrogen and nitrogen.

    b. Draw each molecule that you construct.

    c. Record next to each drawing the chemical formula for the molecule.

6. Follow your teacher's demonstration to construct a molecule using two oxygen atoms. Remember, all the bonding sites must be connected.

7. Construct two molecules: one using 2 hydrogen atoms and one using 2 nitrogen atoms.

8. Draw a diagram of each of the molecules you made for Steps 6 and 7.

9. Next to each diagram record the chemical formula for the molecule.

10. Take apart all of the models, and return all of the pieces to the set.

Part B : Making More Complex Molecules

11. Construct and draw at least four more molecules according to the following two rules:

    • Each molecule must contain between two and five atoms.

    • All the bonding sites (the protruding "sticks") of an atom must be connected to those of another atom.

    After drawing each molecule, pull it apart before constructing the next.

12. Construct and draw two more molecules following only one rule:

    • All the bonding sites must be connected to those of another atom.

13. Take all the molecules apart, and return all the pieces to the set.

14. Compare your drawings with those of the other pair in your group.

15. Construct and draw a model of a molecule with the formula CO_2.

ANALYSIS

1. How many different elements were you working with?

2. What was the role of the "sticks" on each atom model?

3. Was it possible for an atom to make more than one bond? Explain and give an example.

4. How many bonds could each of the following make with hydrogen? Copy the table below into your science notebook. Use the atomic numbers to help you find the elements on the periodic table.

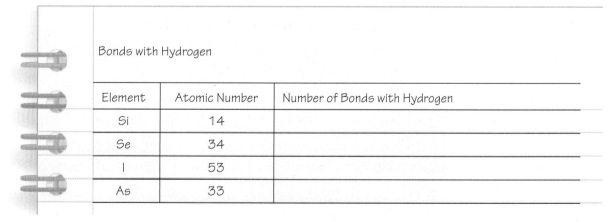

Bonds with Hydrogen

Element	Atomic Number	Number of Bonds with Hydrogen
Si	14	
Se	34	
I	53	
As	33	

5. If you had two oxygen atoms and one hydrogen atom, could you form a molecule? Explain.

6. Make a drawing to show the difference between an atom and a molecule.

7. Which model provides more information—a chemical formula or a sketch of the molecule?

LABORATORY

In Activity 12, "Evaluating Materials," and Activity 13, "Product Life Cycle," you compared plastic and glass bottles and aluminum cans to evaluate which was the best material for drinks. However, within these categories, there are more choices. For example, not all plastics are the same. Even plastics that look alike can have different properties and they can be used for different purposes.

You may have noticed that two plastic cubes can be the same size, shape, and color, but one is heavier. This could be because they are made of two types of plastic with different chemical and physical properties. Knowing the properties of plastics is helpful when deciding which plastic to use to manufacture a product.

CHALLENGE

How do the physical and chemical properties of plastics affect their uses?

Plastic is one of the most diverse synthetic materials in existence.

MATERIALS

For each group of four students

1 strip and 1 square of:
blue polypropylene (PP)
green polyvinyl chloride (PVC)
red high-density polyethylene (HDPE)
yellow polystyrene (PS)
1 vial of alcohol
1 vial of water
1 vial of alcohol-water mixture
1 vial of saltwater
1 paper clip
1 pair of plastic forceps

For each student

1 pair of safety goggles

SAFETY

Wear safety goggles at all times during this lab. Do not allow solutions to touch your skin or clothing. Clean up any spills immediately. If accidental contact occurs, inform your teacher, and rinse exposed areas.

PROCEDURE

Part A: Investigating Plastics

1. Examine the four different types of plastic strips and squares. They have been coded by color so you can tell them apart. Your group will work together to determine the properties of each type of plastic.

2. Read the procedure for each test shown in the table, "Testing Properties of Plastics," on the next page.

3. In your notebook, construct a data table "Properties of Plastics" to record the results of the tests. Be sure to add a column for the heat and acetone tests your teacher will conduct.

4. With your group, determine the properties of each of the four types of plastics using the tests in the table.

Testing Properties of Plastics

Property	Test
Flexibility	1. Gently bend the plastic strip back and forth.
	2. Observe its flexibility (ability to bend).
	3. Record your observations.
	Hint: You may want to rank the relative flexibility of each plastic on a scale of 1–4, with 1 representing the least flexible.
Crease color	1. Gently bend the strip of plastic in half.
	2. Observe the color of the crease that is produced.
	3. Record your observations.
Hardness	1. Using the end of a paper clip, gently try to draw a line in the plastic strip.
	2. Record your results.
	Hint: You may want to rank the relative hardness of each plastic on a scale of 1–4, with 1 representing the piece that was scratched the least.
Density relative to alcohol	1. Place a plastic square in the vial labeled "Alcohol," cap it, and gently shake the vial.
	2. Observe whether the plastic floats or sinks.
	3. Use forceps to remove the piece from the vial.
Density relative to alcohol-water mixture	1. Shake the vial labeled "Alcohol-Water" well to create an alcohol-water mixture.
	2. Place a plastic square in the vial, cap it, and gently shake the vial.
	3. Observe whether the plastic floats or sinks.
	4. Use forceps to remove the piece from the vial.
Density relative to water	1. Place a plastic square in the vial labeled "Water," cap the vial, and shake it gently to wet the plastic.
	2. Observe whether the plastic floats or sinks.
	3. Use forceps to remove the piece from the vial.
Density relative to saltwater	1. Gently shake the vial labeled "Saltwater" until no salt crystals are visible in the water.
	2. Place a plastic square in the vial, cap the vial, and shake it gently to wet the plastic.
	3. Observe whether the plastic floats or sinks.
	4. Use forceps to remove the piece from the vial.

LABORATORY

In the last activity, you observed that different types of plastics have specific properties. For example, the polyvinyl chloride (PVC) used to make food packaging softens and bends when exposed to heat or liquid acetone, but the high-density polyethylene (HDPE) used to make milk jugs does not. Their properties differ because they are made of different molecules. Materials engineers can use **chemical reactions** to create products with particular properties. A chemical reaction occurs when the atoms and molecules of two or more substances rearrange to form new substances.

In this activity you will mix two **reactants**, or inputs, which react chemically to create a new **product**, or output. Then you will compare the physical and chemical properties of the substances before and after they have reacted chemically.

CHALLENGE

How are reactants changed by a chemical reaction? How are the products different?

These materials scientists study the creation of new materials. The scientist above is preparing a material used to repair bones. The scientist on the right is testing a new form of bullet-proof glass to see if it meets safety requirements.

MATERIALS

For each group of four students

- 1 bottle of polyvinyl alcohol (PVA) solution
- 1 bottle of sodium borate solution

For each pair of students

- 4 white "hydrogen atoms"
- 2 black "carbon atoms"
- 1 red "oxygen atom"
- 7 white "bonds"
- 2 30-mL graduated cups
- 1 plastic spoon
- 1 stir stick
- paper towels
- warm soapy water

For each student

- 1 pair of safety goggles

SAFETY

Wear safety goggles at all times during this lab. Do not allow solutions to touch your skin or clothing. Clean up any spills immediately. If accidental contact occurs, inform your teacher, and rinse exposed areas.

PROCEDURE

1. In your science notebook, create a table to record your observations of the reactants before the reaction and the results after the reaction is completed.

   Hint: Read through the entire procedure before making your table so you know what you will need to record.

2. Pour 10 mL of polyvinyl alcohol (PVA) into an empty 30–mL graduated cup. As you pour, be sure to observe the PVA and then record in your table its color, how well it pours, whether it can be stirred, and if it appears sticky.

3. Pour 2.5 mL of sodium borate into the other empty graduated cup. As you pour, be sure to observe its properties and record them in your table.

4. One partner should slowly add all of the sodium borate to the PVA while the other stirs constantly with the stir stick. Observe the changes, and keep stirring until nothing further happens. Record all changes that occurred as you stirred.

5. Observe the properties of the new substance that results. Record your observations in your data table.

6. Transfer your new product from the cup onto a paper towel using the spoon. Immediately wash the cups. Then investigate and describe additional properties, such as:

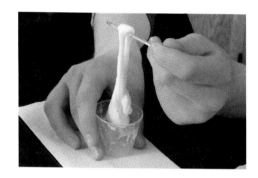

Stickiness: Does it stick to your hands? To the desk? To the paper towel?

Stretchiness: What happens when you pull it slowly? When you pull it quickly?

Bounciness: Try bouncing a small piece.

7. In your table summarize the properties of this new substance.

8. Follow your teacher's directions for cleanup.

ANALYSIS

1. How do the physical properties of the final product compare to the properties of:

    a. polyvinyl alcohol (PVA), one of the reactants?

    b. sodium borate, the second reactant, which you added to the PVA?

2. What evidence can you provide that a new substance formed?

3. Plastics are a category of materials. Compare the plastics that you worked with in this activity to the properties of the plastics you tested in Activity 18, "Properties of Plastics." From these two investigations, what can you say about the properties of plastics?

Plastics, including the substance you made in Activity 19, "Creating New Materials," have different properties, but they all belong to a group of materials called polymers. **Polymers** are compounds made of thousands of repeating smaller molecules. The molecules that repeat in a polymer are called monomers. Notice their names. Monomer starts with the prefix *mono* which means "one" (in Greek). Polymer starts with the prefix *poly* meaning "many." So, a polymer is made of many monomers.

In this activity you will construct paper-clip models to help you understand the properties of polymers. Scientists use models to help explain things we cannot see. But keep in mind that a scientific model, like the molecular model you have worked with, does not have to look like the real thing— it just has to act like it in one or more important ways.

CHALLENGE

How can you use models to represent changes that occur during a chemical reaction?

In what ways is this architectural model like the building it represents? In what ways does it differ?

MATERIALS

For each group of four students

1 wide-mouthed plastic bottle
48 silver paper clips
6 colored paper clips
2 clear plastic cups
1 plastic spoon

For each student

1 Student Sheet 20.2, "Polymers in Daily Life"

PROCEDURE

Part A: Examining a Monomer

1. In your science notebook, create a table to record how well a monomer, a polymer, and a cross-linked polymer can be poured, stirred, and pulled, as shown by the models you will make. Read through the entire procedure before constructing the table so you will know what you will need to record.

2. Work with your group to investigate the properties of the model monomers. Put 24 unconnected silver paper clips in the wide-mouthed bottle. Each paper clip represents one monomer.

3. Slowly pour the monomers from the bottle into the plastic cup. (If necessary, gently shake the bottle.) Repeat this two or three times. Describe how quickly the clips come out of the bottle. Record your observations in your data table.

4. Use the plastic spoon to stir the monomers in the cup. Record your observations.

5. Reach into the cup and pull out a single monomer. Record in your table your observations about pulling out the monomer.

Part B: Forming a Polymer

6. Each member of your group will now link six paper clips from the remaining 24 clips into a straight chain, as shown in the diagram below. Each clip represents an individual monomer.

Model of a polymer

7. Link your four chains together to make one long chain of 24 paper clips. You have just made a model of a polymer like the polyvinyl alcohol (PVA) you used in Activity 19, "Designing New Materials." (You would need thousands of paper clip monomers to make a realistic paper clip polymer.)

Model of a longer
polymer molecule

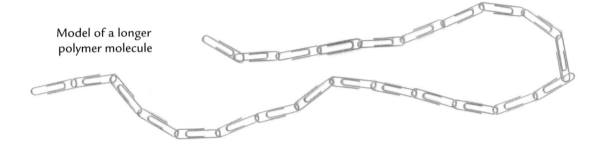

8. Put your polymer in the wide-mouthed bottle. Leave one or two paper clips hanging out of the top. Now pour the polymer into a plastic cup two or three times. Record your observations.

9. Use the plastic spoon to stir the polymer in the cup. Record your observations.

10. Reach into the cup, and pull out a single paper clip. Record your observations.

Part C: Cross-Linking a Polymer

11. Separate the polymer back into four chains of six paper clips each. Each part represents individual polymer molecules. Place the chains in four parallel rows as shown in the diagram below.

12. Use two colored paper clips to connect, or cross-link, the first and second chain. Continue to do this with all four of the chains, as shown in the diagram below. You have just made a model of a cross-linked polymer, like cross-linked polyvinyl alcohol (PVA). You have constructed a model of a chemical reaction that chemically bonds polymers together into cross-linked polymers. The colored paper clips represent the sodium borate molecules that linked the polymer polyvinyl alcohol chains together in the chemical reaction in Activity 19, "Designing New Materials."

13. Test how well your cross-linked polymer can be stirred, pulled, and poured. Record your observations in your data table.

14. Separate all of the paper clips, and put the 24 silver paper clips back in the plastic cup.

ANALYSIS

 1. Models provide ways to represent complex systems. In Activity 19, "Creating New Materials," and this activity you made a total of three models of polymers. Analyze each of the models you built.

    a. In your science notebook, make a table like the one below.

    b. Fill in the table using observations from this activity.

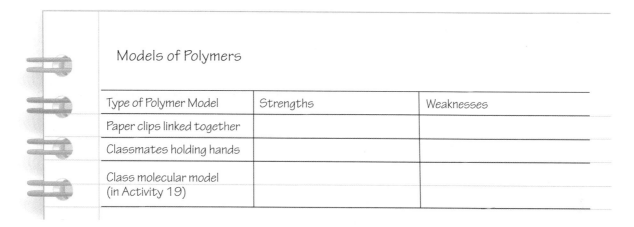

Models of Polymers

Type of Polymer Model	Strengths	Weaknesses
Paper clips linked together		
Classmates holding hands		
Class molecular model (in Activity 19)		

2. Compare the models you built in this activity:

    a. Which was the most helpful when you analyzed the physical properties of a polymer?

    b. Which was the most helpful when you analyzed the chemical reaction that occurred?

3. Using examples from this and Activity 19, "Designing New Materials," explain the relationships between a monomer, a polymer, and a cross-linked polymer. Include a sketch to illustrate your explanation.

4. How does cross-linking affect the properties of a polymer?

5. All plastics are polymers. Based on what you observed with the models, what advantages do you think polymers have over monomers?

READING

Can you imagine a world without plastics? Plastic soft drink containers, bags, pens, DVDs, and computer and television parts are just a few things made of plastics that would be different. For thousands of years, however, people lived without plastics. But today, materials scientists and engineers have created plastics to make everyday products that in the past were made from glass, metal, and wood. In this activity, you will read how a plastic, a synthetic polymer, is made through a chemical reaction.

CHALLENGE ➔ **What is the chemical structure of plastics?**

Bakelite was the first synthetic plastic, invented by Belgian scientist Leo Baekeland in 1907. In the 1920s, the versatile Bakelite was manufactured to make all sorts of products from auditorium walls to radios.

MATERIALS

For each student
1   Student Sheet 21.1, "Three-Level Reading Guide: Polymer Parts"
1   Student Sheet 19.1, "Comparing Properties of Polymers"

READING

Use Student Sheet 21.1, "Three-Level Reading Guide: Polymer Parts," to guide you as you complete the following reading.

Plastics are Polymers

What makes plastics different from other materials such as glass and aluminum? The answer is found in the wide variety of plastic compounds that can be made from chains of carbon atoms. Scientists make new plastics by designing compounds with a wide variety of properties.

The majority of plastics used to make products are synthetic. This means that they are made in laboratories and factories, and do not exist in nature. The first plastic was developed in 1907. Some natural polymers include the cellulose that makes up wood and cotton, the protein that forms strands of human hair, and raw rubber that is collected from rubber trees.

Plastics are part of a larger category of compounds called polymers. A **polymer** is a substance made up of thousands of repeating small molecules. The prefix "poly-" means "many," and the word "polymer" means "many parts." The small molecules that repeat in a polymer are called monomers. The prefix "mono-" means "one," and so a monomer is "one part." You modeled the formation of a polymer from many monomers when you attached paper clips to make a long chain. Each paper clip represented the monomers that bond together to form a polymer. The long chain of paper clips represented the polymer.

Take polyethylene, for example. The plastic that was color-coded red in Activity 18, "Properties of Plastics," was polyethylene. Polyethylene means "many ethylenes," and it is a chain of ethylene molecules. The ethylene molecule is the monomer.

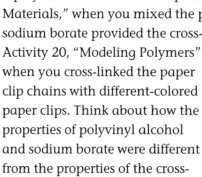

ethylene
· single molecule
· monomer

polyethelene
· thousands of the same molecule linked together
· polymer

Adding the prefix *poly-* to the name of a monomer forms the names of many synthetic polymers. Think about the other plastics you used in Activity 18: polystyrene—a chain of styrene molecules; polyvinyl chloride—a chain of vinyl chloride molecules; high-density polyethylene—a chemically bonded chain of ethylene molecules; and polypropylene—a chain of propylene molecules.

Synthetic plastics, like the four you investigated in Activity 18, have been in use for less than 100 years. However, people have been using natural polymers like wood, natural rubber, and wool for centuries.

Investigating the Structure of Polymers

Herman Staudinger

Scientists began to investigate the atomic and molecule structure of natural polymers so they could learn how to make synthetic polymers. In 1920, the German chemist Herman Staudinger proposed that polymers were made of long chains of many small molecules. He thought that the length of the chain was related to the physical properties of the polymer. At the time, his ideas were considered radical, and many scientists did not take them seriously. But he continued to collect data that supported his ideas. From his work, and the work of other scientists, dozens of synthetic plastics were developed. Staudinger's research on the properties and structure of plastics was so important that he received the Nobel Prize in 1953.

Today, scientists know that changing the length of a polymer chain is not the only way to change its properties. Another way is to cross-link a polymer. You modeled this process in Activity 19, "Designing New Materials," when you mixed the polyvinyl alcohol with sodium borate. The sodium borate provided the cross-links. You also modeled cross-linking in Activity 20, "Modeling Polymers" when you cross-linked the paper clip chains with different-colored paper clips. Think about how the properties of polyvinyl alcohol and sodium borate were different from the properties of the cross-linked polymer.

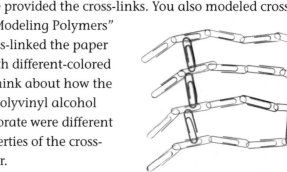

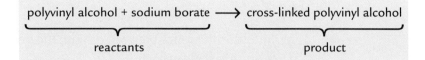

polyvinyl alcohol + sodium borate ⟶ cross-linked polyvinyl alcohol

reactants   product

Why does cross-linking a polymer change its properties? New chemical bonds form and change the structure of the molecules. The polyvinyl alcohol and sodium borate are reactants, and the result of their chemical reaction leads to the formation of a new product. The molecules and physical properties of the product are different than either of the reactants.

As Staudinger found, the number of cross-links is related to the physical properties of a cross-linked polymer, just as the length of the polymer chain was related to the physical properties of the polymer. If there are few cross-links, the cross-linked polymer has "memory." After it is stretched, it "remembers" to return to its original shape, like a rubber band. If a plastic has more cross-links, the result is a harder substance that cannot be stretched and does not return to its original shape.

One problem with cross-linking is that it is often difficult to reverse. In fact, the more cross-links there are in a polymer, the harder it is to break down the polymer chemically. This means that cross-linked polymers are usually difficult to recycle.

A polymer that is commonly cross-linked to improve its uses is rubber. Natural rubber gets sticky in hot weather and brittle in cold weather, and it falls apart very easily. But when rubber is cross-linked, its properties change. Cross-linking rubber makes it more stable and elastic. Most of the rubber products in the world around you, from food containers to car tires, are made of cross-linked rubber. While this makes better products, a trade-off is that it causes disposal problems.

Cross-linked rubber is so stable that it does not degrade. This can make recycling cross-linked polymers difficult. However, there are ways to reuse the material. For example, old tires can be shredded and made into chips. These chips are used on playgrounds, running tracks, and in road construction. Scientists and engineers have also developed ways to use old tires as a source of energy.

It is estimated that two to three billion tires sit in landfills across the United States. Is this an environmental disaster or an opportunity to find new ways to deal with them?

ANALYSIS

1. What is the difference between a synthetic and a natural polymer? Give one example of each.

2. Why do two polymers, such as polystyrene and polyethylene, have different properties?

3. Explain why cross-linking a polymer like polyvinyl alcohol or rubber changes its properties. Include a diagram showing the relationships between a monomer, a polymer, and a cross-linked polymer.

INVESTIGATION

In the beginning of this unit you considered materials used to make a single-material product, a drink container. But what about the materials that go into a more complex product—for example, a computer?

A computer contains many pieces that must be manufactured and put together. Think about all of the components—parts—in all of the computers in the world that make computers work. What raw materials are needed to make the components? How much waste is created? What impact does that waste have on our environment?

In this activity you will analyze the materials used and the amounts of waste produced to manufacture a computer.

CHALLENGE ⟹ **What is the environmental impact of manufacturing a computer?**

Manufacturing a computer requires assembling many parts, each made from unique materials.

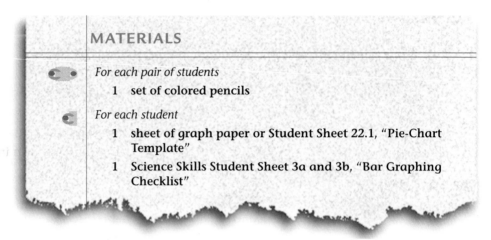

MATERIALS

For each pair of students
1 set of colored pencils

For each student
1 sheet of graph paper or Student Sheet 22.1, "Pie-Chart Template"
1 Science Skills Student Sheet 3a and 3b, "Bar Graphing Checklist"

PROCEDURE

1. With your partner, read the information in Table 1, "Materials in a Desktop Computer," below. Discuss the information in the table.

Table 1: Materials in a Desktop Computer (weighing approximately 27 kg (60 lb))		
	% of Total Weight	% Recyclable
Aluminum	14	80
Copper	7	90
Glass	24	0
Iron compounds	20	80
Lead	6	5
Plastic	25	20
Zinc	2	60
Other metals	2	—

2. With your partner read the information in Table 2, "Waste Products from Manufacturing Selected Computer Components," below. Discuss the information in the table.

Table 2: Waste Products from Manufacturing Selected Computer Components			
Component	Component Weight (kg)	Total Waste Produced during Manufacturing (kg)	Hazardous Waste Produced during Manufacturing (kg)
Computer chip	< 0.5	40	3
Circuit board	2	21	18
Monitor	20	1	0.9

3. With your partner decide which of you will construct a pie chart for the data in Table 1, and who will construct a bar graph for Table 2. You might want to try sketching ways to represent the information before constructing your final chart or graph. Be sure to label your work and give it a title.

4. Show your work to your partner. Together write down the conclusions that can be drawn from the information shown in the pie chart and the bar graph.

ANALYSIS

1. What are the top three materials by weight in a computer?

2. You are a materials scientist asked to present the information in Tables 1 and 2 to a group of computer manufacturers who want to reduce the effect of the computer life cycle on the environment. What information from your data would help them? Make a list of statements summarizing the information your graphs and charts show.

3. Based on your list from Analysis Question 2, what two statements do you think are the most important to discuss with the manufacturers? Explain why they are the most important.

READING

As you saw in the last activity, a computer is made of many parts, each manufactured from one or more materials. One essential part of a computer, and of many other electronic devices, is a **circuit board.** It works like a wiring system to transfer electricity to each operating part of the computer. To do this a circuit board contains a network of copper paths. These paths conduct the flow of electricity within the computer. A chemical process called **etching** is used to create the copper paths on the circuit board. In this activity you will find out how this works by etching your own circuit board.

CHALLENGE

How is a computer circuit board produced?

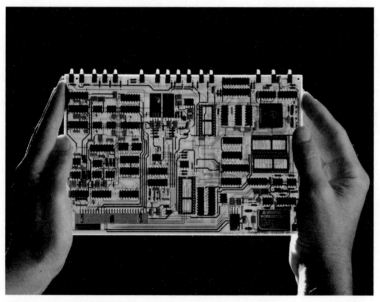

The large circuit board (left) holds many smaller circuit boards, one of which is magnified on the right.

MATERIALS

For each group of four students

1 felt-tip permanent marker
1 piece of copper-coated plastic
1 piece of steel wool
1 pair of forceps
1 battery harness with light bulb
1 9-volt alkaline battery

For each pair of students

1 piece of paper

For each student

1 Student Sheet 23.1, "Three-Level Reading Guide: Etching Circuit Boards"

SAFETY

Wear safety goggles at all times during this lab. Do not allow solutions to touch your skin or clothing. Clean up any spills immediately. If accidental contact occurs, inform your teacher, and rinse exposed areas.

PROCEDURE

Part A: Designing and Etching a Circuit Board

1. Listen carefully as your teacher describes how a circuit board works.

2. Outline the shape of the copper-coated plastic on a piece of paper.

3. Using a pencil, work with your partner to create a circuit board design. It should be a pattern that will conduct electricity from one end of the board to the other. Create a sketch of your design, making sure to use thick lines.

4. Share your design with your group. Decide which design will be etched on the piece of copper-coated plastic.

5. Select someone in your group to clean the surface of the copper-coated plastic piece by rubbing the copper-coated side with steel wool. Cleaning will remove surface dirt and other impurities that might interfere with the etching reaction. Once you clean it, be careful not to touch the copper surface with your fingers. Oil from your fingers will interfere with the etching process.

6. Use the marker to draw your design on the copper-coated side of the circuit board and to write your initials on the plastic side. Be sure to make thick lines with the marker.

7. Let the ink dry for 1 minute.

8. Re-trace your design and your initials and again let the ink dry for 1 minute.

9. Look at the copper chloride etching solution your teacher has prepared and record your observations in your science notebook. Now place your circuit board in the tray. It will soak there overnight.

Part B: Examining the Circuit Board

10. Observe the used copper chloride after the etching process is completed. Describe your observations in your science notebook.

11. Obtain your circuit board from your teacher after it has been rinsed off with water.

12. Rub your circuit board with steel wool to remove any remaining ink.

13. Examine your circuit board, and then test it with the battery-and-lightbulb circuit. Record the results of your test.

Part C: Reading

Use Student Sheet 23.1, "Three Level Reading Guide: Etching Circuit Boards" to guide you as you complete the following reading.

READING: MAKE PRODUCTS, MAKE WASTE

Making Everyday Products

We buy and use products every day. These products include drinks and items we consume and dispose of right away. But we also buy products that serve us for longer periods of time, like sneakers, cell phones, or computers. What happens before you buy a product? It has to be made from materials, and the materials have to come from somewhere.

Take, for example, a computer. To manufacture a computer the parts must be made first. To make the parts raw materials or recycled materials must be obtained. As you saw in the demonstration, copper is one of the raw materials that end up in a circuit board. Mining companies dig out copper-containing rocks, known as copper ore, from deposits in the earth. Refining companies then physically crush the rock and chemically remove the copper from the ore. The copper that is removed and purified is then sold to companies that use copper in their products.

Copper-containing rock can be mined from open pit mines (left) on the earth's surface or from tunnel mines (right) that are blasted into the surface.

Hot liquid metal copper is poured into molds where it will cool.

Making Circuit Boards

During the production of a circuit board, a chemical reaction etches a copper circuit on a piece of plastic. To etch means to use a corrosive solution to make a design in a material by dissolving the material not wanted. The copper that was protected from the etching solution is left on the board and creates a metal path. The metal path determines how electricity flows throughout the computer. This is a process that removes much of the copper on the board, leaving it in the etching solution.

Making Waste

Each step in the process from raw materials to finished circuit board creates some form of waste. After ore is mined to obtain copper, the copper-containing rock is extracted to be used in products. However, more than 98% of the ore does not contain any form of copper, so a lot of waste remains.

As you observed in this activity, after a circuit board is etched the used etching solution and rinse water contain copper. Other steps in the computer manufacturing process create yet more wastes that have copper in them. Solutions containing copper above a certain concentration are considered toxic. In fact, the U.S. Environmental Protection Agency (EPA) reported that in the year 2000, of all the toxic chemicals released by companies in the United States, the most common toxic substance was copper-containing waste. About 1.5 billion pounds of these chemicals were released into the environment that year.

A technician works with a machine (left) that etches copper circuit boards. Mining and manufacturing copper-containing substances can result in waterways that are polluted with copper waste.

Copper Isn't Always Bad

Like other living organisms, the human body needs small amounts of copper and other metals for it to work properly. That's why they are often among the ingredients of vitamin and mineral supplements. The U.S. Food and Drug Administration's (FDA) recommended daily intake of copper for adults is about 2 milligrams (mg). But in much larger amounts, copper, like many other metals, can be toxic. Drinking water that has high levels of copper can cause vomiting, diarrhea, stomach cramps, and nausea. Eating or drinking very high amounts of copper can cause liver and kidney damage. Inhaling copper dust over long periods of time can cause dizziness, headaches, diarrhea, and irritation of the nose, mouth, and eyes. Since high levels of copper can be toxic, proper disposal is crucial.

Today, the United States has laws that prevent companies and individuals from dumping toxic waste directly into the soil, waterways, and sewer systems. This helps keep our environment cleaner and safer. But manufacturing products that we have come to depend on, like circuit boards, still produces toxic waste. Figuring out how to handle this waste in ways that will not harm the environment is a problem many companies and government agencies face every day. If you consider the amount of waste produced by manufacturing products every year, that's a lot of toxic waste that is built up in the course of one year. It often costs companies a great deal of money to dispose of toxic waste safely.

ANALYSIS

1. Describe the changes that occurred during the etching process in:

   a. your circuit board.

   b. the copper chloride etching solution.

2. What do you think should be done with the used copper chloride etching solution?

3. Etching circuit boards creates large amounts of copper-containing toxic waste. What ways can you think of to reduce the amount of copper-containing waste produced in the United States?

   Hint: You may want to look at Student Sheet 13.1, "Green Chemistry Guidelines," to help you think of ways to improve methods of manufacturing.

LABORATORY

Manufacturing circuit boards produces water that contains copper compounds. The concentration of copper in the waste is one factor that will determine how the waste can be disposed. **Concentration** is the amount of one substance in another substance. In this activity you will determine the amount of copper compounds in the used copper chloride solution from Activity 23, "Producing Circuit Boards." It is important to know the concentration of copper in the solution because there are local, state and federal laws that set limits on what types of wastes can be released and at what concentrations. For this reason, manufacturers need to dispose of the used copper chloride solution in ways that do not put high concentrations of copper in rivers or waterways.

One way to dispose of the waste is to reduce the concentration of copper in the waste by diluting it, and then releasing it into a waterway. When waste is **diluted**, it is combined with water. This does not change the waste chemically, but decreases the concentration of waste per volume of water. Once the waste is diluted to below the limit set by law, it can be disposed of in a waterway. Depending on where the manufacturer is located, limits for the maximum concentration of copper that can be released in a single day from a single place may range from 1 to 10 parts per million (ppm). **Parts per million** is a way of expressing the concentration of a substance in one million parts of another substance.

In this activity you will determine the concentration of the used copper chloride solution in parts per million. Knowing the concentration will help you decide if dilution is a way to dispose of the waste.

CHALLENGE

How much copper is in the used copper chloride solution?

MATERIALS

For each group of four students

1 30-mL dropper bottle of each of the following:

100,000 ppm copper chloride solution

water

5% ammonia solution

used copper chloride solution from Activity 23, "Producing Circuit Boards"

1 cup of water

For each pair of students

1 SEPUP tray

1 dropper

1 stir stick

1 sheet of white paper

paper towels

1 copy of Transparency 24.1, "Diluting and Testing Copper Chloride"

For each student

1 pair of safety goggles

1 Student Sheet 24.1, "Determining Concentration"

1 Student Sheet 24.2, "Treating Waste"

SAFETY

Wear safety goggles at all times during this lab. Do not allow solutions to touch your skin or clothing. Clean up any spills immediately. If accidental contact occurs, inform your teacher, and rinse exposed areas.

PROCEDURE

Part A: Preparing a Dilution of 100,000 ppm Copper Chloride

1. Place the copy of Transparency 24.1, "Diluting and Testing Copper Chloride" underneath your SEPUP tray. This will help you see the colors of the solutions as you perform the dilutions.

2. Put 10 drops of 100,000-ppm copper chloride solution in Cup 1 of the SEPUP tray.

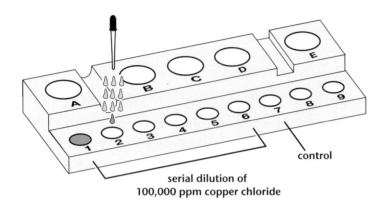

serial dilution of
100,000 ppm copper chloride

3. Use a clear dropper to transfer one drop of 100,000-ppm copper chloride solution from Cup 1 to Cup 2. Return any excess in the dropper to Cup 1, and rinse the inside of the dropper in the cup of water.

4. Add 9 drops of water to Cup 2. Stir the solution with the stir stick. Clean the stir stick.

5. Use the dropper to transfer one drop from Cup 2 to Cup 3. Return any excess in the dropper to Cup 2, and rinse the inside of the dropper.

6. Add 9 drops of water to Cup 3, and stir.

7. Continue this dilution process through Cup 6 by moving a drop of solution from the previous cup to the next cup, adding 9 drops of water, and stirring. Be sure to return any excess solution in the dropper to the previous cup, and rinse the dropper.

8. Add 10 drops of water to Cup 7. This cup will act as a control to ensure that the water you added to Cups 1–6 does not contain copper.

9. Record the color of the solutions in Cups 1–7 in the first column of the data table on Student Sheet 24.1, "Determining Concentration."

10. You will use ammonia solution to indicate if copper is present in the solution in each of the cups. Add 5 drops of ammonia to each of the seven cups, and stir. Be sure to clean the stir stick after mixing each cup to avoid contamination.

11. If after adding ammonia, the solution is green, blue-green, or blue, copper is present in the solution. Record your observations in the second column of your data table.

Part B: Concentration of Copper in Used Copper Chloride Solution

12. Place 10 drops of the used copper chloride solution into Cup 9. Add 5 drops of ammonia, and stir. Record your observations.

13. Determine the concentration of copper in the used copper chloride solution. To do this, compare the color of the solution in Cup 9 to the colors in Cups 1–7. Record the concentration for the cup that has the closest concentration to Cup 9 on Student Sheet 24.1, "Determining Concentration."

14. Dispose of the solutions in your SEPUP tray as directed by your teacher.

ANALYSIS

 1. Which contains a more dilute solution, Cup 1 or Cup 2? Explain.

 2. Was there copper in Cups 1–6? How did you know it was or was not there? Explain, using evidence from this activity.

3. What is the concentration of copper in the used copper chloride solution from Activity 23, "Producing Circuit Boards"? Use the evidence from this activity to support your answer.

4. How many liters of water would you need to dilute 1 liter of used copper chloride solution from 100,000 ppm of copper to less than 1 ppm?

5. Based on your answers to Analysis Questions 3 and 4, how many liters of water would it take to dilute your waste from Activity 23 to 1 ppm, an acceptable concentration to pour down the drain?

6. Is dilution an acceptable way to dispose of the used copper chloride solution? Explain.

EXTENSION

Towns, cities, and states in the United States set limits on the amount of copper that can be disposed of down drains. Find out what the local limit is in your area.

LABORATORY

So far in this unit you have performed two chemical reactions. In Activity 19, "Creating New Materials," you cross-linked polyvinyl alcohol in a chemical reaction that produced a new polymer. In Activity 23, "Producing Circuit Boards," you observed a chemical reaction that etched copper. These are two examples of chemical reactions. You may be amazed to know that there are chemical reactions going on around you and inside of you every day. Whether you are cooking your dinner in a pan or releasing energy from food in your cells, chemical reactions are changing reactants into products. Understanding chemical reactions is helpful when creating materials and in deciding how to reduce the waste created at the same time.

In this activity you will conduct two chemical reactions in closed containers. Scientists call a container a **closed system** if none of the reactants or products can escape from the reaction container. If a chemical reaction takes place in a container that allows any reactants or products to escape, it is called an **open system.** You will investigate what changes and what stays the same when a chemical reaction takes place in a closed system.

CHALLENGE

How does the total mass of the reactants compare to the total mass of the products in a chemical reaction?

Two liquid reactants mix and undergo a chemical reaction that results in the creation of a yellow product.

MATERIALS

For each group of four students

1 balance

1 SEPUP tray to hold copper chloride bottles

1 30-mL bottle of 100,000-ppm copper chloride solution

1 30-mL bottle of sodium hydrogen phosphate solution

For each pair of students

1 10-mL graduated cylinder

1 aluminum washer

2 reaction bottles

For each student

1 Student Sheet 25.1, "Mass of Reactants and Products"

1 pair of safety goggles

SAFETY

Wear safety goggles at all times during this lab. Do not allow solutions to touch your skin or clothing. Clean up any spills immediately. If accidental contact occurs, inform your teacher, and rinse exposed areas.

PROCEDURE

Part A: Chemical Reaction in an Closed System

1. With your partner, place an aluminum washer in the bottom of one of the reaction bottles.

2. Fill the dropper with 1 mL of 100,000-ppm copper chloride solution.

3. Being careful not to squeeze the dropper and mix the two reactants, place the top on the bottle and twist the lid securely.

4. Use the balance to measure the total mass of the bottle, dropper, and reactants to the nearest $\frac{1}{10}$ of a gram. Record this initial total mass on Student Sheet 25.1, "Mass of Reactants and Products."

5. Observe the two reactants and record your observations on Student Sheet 25.1.

6. While holding the reaction bottle securely with one hand, use the other hand to squeeze the dropper, releasing the copper chloride solution into the bottle. Swirl the bottle to mix the copper chloride solution with the aluminum washer.

7. Set the bottle on the table, and observe. On Student Sheet 25.1, record your observations both as the reaction happens and after there are no more signs of a reaction.

8. Determine the total final mass of the reaction bottle to the nearest $\frac{1}{10}$ gram. Record this final mass on your student sheet.

9. Calculate the change in total mass.

Part B: Another Chemical Reaction in a Closed Chamber

10. Now conduct a second chemical reaction in a closed system. With your partner, pour 4 mL of 0.8 M sodium hydrogen phosphate into the bottom of the second reaction bottle.

11. Fill the dropper with 1-mL of 100,000-ppm copper chloride solution.

12. Being careful not to bump or drop any of the copper chloride into the bottle, carefully twist the dropper top securely onto the bottle.

13. Use the balance to measure the total mass of the bottle, dropper, and reactants to the nearest $\frac{1}{10}$ of a gram. Record this initial total mass on Student Sheet 25.1, "Mass of Reactants and Products."

14. Observe the two reactants and record your observations on Student Sheet 25.1.

15. While holding the reaction bottle securely with one hand, use the other hand to squeeze the dropper, releasing the copper chloride solution into the bottle. Swirl the bottle to mix the copper chloride solution with the sodium hydrogen phosphate solution.

16. Set the bottle on the table, and observe. On Student Sheet 25.1, record your observations both as the reaction happens and after there are no more signs of a reaction.

17. Determine the total mass of the reaction bottle to the nearest $\frac{1}{10}$ gram. Record this final mass on your student sheet.

18. Calculate the change in total mass.

19. Clean up according to your teacher's directions.

ANALYSIS

1. What evidence do you have that a chemical reaction took place between:

   a. copper chloride solution and aluminum?

   b. copper chloride solution and sodium hydrogen phosphate?

2. What can you conclude about the effect of a chemical reaction on the mass of reactants in a closed system? Support your answer with evidence from this activity.

 3. Using what you now know about the Law of Conservation of Mass, how would you respond if a company said it had developed a way to make hazardous materials and wastes "disappear"?

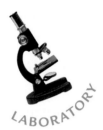

LABORATORY

When the wastebasket is full, what do you do with the waste? Take it out to the garbage can? Most likely this is the easiest option. In Activity 23, "Producing Circuit Boards," you saw that the chemical reaction that produces a circuit board also produces copper chloride waste. What do large manufacturing companies do with waste? What is the best choice for the environment? For years, people have gotten rid of waste through incineration. **Incineration** is the burning of wastes at very high temperatures—greater than 650°C (1,200°F). In this activity, you will explore how well incineration works to eliminate the copper-containing toxic waste.

CHALLENGE ⟹ **When waste is incinerated, what happens to potentially toxic heavy metals?**

A toxic waste incineration facility.

MATERIALS

For each group of four students

1 dropper bottle of water
1 dropper bottle of ammonia

For each pair of students

1 sample of ash from metal paper
1 sample of ash from nonmetal paper
1 SEPUP tray
1 stir stick
1 dropper
1 piece of white paper
1 paper towel

For each student

1 pair of safety goggles
1 Student Sheet 24.2, "Treating Waste"

SAFETY

Wear safety goggles at all times during this lab. Do not allow solutions to touch your skin or clothing. Clean up any spills immediately. If accidental contact occurs, inform your teacher, and rinse exposed areas.

PROCEDURE

Part A: Observing Incineration

1. In your science notebook, make a table like the one shown below.

Testing for Copper

	Color after Adding Ammonia	
Substance	Metal Paper	Nonmetal Paper (control)
Unburned paper		
Smoke		
Ash		

2. Watch as your teacher uses ammonia to test two pieces of paper—one metal and one nonmetal—for copper. Record your observations in your table. The nonmetal paper is being tested as a control.

3. To simulate incineration, your teacher will burn both pieces of paper. Observe as your teacher uses ammonia to test the smoke, one of the products of incineration, for the presence of copper. Record your observations in your table.

Part B: Testing Ash for Copper

4. Place your SEPUP tray on a piece of white paper.

5. Use your stir stick to put one scoop of ash from the metal paper into Cup 1.

6. With your stir stick, break the ash into smaller pieces.

7. Add 20 drops of water to Cup 1, and stir. Clean the stir stick.

8. Use your stir stick to put one scoop of ash from the nonmetal paper into Cup 2.

9. Add 20 drops of water to Cup 2, and stir. Clean the stir stick.

10. Add 5 drops of ammonia to Cups 1 and 2 to test for the presence of copper. Stir Cup 1, clean the stir stick, and stir Cup 2. Record your observations in your table.

11. Dispose of the substances in your SEPUP tray as directed by your teacher.

ANALYSIS

1. Which of the three items in your table, "Testing for Copper,"—paper, smoke, or ash—are products of incineration?

2. Which of the products of incineration contained copper? Explain your evidence.

3. How did incineration change the metal paper?

4. What are the advantages and disadvantages of using incineration to dispose of heavy metal wastes?

5. Look at the information on Transparency 26.1, "Municipal Waste Disposal in the U.S. and Japan," and Transparency 26.2, "Relative Landmasses of the U.S. and Japan." Based on what you know about incineration and the information shown, why do you think these two countries handle waste disposal differently?

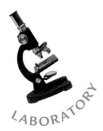

LABORATORY

Deciding how to handle waste produced from manufacturing is challenging. It can be diluted or incinerated, as you saw in previous activities. In some cases, it contains valuable materials that can be **reclaimed** and then reused. To reclaim metal means to get it back so it can be used again. Reclaiming metal from waste reduces the amount of new metal needed for manufacturing.

One way to reclaim copper from used copper chloride is to combine the waste with a solution that **precipitates** the copper. The metal copper precipitates, or falls out of solution because of a chemical reaction. Reclaiming the copper can be a useful way to deal with waste because it reduces the amount of toxic waste that is discarded, and provides copper that can be used again to make new products. Chemists have found that other types of metal are particularly effective in removing copper from waste products. In this activity you will test three metals to find out which one is best at reclaiming copper from waste.

CHALLENGE

Which metal is best at reclaiming copper from the used copper chloride solution?

 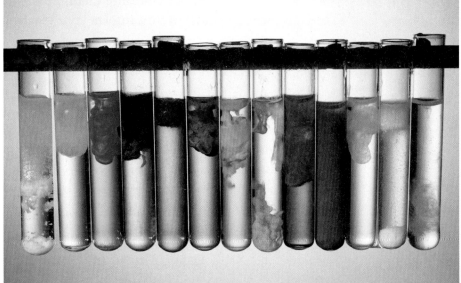

Mixing two chemicals (left) results in a chemical reaction that creates an orange precipitate. Test tubes (right) hold the results of several metal precipitation reactions.

MATERIALS

For each group of four students

1   dropper bottle of used copper chloride solution from Activity 23, "Producing Circuit Boards"
1   dropper bottle of 5% ammonia solution
1   cup of water

For each pair of students

1   SEPUP tray
1   aluminum washer
1   iron washer
1   zinc washer
1   plastic spoon
1   dropper
    paper towels

For each student

1   pair of safety goggles
1   Student Sheet 24.2, "Treating Waste"

⚠ SAFETY

Wear safety goggles at all times during this lab. Do not allow solutions to touch your skin or clothing. Clean up any spills immediately. If accidental contact occurs, inform your teacher, and rinse exposed areas.

PROCEDURE

Read through the entire procedure before you begin, and in your science notebook prepare a data table for recording your observations and results.

1. With your partner carefully examine each of the three metal washers: aluminum, zinc, and iron. Record your observations in your data table.

2. Add 10 drops of used copper chloride solution to Cups 1–4 of the SEPUP tray.

3. Using forceps, place the aluminum washer in Cup 1, the iron washer in Cup 2, and the zinc washer in Cup 3. Cup 4 will serve as a control for comparison purposes.

4. Observe the reaction in each cup for 5–10 minutes. Record your observations of each reaction in your data table. Be sure to include a comparison of the results obtained with each of the different metals.

5. Using the plastic spoon, remove the pieces of metal from the cups, and place them on a paper towel. Clean the spoon with a paper towel after each piece is removed.

6. In your data table, record your final observations of each metal.

7. Record your observations of the solutions left in each cup.

8. Using a dropper, put 5 drops of each of the solutions into a clean cup in the SEPUP tray. Do this by transferring 5 drops from Cup 1 to Cup A, from Cup 2 to Cup B, from Cup 3 to Cup C, and from Cup 4 to Cup D. Be sure to clean the dropper with water after each transfer so the solutions do not mix.

9. Test for copper in each solution by adding 2 drops of ammonia solution to Cups A–D. If copper is present in the solution, a deep blue color or a blue-green precipitate will form when ammonia is added.

10. Record your observations of the ammonia test in your data table. Dispose of the metals and solutions in your SEPUP tray as directed by your teacher.

ANALYSIS

1. Explain the purpose of including Cup 4 and Cup D in your investigation.

2. Prepare a written report summarizing your investigation. Put your report on a clean sheet of paper. Include your name, the date, and a title for your report. Your report should have the following three components:

   a. A statement of the problem you were trying to resolve.

   b. A description of the materials and procedure you used to solve the problem.

   c. An analysis of the results, which should include:

   - a copy of your data table.
   - a summary of the results shown by the data in your data table.
   - an answer to this question: Which metal seemed to work best at removing the copper from solution? (Describe your evidence completely in your answer.)
   - any problems you may have had with the investigation.
   - any additional questions related to the problem that you would like to investigate.

3. Companies that make circuit boards often reclaim copper from copper-containing solutions. This allows them to reuse the copper, or sell it. Based on your results from this investigation and the information below, which metal would you recommend a company use to reclaim copper? Support your answer with evidence, and identify the trade-offs of your decision.

More Information on Metals

Metal	Approximate Cost per Pound in 2012 (U.S. dollars)	Maximum Wastewater Concentration (ppm)	Health Benefits	Health Hazards
Aluminum	$1.00	Not Restricted	Trace amounts may help enzymes function.	High levels may cause bone disease.
Copper	$3.80	1	Essential for nervous system functions and energy metabolism, the recommended daily intake for an average adult is 2 mg.	Large amounts ingested over time cause liver and kidney damage.
Iron	$0.06	100	Essential for formation of red blood cells, the recommended daily intake is 18 mg for an average adult.	Large amounts ingested over time may cause inflammation and damage to organs.
Zinc	$0.90	2.4	Small amounts are needed for functioning of enzymes and forming proteins. The recommended daily intake for an average adult is 15 mg.	Large amounts ingested over time may cause inflammation and damage to organs.

EXTENSION

What other metals can precipitate copper from the used copper chloride solution? Design an experiment to find out. After your teacher approves your investigation, conduct the experiment, and present the results to the class.

28 Another Approach to Metal Reclamation

LABORATORY

In the last activity, you conducted a chemical reaction with solid metals to precipitate copper metal from the used copper chloride solution. The brown deposit that formed was solid copper. Reclaiming copper from waste solutions has two advantages. First, it reduces the volume of toxic copper compounds that are thrown away as copper is replaced in solution with another, less toxic metal. Second, copper is a valuable metal that can be reused or sold.

Solid metals are not the only reactants that precipitate copper. Certain solutions can also form copper precipitates when they react with the used copper chloride solution. As you work to determine the best way to treat the waste from circuit-board manufacturing, you will evaluate two more chemical reactions that reclaim copper from the used copper chloride solution.

CHALLENGE

Which compound in solution is best for reclaiming copper metal from the used copper chloride solution?

A goldsmith sorts printed computer circuit boards to reclaim the precious metal before the boards are recycled.

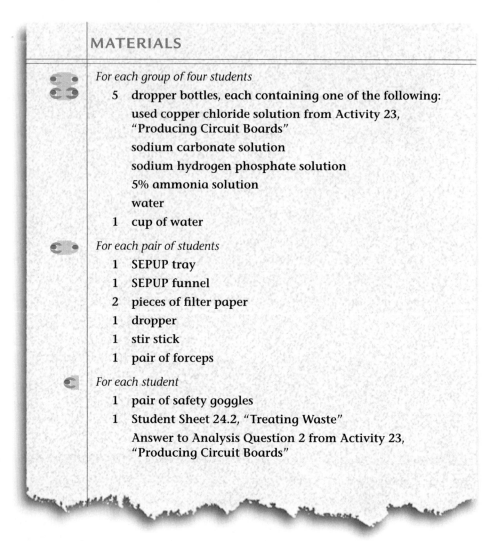

MATERIALS

For each group of four students

  5 dropper bottles, each containing one of the following:
      used copper chloride solution from Activity 23, "Producing Circuit Boards"
      sodium carbonate solution
      sodium hydrogen phosphate solution
      5% ammonia solution
      water

  1 cup of water

For each pair of students

  1 SEPUP tray
  1 SEPUP funnel
  2 pieces of filter paper
  1 dropper
  1 stir stick
  1 pair of forceps

For each student

  1 pair of safety goggles
  1 Student Sheet 24.2, "Treating Waste"
      Answer to Analysis Question 2 from Activity 23, "Producing Circuit Boards"

SAFETY

Wear safety goggles at all times during this lab. Do not allow solutions to touch your skin or clothing. Clean up any spills immediately. If accidental contact occurs, inform your teacher, and rinse exposed areas.

PROCEDURE

Part A: Precipitation of Metals

1. In your science notebook, prepare a data table like the one shown on the next page.

2. Add 15 drops of used copper chloride solution to Cups 1 and 2 of the SEPUP tray.

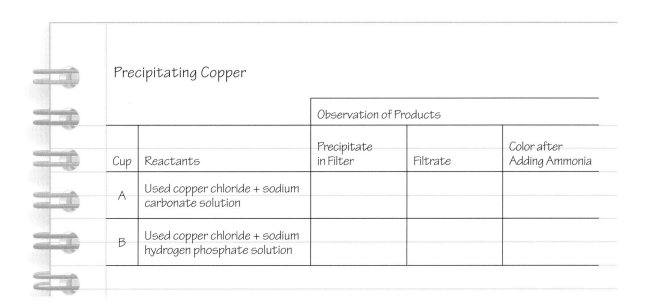

Precipitating Copper

Cup	Reactants	Observation of Products		
		Precipitate in Filter	Filtrate	Color after Adding Ammonia
A	Used copper chloride + sodium carbonate solution			
B	Used copper chloride + sodium hydrogen phosphate solution			

3. Add 20 drops of sodium carbonate solution to Cup 1, and stir. Rinse the stir stick.

4. Add 20 drops of sodium phosphate solution to Cup 2, and stir.

5. Examine the results of the reaction in Cups 1 and 2.

Part B: Filtration

6. Now you will filter out the copper precipitate. Use the illustration below as a guide to fold the filter paper and set up the funnel.

7. Place the funnel over large Cups A and B of the SEPUP tray.

   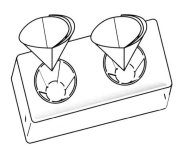

Step 1
Fold filter paper in half.

Step 2
Fold filter paper in half again.

Step 3
Open with three thicknesses of paper on one side of the cone and one thickness on the other.

Step 4
Place in funnel and add 3–5 drops of water from the dropper bottle to hold it in place.

8. The solid that formed when you mixed the liquids in Steps 3 and 4 is a precipitate. It can be removed by filtering. Use a clean dropper to transfer both the precipitate and the solution from Cup 1 to the filter paper above Cup A. Rinse the dropper thoroughly.

   Hint: If the solid is difficult to remove, add a few drops of water to Cup 1. Use the dropper to remove the water and the precipitate, and transfer it to the filter paper.

9. Use a clean dropper to transfer the precipitate and solution from Cup 2 to the filter paper above Cup B.

10. Wait a few minutes as the solutions pass through the filter paper. After most of the liquid has filtered through, move the funnel so that it rests over Cups C and D.

11. Use forceps to gently pick up the filter paper in Cups A and B, and inspect the precipitate. Record your observations of the precipitate.

12. The filtered liquids left in Cups A and B are now called the filtrates. In your data table, record your observations of the filtrates.

13. Add 5 drops of ammonia to Cups A and B, and stir. Record your observations and the results of the ammonia test in your table.

14. Dispose of the filter papers and solutions in your SEPUP tray as directed by your teacher.

ANALYSIS

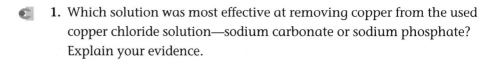

1. Which solution was most effective at removing copper from the used copper chloride solution—sodium carbonate or sodium phosphate? Explain your evidence.

2. The table, "Summary of Precipitation Reactions," on the next page, shows information about each of the substances you used to precipitate copper. Based on your answer to Analysis Question 1, your results from Activity 27, and the information on the next page, which precipitation reaction would you recommend a company use to reclaim copper?

   Be sure to support your answer with evidence, and discuss the trade-offs.

Summary of Precipitation Reactions

Metal	Approximate Cost per Pound (U.S. dollars in 2012)	What Are the Products of the Reaction?	What Can Be Done with these Products?
Aluminum	$1.00	Copper Aluminum chloride	Reuse copper Easy disposal of aluminum chloride through release into environment
Iron	$0.06	Copper Iron chloride	Reuse copper Restricted disposal of iron chloride—must be treated, stored, or diluted
Zinc	$0.90	Copper Zinc chloride	Reuse copper Highly restricted disposal of zinc chloride—must be treated or stored
Sodium Carbonate	$0.10	Copper carbonate Dissolved salt	Reuse copper carbonate Easy disposal of dissolved salt through release into environment
Sodium Phosphate	$0.30	Copper phosphate Dissolved salt	Reuse copper phosphate Easy disposal of dissolved salt through release into environment

3. Making 1,000 circuit boards can produce more than 18,500 liters (5,000 gallons) of copper-containing wastes. How do you think this toxic waste should be handled? Review your results from Activities 24–28, and the information you have collected on Student Sheet 24.2, "Treating Waste," and support your answer with evidence. Be sure to consider dilution, incineration, precipitation, and any other option that would reduce the environmental harm from the production of circuit boards.

4. Reflection: Look back at your answer to Analysis Question 2 from Activity 23, "Producing Circuit Boards." Now that you've completed the unit, has your idea of what to do with the waste changed? Explain.

TALKING IT OVER

The Sunnyvale school district has been awarded a Green Computer Grant. To use the grant money, the school district must purchase "green" computers. The term "green" describes activities or products that disturb our environment less than current activities or products do. "Green" houses, for example, would have solar panels for energy, and be made from recycled building materials. "Green" electronics have been engineered in ways that produce less waste and thus reduce the environmental impact of their product life cycle. The Sunnyvale school district must show how the computers they decide to purchase have "green" features.

You are a materials scientist asked by the Sunnyvale school district to analyze proposals from computer companies about their products. You will recommend which computers to purchase based on the computer's green features and your knowledge of the products' life cycles.

CHALLENGE ⟹ **Which "green" computers should the school district purchase?**

Deciding which computer to buy can be based not only on the computer's features, but also the environmental impact of the entire computer life cycle.

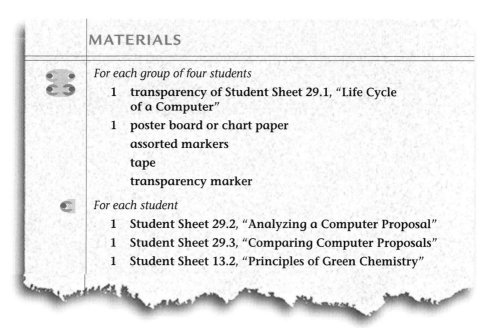

MATERIALS

For each group of four students

1 transparency of Student Sheet 29.1, "Life Cycle of a Computer"

1 poster board or chart paper

assorted markers

tape

transparency marker

For each student

1 Student Sheet 29.2, "Analyzing a Computer Proposal"

1 Student Sheet 29.3, "Comparing Computer Proposals"

1 Student Sheet 13.2, "Principles of Green Chemistry"

PROCEDURE

1. With your group review Transparency 29.1, "Life Cycle of a Computer" and identify each of the life cycle stages listed below. Use a transparency marker to label each stage on the transparency.

   - raw materials
   - manufacturing
   - useful life
   - end of life
   - recycling

2. With your group you will perform a life cycle analysis for a hypothetical new material. To analyze this proposed change, you will predict how using the new material will affect each stage of the life cycle. To do this

   - Read the news flash that follows.

NEWS FLASH

New Polymer to Revolutionize Computer Manufacturing

Scientists and engineers have announced the creation of a new plastic made from plant-based polymers. It is hoped that this material will replace the synthetic polymers currently used to make computer monitors. Since the new plastic is made from plant-based materials, this would reduce the need for the raw material, petroleum. When recycled, the polymer can be broken down into a material that can be used to make computer monitors a second and third time, much like the process used to recycle glass bottles. This is an improvement over plastics currently used to make computer monitors since the current plastics cannot be reused to manufacture new monitors.

- With your group use a transparency of Student Sheet 29.1, "Life Cycle of a Computer," to think about which step(s) would change using the new material. Share your ideas with the class.

3. Now you will perform a life-cycle analysis for "green" computers. Your teacher will assign your group one of the four computer proposals described on the pages that follow.

4. With your group, read your assigned proposal. Fill out Student Sheet 29.2, "Analyzing a Computer Proposal," to help you identify how each feature of the proposal will change the life cycle of the computer.

5. Your group will work together to present a life-cycle analysis to the class. In your presentation you should be prepared to:

- Describe each feature of the computer proposal.

- Point out on your transparency of Student Sheet 29.1, "Life Cycle of a Computer," how your proposal would modify the life cycle of a computer.

- Explain how each feature changes the life cycle and reduces the environmental impact of the computer.

- Explain which "Principles of Green Chemistry" are incorporated in the proposal.

   Hint: Refer to Student Sheet 13.2

6. Make your presentation to the class, and listen to those of the other groups. As you listen to each presentation, record information on Student Sheet 29.3, "Comparing Computer Proposals." You will use this information to choose a proposal.

   Note: For each of the four computer plans presented below, the system specifications are the same. That means that the memory, processing speed, and software programs are identical.

Proposal A Features

- Each computer has a cathode ray tube (CRT) monitor.

- The glass used in the monitor is from recycled glass products.

- Company reuses copper from circuit-board etching to produce more circuit boards.

- Computers are shipped in bulk. This reduces the amount of packing material needed to individually ship each computer.

Proposal B Features

- Each computer has a cathode ray tube (CRT) monitor.

- Old computers are shipped back to the computer company. The company takes apart the old computers and reclaims metal components, such as the copper from the circuit board and the wires, to reuse in new computers.

- Nontoxic manufacturing wastes are sent to landfills. Hazardous materials are labeled, packaged, and sent to hazardous-materials facilities.

- The plastic cases that hold the monitors are made from a plant-based plastic.

Proposal C Features

- Each computer has a flat screen liquid-crystal display (LCD) monitor that uses about 50% less electricity and 30% less materials than the standard CRT monitor.

- Reclaimable metals are precipitated from waste solutions and are reused in the manufacturing process.

- 15% of the plastic components of the computer are made of recycled plastic.

- The company will take back the computers once they are no longer being used, dismantle them, and use the metal components for further computer manufacture.

Proposal D Features

- Each computer has a flat screen liquid-crystal display (LCD) monitor that uses about 50% less electricity and 30% less materials than the standard CRT monitor.

- Computers are shipped in bulk, reducing the amount of packing material needed to individually ship each computer.

- 15% of the metal components of the computer are made of recycled metal.

- The company offers a coupon for 50% off a new computer if the current computer is kept and upgraded for at least eight years (instead of buying new computers).

ANALYSIS

1. Which proposal would you recommend the district choose for its Green Computer Grant? State your opinion, citing evidence from Student Sheet 29.3, "Comparing Computer Proposals," and previous activities. Include a discussion of the trade-offs involved in your decision.

2. With your group, explain how the science you learned in this unit helped you analyze your proposal. To do this, choose one feature of your proposal and explain which concept you learned helped you to understand that this feature would improve the life cycle of a computer.

3. The proposals your group analyzed did not include the cost of each computer. The school board members did not provide this information earlier because they wanted you to evaluate the plans based only on the chemistry of the materials and the products' life cycles.

   • Read the list price for each computer proposal below.

   • Knowing the price of each computer, does your answer to Analysis Question 1 change? Explain.

Proposal Costs		
Proposal	**Cost per Computer**	**Purchase Plan**
A	$1,250	Year one—120 computers purchased
B	$1,650	Year one—60 computers purchased Year two—30 computers purchased Year three—30 computers purchased The price is locked in for all three years.
C	$2,450	Year one—120 computers purchased
D	$1,800	Year one—120 computers purchased

4. **Reflection:** Do you think that there should be green guidelines for families and individuals when they buy products, such as computers?

Water

C

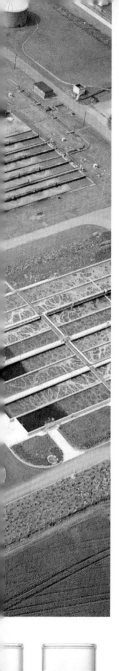

Water

When Micah came downstairs after a long hot shower his mother exclaimed, "I hope you enjoyed your shower today because starting tomorrow you'll have to shorten it. Our water bill has gone up."

"Oh no!" replied Micah as he grabbed breakfast to eat on the way to school. "Long showers help me wake up in the morning. Why would our bill go up? Don't we just get our water straight from the river outside of town?"

Micah's mother was sitting at the table reading the newspaper. "*The Times* just published an article about how the rates are going up because the wastewater treatment service charge has increased."

"What's a wastewater treatment service charge?" asked Micah.

"Water that has been used by residences and businesses, called wastewater, travels to the wastewater treatment plant once it is flushed or washed down the drain. The service charge includes the cost of treating the water at the plant so that it is clean and safe before it is released back into the environment. And remember, you drink that water too."

"Wow," said Micah, " I guess there's a lot I don't know about where our water comes from and what happens before it gets to our faucets."

• • •

Water is essential for life on earth. This is true for all of the plants and animals that live on the land and in the water. We must drink water in order for our cells and bodies to function properly. We also rely on water for various products and services, and for recreation. Because of the central role that water plays in our lives, there are numerous societal decisions and personal health risks associated with poor water quality. How do you know the water you drink is safe? What does your community do to make its water safe to drink? Whose responsibility is it? In this unit you will explore these questions as you investigate the interesting physical and chemical properties of water, what happens to substances once they are dissolved in water, and chemical testing for contaminants.

You have probably tasted bottled spring water. Every year in the United States, people spend billions of dollars on bottled water. Yet most people have access to drinking water directly from the tap. Do you think people can tell the difference between tap water, distilled water (water without dissolved solids), and bottled spring water?

CHALLENGE **Can you tell the difference between different kinds of bottled water and tap water?**

How do you decide to drink bottled or tap water?

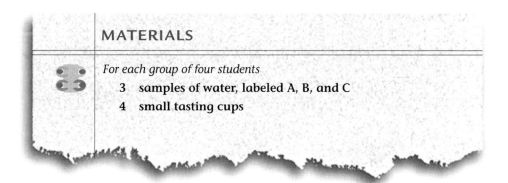

MATERIALS

For each group of four students

3   samples of water, labeled A, B, and C
4   small tasting cups

 SAFETY

Use your own tasting cup only. Remember, never taste any substance in the science classroom unless specifically instructed to do so by your teacher.

PROCEDURE

1. In your science notebook construct a larger version of the data table shown below, "Water Tasting."

Water Tasting				
	Observations			
Water Sample	Appearance	Smell	Taste	Predicted Sample Identity
A				
B				
C				

2. Fill each person's tasting cup half full of water sample A. Be sure to pour from the large cup into each student's small tasting cup.

3. Observe the appearance of the water sample. Smell the sample. Finally, taste your sample. Drink all of the water in the cup.

4. Record your observations of appearance, smell, and taste in your table. Do not share your results with other members of the group.

5. Repeat Procedure Steps 2–4 for water samples B and C.

6. Identify each sample as distilled, spring, or tap water. Record your results in the Predicted Sample Identity column of your data table. Be sure to give a reason for your predictions.

7. When everyone in the group has finished, take turns sharing your results with the rest of the group.

8. Discuss your reasons as well as your choices within your group, and try to reach agreement about the samples. Create a second data table in your science notebook like the one shown below. Record your choices and reasons for each choice in the Predicted identity column.

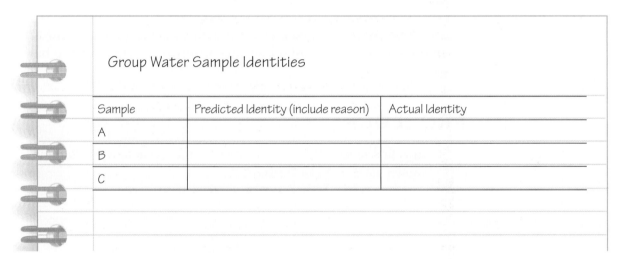

Group Water Sample Identities

Sample	Predicted Identity (include reason)	Actual Identity
A		
B		
C		

ANALYSIS

1. Which water sample tasted best to you, and why?

2. Would you spend the extra money on bottled spring water, after your taste-test experience? Why or why not?

3. Some people might disagree with your decision for Analysis Question 2. What reasons do you think they would give for their opinion?

4. **Reflection:** What other information about spring, tap, and distilled water would you like to investigate further before you decide which water to drink?

EXTENSION

Study and compare the information on the labels of various samples of bottled spring water.

READING

Carla and her grandparents lived in a neighborhood called Shadow Hills. Carla enjoyed listening to her grandparents talk about the early days in their town, Willow Grove, when the community was mostly farms and woods. As the town grew, housing, schools, factories, and businesses covered much of the land. Some people were unhappy about the growth of the town. Just the other day Carla heard one of her teachers say that she was worried about water pollution from Willow Grove and the nearby city, Metroville. The water pollution could cause substances called **contaminants** to enter the drinking water supply. These contaminants could be undesirable and even harmful. Carla decided it was time for her to learn about the local water.

CHALLENGE

How would you react if you lived in Willow Grove and your drinking water supply were threatened by contamination?

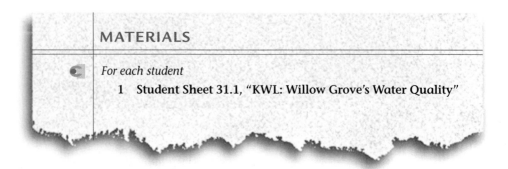

MATERIALS

For each student
1   Student Sheet 31.1, "KWL: Willow Grove's Water Quality"

READING

Use Student Sheet 31.1, "KWL: Willow Grove's Water Quality," to guide you through the following reading.

Willow Grove's Drinking Water

Carla realized that she didn't know where her drinking water came from. Grandma told her that many people in Willow Grove used water piped to their houses from the Willow Grove Water District. But the people who lived in outlying areas, such as the new Shadow Hills neighborhood, and some of the farms still used groundwater from their own wells.

The maps on the next page show the town.

Carla called Willow Grove Water District where a public relations manager told her that the water district tested the water regularly and made sure it met all federal standards. He suggested that Carla do some research to find out the history behind why water companies were required to carefully follow these water quality standards. Then he told her that Willow Grove Water District drew its water from surface water in Willow Lake. Willow Lake once provided the water needed by some of the industries that operated in Willow Grove. Now many of these plants had closed, leaving deserted factory buildings. The water district cleaned up the lake 30 years ago, and the town built a park and walking path along part of the lake.

Concerns About Willow Grove's Water

People in Willow Grove were concerned, however, because the Acme Metals Company in Metroville was expanding. This company used a lot of water, and returned its wastewater to the Fenton River only 30 miles up the river from Willow Grove. The Fenton River flowed from the hills in the west to the east through Willow Grove. Acme Metals said they had installed the latest water-treatment equipment to be sure the water they returned to the river would be clean and safe. Carla's grandparents were worried about

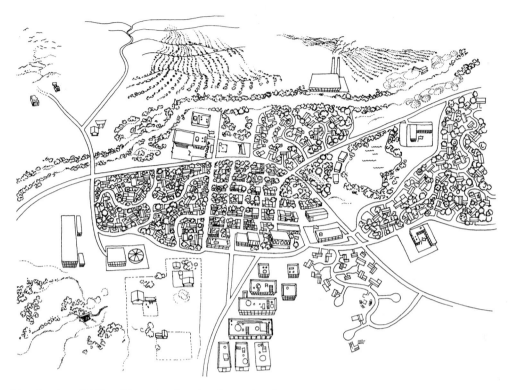

Line drawing of Willow Grove showing elevation and contour.

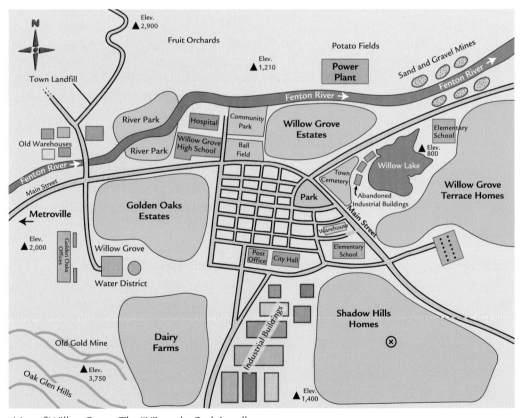

Map of Willow Grove. The "X" marks Carla's well.

whether the company's current water-treatment process could handle the expansion, and if it would pollute the river water with metal and acid wastes.

Then they became worried about the lake too. Last week Carla took her dog for a walk near the lake. Her dog loved to run around the lake and drink the lake water. While walking, Carla noticed a funny smell in one part of the lake. She took her grandfather with her the next day, and he thought it smelled strange too. A few days later, her dog got really sick.

Carla and her family and others in their neighborhood were deciding whether to join Willow Grove Water District. They all worried that their well might be contaminated. They decided to find out as much as they could about the water supply in Willow Grove. Until they felt sure their water was safe, they decided to drink bottled water.

ANALYSIS

1. How could the river or lake water in Willow Grove have become contaminated?

2. Is there any scientific evidence that the river or lake water in Willow Grove was contaminated?

3. What kind of scientific evidence do you think would help Carla and her family decide if the water were safe?

4. If you lived in Willow Grove, would you be worried? Explain.

5. Do you have any concerns about the water in your own community? If yes, explain what your concerns are.

EXTENSION

Do some research to find out about your source of drinking water. You can start by researching the website of your local water district or looking at information on a water bill from the water utility in your area.

*C*arla followed the public relations manager's suggestion to do some research on the history of water quality. She went to the library and found some information on cholera (KA-le-rah) deaths during an outbreak in London, England in 1849. She knew from her history class that 19th century households did not have indoor plumbing. This meant they had to carry their water for drinking, cooking, and washing from a community pump that may have been several blocks away. She also knew that people were concerned about diseases such as tuberculosis, pneumonia, and cholera. If you caught one of these, you would likely die. She decided to find out more about the cholera outbreak in London.

CHALLENGE

How can you use data to make hypotheses about the reason for cholera deaths in London in 1849?

MATERIALS

For each pair of students
1   Student Sheet 32.1, "London Street Map"
    colored pencils
    tape

Cholera spread rapidly through England in 1832 and 1849.

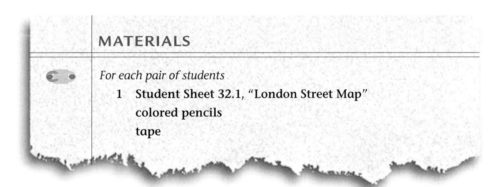

READING

London in 1832

The following is an abridged account of Dr. W. B. O'Shaughnessy's observations of a cholera victim in 1832:

Wanting to acquaint myself with the celebrated cholera, I traveled down to [London] from Edinburgh, prepared, yet unprepared, dear sirs. I saw a face, a girl I never can forget, even were I to live beyond man's natural age.

The girl lay . . . in a low-ceilinged room. I bent to examine her. The color of her skin—a silver blue, lead colored, ghastly tint; eyes sunk deep into deep sockets as though driven back or counter-sunk like nails, her eyelids black, mouth squared as if to bracket death; fingers bent, inky in their hue. Pulse all but gone at the wrist.

This is another description of cholera, based on outbreaks in the United States:

It [is] not easy for survivors to forget a cholera epidemic . . . The onset of cholera is marked by diarrhea, acute spasmodic vomiting, and painful cramps. Consequent dehydration [the victim can lose up to five gallons of liquid in 24 hours], often accompanied by cyanosis [the body turns blue], gives the sufferer a characteristic and disquieting appearance: his face blue and pinched, his extremities cold and darkened, the skin of his hands and feet drawn and puckered . . . Death may intervene within a day, sometimes within a few hours of the appearance of the first symptoms. And these symptoms appear with little or no warning.

(From Charles E. Rosenberg, *The Cholera Years: The United States in 1832, 1849, and 1866.* Chicago: University of Chicago Press, 1962)

In 1849, another outbreak of cholera killed more than 2,200 people—rich and poor, young and old—in just one area of south London. John Snow, a doctor in England, thought that by checking the city's death records and mapping exactly where people were living when they died, he might find some clues about what was causing the disease.

PROCEDURE

1. With your partner, use the list of cholera deaths on the next page to plot the locations of the victims' homes on Student Sheet 32.1, "London Street Map."

2. Use a colored pencil to put a small dot at the approximate address for each death.

3. If there is more than one death at the same location, put the other dots as close as possible to each other. The grid location number will help you find the street addresses.

ANALYSIS

1. Where are the deaths? Are they scattered throughout the area shown on the map, or are they bunched in particular city blocks?

2. Look at information that you know about the victims, such as their ages and occupations. Are there any similarities among the victims?

3. Look carefully at the map. Are there any clues about the cause of the disease?

4. Based on the evidence of deaths shown on the map, state two or three hypotheses that might explain how the disease is spread.

EXTENSION

Visit the *Issues and Physical Science* page on the SEPUP website for more information about cholera and its causes, including the bacteria *Vibrio cholerae*.

Date	Name	Age	Sex	Occupation	Address	Grid
	Deaths from Cholera in London in 1849					
13 Feb	Anne Kelly	3	F	child	156 Broad St., between Marshall & Little Windmill Streets	E-5
23 Feb	Edwin Drummond	48	M	steeplejack	54 Little Windmill St., between Broad & Silver Sts	E-5
18 Mar	Patty Orford	23	F	seamstress	160 Broad St., near corner of Little Windmill St.	E-5
20 Mar	Sue Burton	22	F	seamstress	16 Queen St., near the corner of Little Windmill St.	H-3
27 Mar	Patrick Kelly	39	M	banker	156 Broad St., between Marshall & Little Windmill Streets	E-5
28 Mar	John Kelly	8	M	child	156 Broad St., between Marshall & Little Windmill Streets	E-5
3 Apr	Mary Thornley	45	F	governess	300 Marshall St., between Broad & Silver Streets	E-6
9 Apr	Thomas Topham, Jr.	19	M	butcher	8 New St., across from the brewery	E-4
9 Apr	William O'Toole	41	M	indigent	Poland Street Work House	D-6
13 Apr	Margaret Kelly	37	F	housewife	156 Broad St., between Marshall & Little Windmill Streets	E-5
21 Apr	Richard Raleigh	13	M	student	173 Broad St., between Poland & Marshall Streets	D-5
24 Apr	Katherine Nelson	1	F	child	426 Wardour St., next to the Brewery Yard	D-3
25 Apr	Russ Rufer	30	M	steeplejack	54 Little Windmill St., between Broad & Silver Sts.	E-5
29 Apr	Sarah Kelly	3	F	child	156 Broad St., between Marshall & Little Windmill Streets	E-5
1 May	Sir John Page	55	M	magistrate	255 Broad St., between Berwick & Poland Streets	D-4
2 May	Ann Nelson	19	F	housewife	426 Wardour St., next to the Brewery Yard	D-3
3 May	Agatha Summerhill	26	F	writer	174 Broad St., between New & Little Windmill Sts.	E-5
11 May	Barney Brownbill	31	M	indigent	Poland Street Work House	C-5
11 May	Rose Thornley	53	F	maid	300 Marshall St., between Broad & Silver Streets	E-6
17 May	Winnifred Topham	17	F	factory worker	2 Peter St., at the end	F-4
21 May	Thomas Topham	38	M	butcher	2 Peter St., at the end	F-4
22 May	Winston Page	49	M	doctor	1000 Regent St., near the corner of Hanover St.	D-9
27 May	Neville West	6	M	child	19 Golden Square	G-6
27 May	Beatrice Braxley	23	F	housewife	253 Broad St., between Berwick & Poland Streets	D-4
27 May	Eleanor Raleigh	12	F	student	173 Broad St., between Poland & Marshall Streets	D-5

TALKING IT OVER

In the last activity you mapped the cholera deaths in London in 1849 and made some hypotheses that might explain how the disease had spread. This is just what Dr. Snow did, and it led him to propose that cholera was being carried in the water. He then set out to prove his hypothesis.

CHALLENGE

What kinds of evidence would help Dr. Snow prove his hypothesis on how cholera spreads?

A tavern in London, named for John Snow, a doctor who hypothesized about the reasons why cholera spread in London.

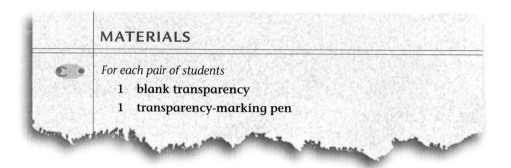

MATERIALS

For each pair of students
1 blank transparency
1 transparency-marking pen

PROCEDURE

1. Read the following background on cholera in London and Dr. Snow's hypothesis.

2. With your partner, read the letters representing written communication between Dr. John Snow and Dr. Joseph Whiting.

3. Work with your partner to answer Analysis Questions 1 and 2 to decide if the data sent to Dr. Snow by Dr. Whiting supports Dr. Snow's hypothesis about the cause of the cholera deaths.

4. With your partner, organize the information from Analysis Questions 1 and 2 on the blank transparency. Be prepared to explain your transparency to the class.

5. After the presentations, complete Analysis Question 3 as directed by your teacher.

READING

Dr. Snow's Hypothesis

Cholera is a disease that causes severe diarrhea and vomiting. In India, cholera has been a health problem since 400 B.C., but it was not well known outside the Far East before 1800. In 1819, however, there were epidemics in Europe and North America. Gradually, the cholera would disappear—only to reappear suddenly in the same or a different place. An ill person might die within a day, sometimes within a few hours of the appearance of symptoms. Even more baffling, some people would get cholera, while others living nearby

Dr. John Snow

would not get sick. Bad air or piled-up trash was often considered to be the cause of cholera.

Investigating the 1849 outbreak in London, Dr. Snow discovered that the majority of deaths occurred mostly in houses located near a certain public water pump in the southern part of the city. Lots of people liked to drink from this pump because of the taste and clearness of its water. Some of the deaths were reported in houses farther away and did not immediately fit the pattern. After studying all of his data, Dr. Snow suggested that cholera was spread in the water supply by invisible bits of human waste from cholera victims.

Dr. Snow was concerned that his mapping of cholera cases in 1849 was not sufficient evidence to prove his hypothesis concerning cholera in the water supply. He tested his hypothesis by carefully reviewing the public records for the 20 years before the cholera outbreak. He discovered that since 1839, about 300,000 people in one area of South London were served by just two water companies, the Lambeth Water Company and the Southwark and Vauxhall (S&V) Water Company. Originally both companies got their water from the Thames River in London. In 1852, the Lambeth Water Company changed its source of Thames water to a section of the river 10 miles upstream because the river water in London contained raw sewage. The other company, S&V, continued to get its water from within London.

When cholera struck again in 1854, Snow reviewed the records for the area served by the two water companies. He asked Dr. John Joseph Whiting to help him gather more evidence related to the water sources for the city of London. He wanted to provide more proof for his hypothesis.

Dr. Snow and Dr. Whiting exchanged their data in letters they wrote to each other. The information that they had painstakingly collected required careful organization before they could infer the cause of cholera. The fictional letters that follow are based on the doctors' correspondence at the time and the evidence they discussed in their actual letters.

FUN.—August 18, 1866.

DEATH'S DISPENSARY.

OPEN TO THE POOR, GRATIS, BY PERMISSION OF THE PARISH.

Cholera was spread through London in contaminated drinking water.

17 August 1854
John Joseph Whiting, M.D.
47 Waterloo Road
London, England

Dear Dr. Whiting,

As you are aware, the dreaded cholera has once again revisited our city. I have a great interest in showing the powerful influence which invisible bits of human waste in the drinking water have on the spread of cholera. The recent outbreak has provided me with the opportunity to test my theories on the grandest scale. The S&V Water Company will not give me data, and so it will be necessary to collect it by going to each house. I am desirous of making the investigation myself, but I feel that I am in need of your assistance in this experiment. My current research includes the following results:

~ *The area of the present outbreak is served by two water companies, S&V and Lambeth.*

~ *Each of the companies supplies both rich and poor; large and small houses; people of both sexes, all ages, all occupations, and every rank and station.*

~ *Two years ago, the Lambeth Water Company moved its water intake pipe upstream from London's sewage-infested water. I am investigating whether this move is related to a decrease in the number of cholera cases. If so, it would support my idea that cholera is spread by human waste in the water.*

To provide evidence for the support of my theories, I need to learn the water supply of each individual house where the fatal attack of cholera occurred. Would you please collect the numbers of deaths that occurred at houses supplied by the S&V Water Company?

If you are agreeable, I will send you the numbers that I have already collected from houses served by the Lambeth Water Company.

Sincerely, your friend,

John Snow, M.D.

30 April 1855
Dr. John Snow, M.D.
18 Sackville Street
London, England

Dear John,

The inquiries that you requested of me were carried out with a good deal of trouble. Many hours were needed to collect the data, as I had to go door to door.

The analysis of my inquiries should leave no doubt as to the correctness of your hypothesis concerning the progress of cholera. I have combined our data and report it to you as follows:

~ S&V Water Company supplied 40,046 houses in which there were 4,093 deaths in 14 weeks.

~ Lambeth Water Company supplied 26,107 houses in which there were 461 deaths in those 14 weeks.

~ The 256,423 houses in the rest of London are served by other water companies and experienced 4,800 deaths.

It has been a pleasure for me to be able to assist you in this experiment of great importance to the community of London.

Sincerely, Your friend,

John Joseph Whiting

Cryptosporidium and *Giardia* are two other types of biological contamination that cause intestinal illness. *Cryptosporidium* is a type of bacteria found in cattle manure along with *E. coli. Cryptosporidium* is a problem because it is difficult to kill with chlorine chemicals. *Giardia,* a tiny parasite, lives naturally in water sources such as rivers and lakes. Most people get sick from *Giardia* by drinking untreated water or water that has not been filtered. This is why it is recommended that you filter your water if you drink from a river or lake while hiking or camping.

STOPPING TO THINK 1

What are the main types of biological contamination, and what are their sources?

Biological Contamination Today

Today, outbreaks of disease from biological contamination still happen. *E coli* contamination is one of the biggest concerns of such U.S. government agencies as the Environmental Protection Agency (EPA) and the Food and Drug Administration (FDA) because outbreaks continue to occur in the United States periodically. Newspaper articles about some recent outbreaks due to biological contamination are represented in the headlines below.

The Daily Tribune
April, 1993
Intestinal Illness Linked to Milwaukee's Water

Metro Times
December, 2011
Illness Linked to Lettuce

Evening Chronicle
November, 1996
Juice Implicated in Death of Infant

The Weekly Gazette
September, 2006
Killer Bacteria Hunted in Spinach Fields

Oil and gas leaking from vehicles onto the road can be washed with rain down the storm drain and into surface water.

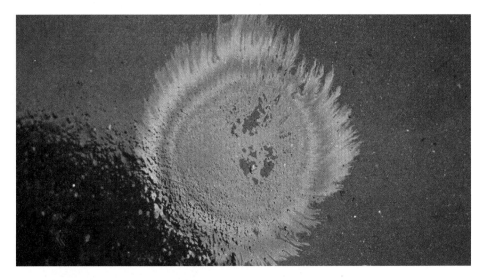

Chemical Contamination

Chemical substances such as fertilizers, gasoline, oil, heavy metals, and acids cause **chemical contamination.** They can enter water supplies from a variety of human activities.

Homeowners and farmers often use fertilizers and chemicals to kill weeds and pests. These chemicals may contaminate the water supply if they mix with rainwater or irrigation water. Some fertilizers contain chemicals that can cause serious health problems and even death if they enter the drinking water supply.

Water pollution caused by vehicles is a big problem. When it rains, oil, gas, and antifreeze that leak from cars are washed from driveways, roads, and parking lots into storm sewers. Gas can also spill onto the pavement from the pump hose at the gas station. To prevent this problem, many filling stations have installed special guards in the gas hose nozzles to keep gas from spilling onto the pavement.

Another major type of chemical contaminant is a group of metals called heavy metals. Heavy metals include copper, lead, silver, and mercury. Heavy metals are part of the natural environment and are found in the soil. In addition to being a part of the natural environment, heavy metal wastes are produced from human activities such as manufacturing, water delivery, and mining.

Chemical, iron, steel, and copper factories produce heavy metal waste. For example, a copper pipe company that makes copper water pipes for houses and businesses produces toxic copper waste. That waste must be disposed of properly so that it does not get into the water supply outside of the plant.

The copper water pipes themselves can also be a source of contaminants in the water. If the copper pipes corrode over time from a chemical reaction between the pipes and the water, copper can get into the water supply.

Industries produce chemical waste during the processing of their products.

Short periods of exposure to copper cause nausea and vomiting. Longer periods of exposure can lead to kidney and liver damage. Lead pipes were used for water service and plumbing in houses and buildings built before 1986. After people learned more about the dangers of exposure to lead in the 1980s, the EPA worked hard to enforce laws to reduce lead in the water from lead pipes.

Over the past two centuries the mining industry has developed various techniques to extract valuable materials, such as coal, silver, and diamonds, from the earth. Many abandoned mines have materials in or around them that contain waste metals and acids left from the mining process. Rain can wash these chemical contaminants into streams and rivers.

STOPPING TO THINK 2

What are some of the ways chemical contamination can get into the water supply?

Contamination and the Environment

Whether biological or chemical, water pollution can harm the environment, make people sick, and even threaten life. Water pollution can cause big problems quickly because water travels easily and is hard to contain. For example, if oil gets washed down a gutter with storm water, it runs to a storm sewer that leads to a river, stream, or lake, which can be many miles away from where the oil was spilled. The oil can harm the fish and wildlife that live in the lake, as well as people who use the lake for recreation or drinking water.

....

STOPPING TO THINK 3

What is it about water that makes water contamination such a big concern?

....

Since water is essential for life and needed for so many different purposes, we must keep it clean. Government agencies, such as the EPA, spend a lot of time and money checking water supplies. They also establish policies to keep water safe. Farms, industries, and companies now are required to follow guidelines for using water responsibly and preventing water pollution. If the water does get contaminated, however, it is important to figure out what and where the contamination is in order to clean it up as safely and quickly as possible. This requires knowledge of the properties of water, the types of water contamination, how to detect the contamination, and the technology used to clean it. You will learn about these topics throughout this unit.

ANALYSIS

1. Based on the information from the reading, determine which type of contamination, biological or chemical, is present in the following scenarios. Explain.

   a. Thousands of cars travel on city roads every day. The tires rub against the road and leave behind small flakes of rubber. When the brakes are used, tiny amounts of copper flake off. Eventually the rubber and copper get washed into streams and rivers.

   b. You wash your car with soap in the driveway. Soapy water drains down the gutter and into the storm drain, and eventually runs into a river, lake, or bay.

   c. Scientists discovered that droppings from seagulls in a restored salt marsh were spreading to shallow ocean waters near a beach. Officials closed the beach to swimming because the bacterial contamination was thousands of times higher than the limit that people could safely be exposed to.

2. Explain how water contaminated from a mine could end up in the ocean 100 miles away.

3. Make a list of things you do every day that require clean and safe water.

4. **Reflection:** Write about some things you and your family regularly do that could threaten the water supply.

EXTENSION

Research the water pollution problems that have occurred recently in your local area. Classify them as either biological or chemical contamination. Start at the EPA website, **www.epa.gov.**

LABORATORY

You probably take water for granted most of the time, maybe because it is so familiar in your daily life. It covers more than 70% of the earth's surface, and more than 60% of your body is water! Salts, sugars, and other substances you need for living and growing are dissolved in the water in your body. But water is not the only liquid familiar to you. Cleaning solutions, cooking oil, and gasoline are some other liquids you encounter routinely.

Water has surprisingly unique properties when compared to other liquids. For one thing, water is the only substance commonly found on earth in three forms—solid, liquid, and gas. These three forms are called **phases** of matter. Solid water is called ice, and water in the gas phase is called water **vapor**, or steam. The differences between the solid, liquid, and gas phases depend on the arrangement and movement of the water molecules, as shown in the diagram below.

CHALLENGE ⟹ **How can physical properties help you identify substances?**

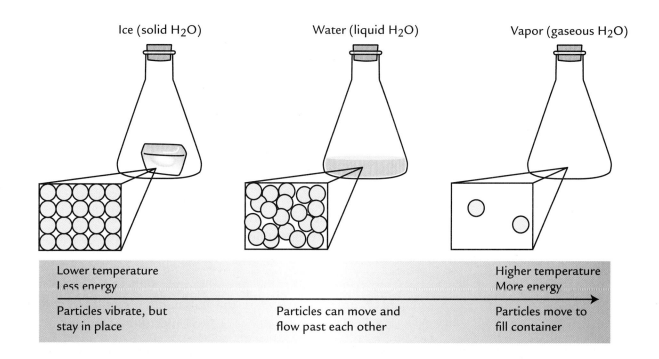

Ice (solid H_2O)   Water (liquid H_2O)   Vapor (gaseous H_2O)

Lower temperature
Less energy

Higher temperature
More energy

| Particles vibrate, but stay in place | Particles can move and flow past each other | Particles move to fill container |

MATERIALS

For the class

    supply of paper towels

For each group of four students

  1 balance
  1 capped vial of "Liquid A"
  1 capped vial of "Liquid B"
  1 dropper bottle of "Liquid A"
  1 dropper bottle of "Liquid B"

For each pair of students

  1 glass slide
  1 10-mL graduated cylinder
  1 piece of plastic wrap or Parafilm

For each student

  1 Student Sheet 35.1, "Comparing Physical Properties of Liquids"
  1 pair of safety goggles

⚠ SAFETY

In this activity, you will be allowed to touch the liquids. Never touch chemicals unless specifically told that it is safe to do so. Wear safety eyewear, and do not taste or drink the chemicals. Follow all classroom safety rules. Wash your hands when you finish.

PROCEDURE

Part A: Observing and Predicting

1. Working with your partner, visually examine the vials of each liquid. Record your observations in the row labeled Appearance in Data Table 1, "Observations of Two Unidentified Liquids," on Student Sheet 35.1, "Comparing Physical Properties of Liquids."

2. Open the vials carefully. Breathe normally, and gently wave the air above each liquid toward your nose. Close the vials tightly. Record your observations in Data Table 1, "Observations of Two Unidentified Liquids."

3. From the dropper bottles place a drop or two of each liquid on your finger. Rub it between your finger and thumb, and record your observations in Data Table 1.

4. Place a drop of each liquid on a piece of plastic wrap. Do not let the drops mix or touch each other. With a stir stick, see if you can stir or move each of the drops. Record your observations.

5. Place a drop of each liquid on the glass slide. Do not let the drops touch each other. Observe as the drops evaporate, and record your observations.

6. By now, you might have some ideas about the identities of the two liquids. Record your ideas in Data Table 1, "Observations of Two Unidentified Liquids."

Part B: Taking Measurements

Be sure to record the number of and kind of unit for all measurements you take in Procedure Steps 7–9.

7. You will determine the density of each of the liquids. Decide which pair in your group of four will work with Liquid A and which will work with Liquid B.

    a. Weigh the 10-mL graduated cylinder, and record the mass of the cylinder in grams.

    b. Your teacher will tell your group what volume of liquid to work with. With your partner, from the dropper bottle put approximately this volume of your assigned liquid into the graduated cylinder. Measure the actual volume you put in the cylinder, and record it in Data Table 2, "Our Group's Density Calculations," on Student Sheet 35.1.

    c. Weigh the cylinder containing the liquid, and record its mass in grams in Data Table 2, "Our Group's Density Calculations."

    d. Calculate the mass of the sample of liquid itself, and record it in Data Table 2, "Our Group's Density Calculations."
    Hint: You know the mass of the empty cylinder and the mass of the cylinder plus the liquid.

    e. Record in Data Table 2, "Our Group's Density Calculations," the data the other pair in your group collected for the volume and mass of the other liquid.

    f. Calculate the densities of both liquids, and record them in Data Table 2, "Our Group's Density Calculations."

    Hint: Recall from Unit A, "Studying Materials Scientifically," that density is the ratio of mass to volume of a substance:

$$\text{Density (d)} = \frac{\text{mass (m)}}{\text{volume (v)}}$$

8. Observe the boiling samples prepared by your teacher. Record in Data Table 1, "Observations of Two Unidentified Liquids," the temperature of each liquid as it boils. Remember to record both the number and the units.

9. Observe your teacher's demonstration of samples of Liquid A and Liquid B that were stored in the freezer. Record both qualitative and quantitative observations in Data Table 1, "Observations of Two Unidentified Liquids."

ANALYSIS

 1. Review the data table below.

Some Properties of Five Liquids					
	Water	**Methanol**	**Ethanol**	**Isopropanol**	**Acetone**
Appearance	Clear, colorless liquid	Clear, colorless liquid	Clear, colorless liquid	Clear, colorless liquid	Clear, colorless liquid
Smell	None	Yes	Yes	Yes	Yes
Shape of a drop on plastic	Round	Flat	Flat	Flat	Flat
Density (g/mL)	1.000	0.791	0.789	0.786	0.790
Boiling point (°C)	100	65	78	82	56
Melting point (°C)	0	−94	−117	−90	undefined

a. Based on your data and the table above, what could liquids A and B be?

b. Why do you think so?

c. How certain are you?

 2. In this activity you compared two liquids.

a. What properties and measurements were the most helpful in identifying the two liquids?

b. Explain your answer.

 3. A liquid forms rounded droplets because of its degree of cohesiveness.

a. Which of the two liquids was more cohesive?

b. Explain the observations that support your answer.

4. Why should you keep liquid samples capped or covered while studying them?

5. Which do you predict would evaporate more quickly at room temperature: methanol or acetone? (Refer to the data in the table.) Explain why.

6. Copy the lists of words below. Then, for each list, follow steps a, b, and c.

List 1	List 2	List 3	List 4
liquid	density	odor	property
solid	boiling point	feel	cohesive
gas	quantitative property	color	liquid
cohesive	color	temperature	comparison
phase	melting point	qualitative property	clear

   a. Look for a relationship among the words in List 1. Cross out the word or phase that does not belong.

   b. In List 1 circle the word or phrase that includes the other three.

   c. Explain how the word or phrase you circled is related to the others.

   d. Repeat steps a–c for each of the remaining lists.

MODELING

In the last activity, you compared the properties of water and a common alcohol. Why do these two substances have some properties in common, while other properties are different?

To answer this question, you will learn about the smallest particles that make up water and alcohol. Imagine dividing a large raindrop into smaller and smaller drops. The tiniest bit of a drop that would still be water is called a **molecule** (MALL-ih-kyool). Molecules are extremely small. Even a tiny drop of water contains billions of billions of molecules! These molecules are made of **atoms**, which are even tinier than molecules. In this activity, you will build and examine models of several types of molecule, including a molecule of water.

CHALLENGE

What are the similarities and differences between molecules of water and molecules of alcohol?

Though it can be solid, liquid, or gas, water is always made of the same kind of molecule—H_2O.

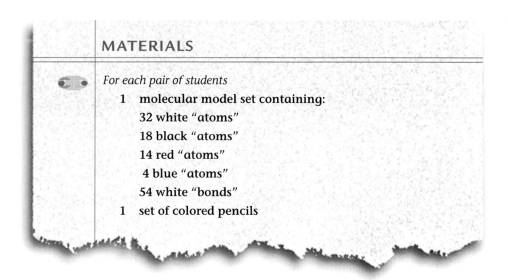

MATERIALS

For each pair of students

1 molecular model set containing:
    32 white "atoms"
    18 black "atoms"
    14 red "atoms"
     4 blue "atoms"
    54 white "bonds"
1 set of colored pencils

Color of Atom	Element	Symbol
⬜	hydrogen	H
⬛	carbon	C
⬛	oxygen	O
⬛	nitrogen	N

PROCEDURE

Part A: Making Simple Molecules

1. With your partner, look at the various pieces in your modeling kit. The colored balls represent atoms of specific elements, as shown in the table above. Each "stick" on an atom represents a bonding site, where the atom can bond with another atom. Each white tube represents a bond that can hold atoms in a molecule together.

2. Discuss with your partner any differences (besides color) you see among the plastic balls.

3. Hydrogen is an element, so it contains only one kind of atom— hydrogen atoms. However, in nature, two hydrogen atoms bond together to make hydrogen molecules and we always find hydrogen in molecular form. Hydrogen, a flammable gas, is composed of these hydrogen molecules.

    a. Use two hydrogen atoms to make a model of hydrogen molecule. Be sure to use a white bond to connect the stick on one hydrogen atom to another.

    b. H_2 is the **chemical formula** for this molecule. In your science notebook, draw a diagram of your model, and label the atoms in it.

4. Oxygen gas makes up 21% of the air you breathe. This oxygen gas is also composed of molecules that contain two atoms.

   a. Use two oxygen atoms to make a model of an oxygen molecule. Hint: When you make a molecule, all bonding sites (sticks) on each atom should be attached with bonding tubes to the sticks on another atom.

   b. What do you think would be the formula for this molecule?

   c. Draw and label a diagram of your model of an oxygen molecule.

5. Nitrogen gas makes up 78% of the air you breathe. It is also composed of molecules that contain two atoms.

   a. Use two nitrogen atoms to make a model of a nitrogen molecule. Hint: When you make a molecule, all bonding sites (sticks) on each atom should be attached with bonding tubes to the sticks on another atom.

   b. What would be the formula for this molecule?

   c. Draw and label your model of a nitrogen molecule.

Part B: Building More Molecules

6. Carbon, hydrogen, oxygen, and nitrogen are the most common elements found in living matter. Furthermore, C, H, and O are the *only* elements found in many important molecules, such as alcohols and sugars.

   Build models of water and two alcohols, methanol and ethanol. The chemical formula for each of these substances is in the table "Some Common Liquids" below.

Some Common Liquids	
Substance Name	**Chemical Formula**
Water	H_2O
Methanol	CH_3OH
Ethanol	C_2H_5OH

7. In your science notebook, write the name and chemical formula and draw a sketch of each molecule.

8. Refer to your models as you work on the Analysis Questions.

9. Take all of the molecules apart, and return all pieces to the set.

ANALYSIS

1. How many different elements were you working with?

2. What was the role of the "sticks" on each atom model?

3. Draw two atoms of hydrogen next to your sketch of a molecule of hydrogen gas (H_2). Label the two atoms of hydrogen with a chemical formula that you think is appropriate for them alone (when they are not bonded).

4. What does the 2 in the molecular formula H_2O stand for? Explain.

5. In this activity, you modeled ethanol, hydrogen, methanol, nitrogen, oxygen, and water. Why are oxygen gas, hydrogen gas, nitrogen gas, and carbon called **elements**, while water and ethanol are called **compounds**?

6. Methanol and ethanol are both alcohols.

    a. Compare: How are the molecules of methanol and ethanol similar?

    b. Contrast: How are the molecules of methanol and ethanol different?

7. a. Why is the formula for methanol usually written as CH_3OH instead of CH_4O?

    b. Looking at its structure, propose two ways other than C_2H_5OH to write the formula for ethanol. Describe the advantages and disadvantages of each.

8. Compare and contrast water with the two alcohols you modeled. How are they the same? How are they different?

9. a. What are the strengths of this modeling kit in helping you to understand what matter is made of?

    b. What do you consider to be the limitations of this modeling kit?

LABORATORY

You have learned that water contaminants may be either biological or chemical. If the contaminants are caused by humans and are harmful to humans or other organisms they are considered pollutants. In the next group of activities, you will investigate chemicals in water. Before learning how to make water clean, you will explore how chemicals can be hidden in water.

Have you ever mixed a spoonful of sugar into water or tea? The sugar seems to disappear as it mixes completely into the liquid. Scientists say that sugar **dissolves** in water, or that sugar is **soluble** (SAWL-yoo-bull) in water. Scientists would call water the **solvent** (SAWL-vent) and sugar the **solute** (SAWL-yoot). When a solute dissolves in a liquid like water, the resulting mixture is called a **solution**. In other words, a solution forms when a solute dissolves in a solvent. In this activity, you will investigate four solid substances as they mix with water.

CHALLENGE ⟹ **What makes a mixture of a solid and a liquid a solution?**

Sugar dissolves when it is mixed into tea.

MATERIALS

For each group of four students

1 vial each of:

   sodium chloride

   copper chloride

   cornstarch

   iron chloride

1 dropper bottle of water

1 SEPUP tray

For each pair of students

1 SEPUP funnel

2 filter papers

1 stir stick

1 dropper

1 magnifier

supply of paper towels

For each student

1 Student Sheet 37.1, "Observing and Comparing Substances and Solutions"

1 pair of safety goggles

SAFETY NOTE

Wear safety goggles at all times during this lab. Do not allow the solutions to touch your skin or clothing. Clean up any spills immediately. If accidental contact occurs, inform your teacher, and rinse exposed areas. Wash your hands after completing the activity.

PROCEDURE

Part A: Observing, Predicting, Mixing

1. Obtain your group's samples of four solids: sodium chloride, copper chloride, cornstarch, and iron chloride. Use the small scoop on the end of the stir stick to place 1 scoop of each solid on a paper towel.

2. With the magnifier examine each solid. Record your observations in Table 1, "Observing and Comparing Solids," on Student Sheet 37.1, "Observing and Comparing Substances and Solutions."

3. Record your predictions of whether each solid will dissolve in water in the Prediction column of Table 1, "Observing and Comparing Solids."

4. In the last column of Table 1, "Observing and Comparing Solids," describe any similarities and differences you see among the four solids.

5. Using Table 2, "Making and Comparing Mixtures," on Student Sheet 37.1, "Observing and Comparing Substances and Solutions," as a guide, add *level* scoops of each solid to the small cups in the SEPUP tray. Make sure you put the correct number of scoops in the correct cup.

6. Add 10 drops from the dropper bottle of water to each of Cups 1–8. Also add 10 drops of water to Cup 9.

7. Stir each cup for exactly one minute. Rinse and dry the stir stick before you begin stirring a new cup.

8. Let the cups sit undisturbed for two minutes. Record your observations of the contents of each cup.

Part B: Filtering the Mixtures

9. See if you can separate the solids from the liquids using a filter. One student pair should filter the sodium chloride and copper chloride in Cups 1 and 3. The other pair should filter the cornstarch and iron chloride in Cups 5 and 7.

10. Place your filter funnel over large Cups A and B in the SEPUP tray if you will be filtering the sodium chloride and the copper chloride, or over large Cups D and E if you will be filtering the cornstarch and iron chloride.

11. Follow your teacher's instructions on how to fold your filter papers, moisten them, and secure them in the filter funnels, as shown below.

  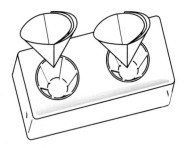

Step 1
Fold filter paper in half.

Step 2
Fold filter paper in half again.

Step 3
Open with three thicknesses of paper on one side of the cone and one thickness on the other.

Step 4
Place in funnel and add 3–5 drops of water from the dropper bottle to hold it in place.

12. When filtering, use the dropper to transfer as much of the liquid portion of the solution as you can; there is no need to transfer all of the undissolved solid (if there is any).

   a. If you are filtering the sodium chloride and copper chloride:

   • transfer the mixtures from Cups 1 and 2 to the filter above Cup A.

   • rinse the dropper, and transfer the mixtures from Cups 3 and 4 to the filter above Cup B.

   b. If you are filtering the cornstarch and iron chloride:

   • transfer the mixtures from Cups 5 and 6 to the filter above Cup D.

   • rinse the dropper, and transfer the mixture from Cup 7 to the filter above Cup E. Wait for all of the liquid to go through the filter, and observe. Then transfer the mixture from Cup 8 to the filter above Cup E.

13. Observe both the material trapped by the filter papers and the liquids that have dripped through the filter. Record your observations in Table 3, "Filtering Mixtures," on Student Sheet 37.1, "Observing and Comparing Substances and Solutions."

14. Remove the filter funnels, dispose of the used filter papers as directed by your teacher, and rinse the filter funnels and SEPUP tray.

ANALYSIS

1. In this investigation, which substance(s) are solutes and which are solvent(s)?

 2. A substance that dissolves in water can be described as soluble in water.

   a. List the four solids in order from most to least soluble in water.

   b. Explain what evidence enabled you to order the substances by solubility.

3. **a.** Must a mixture be clear to be a solution? Explain.

   b. Must a mixture be colorless to be a solution? Explain.

4. Imagine that all four of the tested solids are considered water pollutants. Which would be easiest to remove from the water? Explain your answer.

In Activity 37, "What Dissolves?" you learned that when you mix a substance into another and it dissolves completely, the result is called a solution. Liquid solutions are always clear, and so you can see through them. However, they may or may not have a color.

Some liquids are better solvents than others. Whether or not one substance dissolves in another depends on the chemical properties of both the solvent and the solute. Many of the substances that enter or leave your body are dissolved in water. Dissolved substances can be helpful or harmful, depending on their chemical nature.

CHALLENGE ➡ **Do substances dissolve better in water or in ethanol?**

One of these solutions in water is colorless, while the others are not. All of them are clear.

MATERIALS

For each group of four students

1   30-mL dropper bottle of water
1   30-mL dropper bottle of ethanol
1   vial each of:
     sugar
     sodium chloride
     iron chloride
     lauric acid
     copper sulfate
     neroline yara yara
     cornstarch

For each pair of students

1   SEPUP tray
1   stir stick
     supply of paper towels

For each student

1   pair of safety goggles
1   Literacy Student Sheet 1a, "Keeping a Science Notebook"

SAFETY

Wear safety goggles at all times during this lab. Do not allow the solutions to touch your skin or clothing. Clean up any spills immediately. If accidental contact occurs, inform your teacher, and rinse exposed areas. Wash your hands after completing the activity.

PROCEDURE

Part A: Predicting and Planning an Investigation

1. Look at the names of the substances to test, listed on the next page. In your science notebook:

   a. list the substances, and predict whether each substance will dissolve better in water or in ethanol.

   b. record your reason for each prediction.

> ### Substances to Test
>
> Cornstarch   Lauric acid
>
> Sugar   Copper sulfate
>
> Sodium chloride   Neroline yara yara
>
> Iron chloride

2. Use Literacy Student Sheet 1a, "Keeping a Science Notebook," and work in your group of four students to develop a purpose and a procedure that will give you evidence for answering the Challenge. Keep in mind that two SEPUP trays are available to your group and that you may work as two separate pairs of students for most of the activity, and then pool your results.

3. Be sure to include a data table that each of you will construct in your science notebooks for recording all of your group's results.

Part B: Conducting Your Investigation

4. After obtaining approval from your teacher for the purpose and procedure you developed, conduct the investigation, and record your observations.

5. Trade trays with the other team in your group, and record your observations of their mixtures in your data table.

6. Follow your teacher's directions for cleaning your trays.

ANALYSIS

1. Which solvent/solute pairs dissolved completely? What is your evidence?

2. a. Which solvent/solute pairs seemed not to dissolve at all? What is your evidence?

   b. In these cases how might you test to be sure you are correct that none of the solute dissolved?

3. Which solvent/solute pairs dissolved partially? What is your evidence?

4. Thinking back to Activity 37, "What Dissolves?" explain the connection between the terms "solubility" and "saturation."

5. In your science notebook, create a concept map for the following list of terms from this activity and Activity 37, "What Dissolves?" to summarize your understanding of a solution:

soluble

dissolve/dissolves

solute

solvent

saturated

solution

Follow these steps:

   a. Write the word "solution" in the middle of your paper, and circle it.

   b. Discuss with your group how the other words are related to the word "solution." Sort your words into categories based on these relationships.

   c. Decide on the first set of words you want to add to the concept map, and plan where to place these words on your paper. Then place the words, and circle them.

   d. Draw a line between the word "solution" and your first set of words. On the line, use brief phrases to describe the relationship between the words.

   e. Repeat steps c and d until you have added all of the words to your concept map.

 6. List at least two ways that water's ability to dissolve substances:

   a. can be helpful to people and other living organisms.

   b. can be harmful to people and other living organisms.

EXTENSION 1

If you did not filter your solutions during the investigation, pick those that you want to test to be certain that they are or are not solutions. Use only solutions of water, not alcohol because alcohol solutions are difficult to filter.

EXTENSION 2

Complete Student Sheet 38.2, "What's the Solution?"

MODELING

Imagine taking all of the water at the earth's surface and pouring it into a single container. About 97% of it would be saltwater from the oceans, seas, and salt lakes. The other 3% would be from all of the earth's freshwater, including water frozen in ice sheets, icebergs, groundwater, and water vapor in the air. The surface water in lakes, rivers, and streams makes up only 0.03%!

As you learned in Activity 35, "Mystery Liquids," water exists on the earth as a solid, liquid, or vapor. Water can also change from one of those forms to another. For example, you know that liquid water can turn to ice during **freezing**. Ice can turn back into liquid water during **melting**. During **evaporation**, water turns from a liquid into a vapor. During **condensation**, water turns from a vapor into a liquid. When the vapor in clouds condenses and falls to the earth, the water that falls is **precipitation**.

The **water cycle** is the path that water takes on the earth as it evaporates from surface water, condenses, precipitates, and returns to surface water and groundwater sources. The water cycle determines how water is distributed on earth.

In this activity you will follow and observe the changes in a molecule of water in a water droplet. Your observations will start when the molecule first collects with other molecules to form a droplet falling as precipitation. This is when water is naturally purest. As it travels, however, it can pick up contaminants.

CHALLENGE ➡ **How does water move from place to place and pick up contaminants as it moves?**

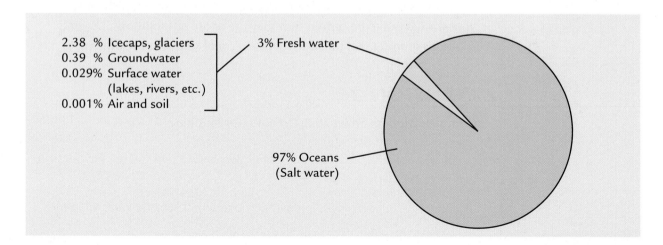

2.38 % Icecaps, glaciers
0.39 % Groundwater
0.029% Surface water (lakes, rivers, etc.)
0.001% Air and soil

3% Fresh water

97% Oceans (Salt water)

MATERIALS

For each pair of students

- 1 set of six Water Cycle Cards
- 1 white number cube
- 1 blue number cube
- colored pencils

For each student

- 1 Student Sheet 39.1, "Talking Drawing: Contaminants and the Water Cycle"
- 1 Student Sheet 39.2, "My Water Cycle Story"

PROCEDURE

Use Student Sheet 39.1, "Talking Drawing: Contaminants and the Water Cycle," to help prepare you for this activity.

1. With your partner, review the six Water Cycle Cards.

2. Your water travels will begin with the Precipitation Card.

3. Record the card title "Precipitation" in the card-title column on Student Sheet 39.2, "My Water Cycle Story."

4. With your partners, look at the Precipitation Card to see where your water molecules can be. Make a choice, and record it in the second column of Student Sheet 39.2, "My Water Cycle Story." In the third column, identify the state of your water (solid, liquid, or water vapor). Since the water is pure at this point, write "none" in the fourth column, which is about contaminants.

5. Roll the white number cube. Look for the number you rolled on the Water Cycle card to find out where your water will go next.

   Note: Water can cycle back to the same place, so you might not use all six cards. When you get to one you have had before, choose another form for the water.

6. Roll the blue number cube. Look for the number you rolled on the Water Cycle card to determine what type of contaminant the water picks up. Record the contaminant in the fourth column of Student Sheet 39.2, "My Water Cycle Story." If no contaminant was picked up, write "none" in the fourth column.

7. Repeat Procedure Steps 4–6 until you have completely filled in Student Sheet 39.2, "My Water Cycle Story."

8. Each row of Student Sheet 39.2 is one part of the story of your water molecules. With your partner:

Discuss where your water molecules are in each part of your story. Remember, your water first started as precipitation with almost no contaminants. If you are still having trouble, you may want to consult Student Sheet 39.3, "Story Ideas."

Describe what happened to your water molecules from one part of the story to the next. Be sure to explain what contaminants the water picked up and exactly how your molecules changed.

Hint: Did it move? If so, how? Or did something else happen, like a temperature change? Did it pick up contaminants? If so, which ones? From where?

9. Based on your discussion, complete the "how it happened" part of the fourth column and the last column of Student Sheet 39.2, "My Water Cycle Story."

ANALYSIS

1. On Student Sheet 39.1, "Talking Drawing: Contaminants and the Water Cycle," you recorded your initial ideas about the water cycle. Use a different colored pencil to complete that student sheet based on what you learned during the activity.

   a. Use the following words to identify where water can be found in the picture:

atmosphere	land
organisms	groundwater
ocean	precipitation

What parts of the water cycle do you see in this photograph, and how could the water get contaminated?

    b. Draw at least six arrows showing the movement of water from one place to another.

    c. On each of the six arrows you drew, write in one contaminant that could possibly be picked up by the water at that point. Label all of the places where contaminants are left behind and where the water is naturally purest.

    d. Label places where each of the following changes in state is occurring:

        condensation

        freezing

        melting

        evaporation

    e. What changes did you have to make to Student Sheet 39.1, "Talking Drawing: Contaminants and the Water Cycle," so that you would have a complete and correct drawing?

2. Explain why the water lost contaminants when it moved into the atmosphere.

3. At what points in the water cycle did the water molecules not pick up any contaminants? Explain why.

4. The term water cycle describes the movement of water on earth and in the earth's atmosphere. Do you think that your diagram on Student Sheet 39.1, "Talking Drawing: Contaminants and the Water Cycle," is a good summary of the water cycle? Why or why not?

5. In this activity you used cards and number cubes to model the water cycle and contaminants that water picks up. In what ways did this activity model the water cycle well? What parts of the water cycle did it not include?

6. Suppose you are a scientist trying to decrease water pollution or to clean up some polluted water. What information from the water cycle model might help you?

7. Expand your notes from Student Sheet 39.2, "My Water Cycle Story," into a story that describes the journey of your water molecules. Your story should follow your water through at least five places. Be as creative and scientifically accurate as you can. Be sure to:

Describe or draw how your water molecules moved from one place to another.

Identify any changes in state (solid, liquid, gas) that occur.

Describe any contaminants the water picks up as it travels and how the contaminants got there.

40 Parts Per Million

INVESTIGATION

In Activity 37, "What Dissolves?" you dissolved different amounts of several solids in 10 drops of water. The water was the solvent, and the dissolved solids were the solutes. Scientists describe the amount of a solute dissolved in a solvent as the **concentration** of a solution. The solution with five scoops of sodium chloride in it was more **concentrated** than the one with one scoop. The solution with one scoop of sodium chloride was more **dilute.** You are probably familiar with these words from using frozen juice concentrates: you start with concentrated orange juice, and dilute it with water before drinking it. The concentrated orange juice has less water, and more orange juice, than the diluted juice you drink.

Scientists don't use scoops and drops as a measure of the amount of solute and solvent in a solution. They use other kinds of measurements to express the concentration of a solution. In this activity you will investigate parts per million and parts per billion as ways scientists describe the concentration of very small amounts of a solute in a solvent, such as water. **Parts per million** and **parts per billion** describe the concentration of a substance, such as a solute, in one million or one billion parts of another substance. You will perform a serial dilution, which is the process of making a solution gradually more dilute.

CHALLENGE → **How much is one part per million of a solute, such as food coloring, and when is it a useful measurement tool?**

These cans of concentrated orange juice must be diluted with water before they are ready to drink. The orange juice in the cans is concentrated, while the orange juice in the pitcher after adding the water is dilute.

MATERIALS

For each group of four students
   1   dropper bottle of red food coloring (10% solution)

For each pair of students
   1   SEPUP tray
   1   dropper
   1   dropper bottle of water
   1   Student Sheet 40.1, "Serial Dilution Template"

⚠ SAFETY

Do not allow the food coloring to touch your skin or clothing because it will stain. Clean up any spills immediately.

PROCEDURE

1. Place Student Sheet 40.1, "Serial Dilution Template," under the SEPUP tray.

2. Fill large Cups A and B with water for washing the dropper.

3. Put 10 drops of 10% red food coloring into small Cup 1, and put one drop into small Cup 2, on the lower level of your SEPUP tray.

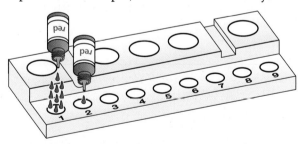

4. To Cup 2, add 9 drops of water. Mix the solution by drawing it up into the dropper. Then gently squeeze the bulb until the dropper is empty, carefully putting the liquid back into Cup 2.

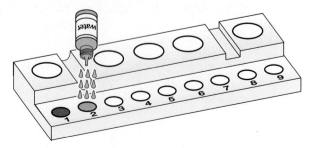

5. Rinse the dropper once in Cup A and then once in Cup B.

6. Using the dropper, transfer one drop of the solution in Cup 2 to Cup 3. Return any excess to Cup 2.

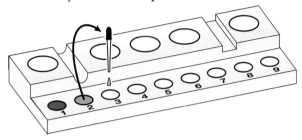

7. Add 9 drops of water to Cup 3. Use the dropper to mix the solution in Cup 3, and transfer one drop to Cup 4. Return any excess to Cup 3. Rinse your dropper as you did in Procedure Step 5.

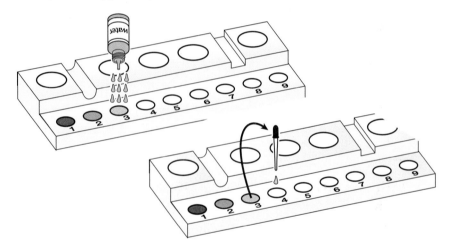

8. Add 9 drops of water to Cup 4. Mix. Transfer one drop to Cup 5. Add 9 drops of water to Cup 5. Mix. Rinse your dropper as you did in Procedure Step 5.

9. Continue this process through Cup 9, each time taking a drop of the solution from the previous cup and adding 9 drops of water. Rinse your dropper each time as you did in Procedure Step 5.

10. Record the color of the solution in each cup in a data table in your science notebook. A sample data table is shown on the next page.

11. Determine the concentration of the solution for each cup as a part of food coloring per total parts of solution, and record it in your data table.

Serial Dilution

Cup	Color	Concentration (parts of food coloring per parts of solution)	
		parts per ____ %	
1		1 part per 10 10%	
2		1 part per ____	
3		1 part per ____	
4			
5			
6			
7			
8			
9			

ANALYSIS

1. Which is more dilute, Cup 1 or Cup 2? How do you know this?

2. If Cup 1 has a concentration of one part in 10, and Cup 2 has $\frac{1}{10}$ the concentration of Cup 1, what is the concentration of Cup 2?

3. Which cup has a concentration of one part of food coloring per one million parts of solution?

4. What is the number of the cup in which the solution first appeared colorless? What is the concentration of the solution in this cup?

    Hint: Express the answer for concentration as 1 part per ____.

5. Do you think there is any of the food coloring in Cup 8, even though it appears colorless? Explain.

6. Explain how you could do an experiment to provide evidence to back up your answer to Analysis Question 5.

7. Describe something a scientist might study and report using parts per million as a measurement tool.

8. Assume someone told you that if your water looks clear and does not smell bad, it is safe to drink. Would you follow this advice? Why or why not?

EXTENSION 1

Mix one scoop of cinnamon with 9 scoops of salt in Cup 1 of a SEPUP tray. Continue to serially dilute the cinnamon with salt until you reach Cup 9. What do you observe? What happens to the particles of cinnamon compared to the salt?

EXTENSION 2

Calculate the percent, fraction, and ratio of cinnamon to salt in the mixture in each cup.

Hint: A data table may be a helpful way to organize your calculations.

EXTENSION 3

Pick one of the comparisons from Transparency 40.3, "Some Interesting Comparisons," and make a drawing or diagram of the comparison.

Federal Water Quality Standards

1. **APPEARANCE/TURBIDITY:** Water should be clear and free of any suspended materials.

2. **ODOR:** Odor should not exceed a threshold value of 3—noticeable but acceptable.

3. **pH:** A pH level between 6.5 and 8.5 is acceptable. pH is a measure of how acidic or basic a substance is. The federal water quality standards require testing for pH, because water with a high or low pH can be harmful to the environment, especially aquatic plants and animals. Such water can also corrode pipes and release harmful metals from the pipes into the drinking water supply.

4. **IRON:** Iron levels should not exceed 100 parts per billion (ppb). Levels over 300 ppb affect the appearance and taste of the water.

5. **NITRATE:** Nitrate levels should not exceed 10 ppm. Higher levels may cause serious problems in infants, including brain damage or death. Nitrates prevent the hemoglobin in the blood of infants and some sensitive adults from carrying enough oxygen through the body.

6. **COPPER:** Copper levels should not exceed 1.3 ppm. Short periods of exposure to levels over 1.3 ppm can cause nausea and vomiting. Longer periods of exposure over many years can cause kidney or liver damage.

Part A: Observing the Water

1. Test the turbidity of the three water samples from Willow Grove, using the distilled water provided for comparison. **Turbidity** is the presence of cloudiness in water caused by impurities. The impurities are suspended in the water, preventing light from going all the way through, and so the water appears cloudy. To determine turbidity, observe the water to see whether it is clear or if it is cloudy from the presence of particles suspended in it.

2. Test the odor of the three water samples from Willow Grove, using the distilled water provided for comparison.

Part B: Testing the pH

3. Put 10 drops of each water sample and 10 drops of distilled water into separate cups in the SEPUP tray.

4. Add one drop of universal indicator solution to the three water samples and the distilled water in the SEPUP tray. Use the chart below to find the pH of the sample. Rinse the tray.

Indicator Color Chart	
Color	**Approximate pH Range**
Red/red-orange	0–3
Orange	3–5
Pale orange/yellow	5–6.5
Yellow-green/green	6.5–8.5
Blue-green	8.5–10.5
Blue	10.5–14

Part C: Testing for Iron

5. Put 10 drops of each water sample and 10 drops of distilled water into separate cups in the SEPUP tray.

6. Add one drop of 0.1 M potassium thiocyanate to the three water samples and the distilled water in the SEPUP tray. Record the color of the solution in each cup.

7. Add one drop of hydrochloric acid to each cup, and record your observations.

8. A reddish orange color indicates the presence of iron. (Note: The smallest concentration of iron this test can detect is 500 ppm.) Rinse the tray.

Part D: Testing for Nitrates

9. Add 3 mL of one of the three water samples to the 20-mL graduated plastic tube (fill to the bottom small line).

10. Add 10 drops of 0.5 M hydrochloric acid solution.

11. With your stir stick, add two level scoops of nitrate indicator powder.

12. Replace the cap, and shake until the powder is completely dissolved. Wait one minute.

13. A purple color indicates the presence of nitrates.

    Hint: Compare to the control if you are not sure of the test result. (Light purple indicates low amounts of nitrates. Medium to dark purple is cause for concern.)

14. Repeat Procedure Steps 9–13 for the other two samples and for the distilled water. Rinse the tray.

Part E: Testing for Copper

15. Put 10 drops of each water sample and 10 drops of distilled water into separate cups in the SEPUP tray.

16. Add 5 drops of 5% ammonia to the three water samples and the distilled water in the SEPUP tray. If a light blue color appears, copper levels are over 2 ppb. Rinse the tray when finished.

ANALYSIS

1. Compare your results to other groups' results. Are they the same? Explain. Based on your comparison, are there any you would like to retest?

2. Prepare a full investigation report for the water testing according to the guidelines on Literacy Student Sheet 1b, "Writing a Formal Investigation Report." Write your report on a clean sheet of paper.

   The analysis section of your report should include the following parts about this investigation of water quality:

   a. a discussion of how all water samples compare to the federal standards.

   b. your ideas about what could have caused any contamination you found in the water.

   c. your ideas about treatment of any of the samples to make them more suitable for use.

   d. a summary of your recommendations to the town of Willow Grove as to whether each water sample is suitable for its current uses. Give reasons for your decision. Discuss any overall problems raised by your results and suggest how the community should respond to your findings.

EXTENSION

Research the possible effects of other chemicals, such as heavy metals, in the water supply.

LABORATORY

In the last activity, you tested water samples from three different sources in Willow Grove. Willow Lake, which supplies drinking water to 50% of Willow Grove residents, was turbid. Turbidity can be due to solid contaminants in the water. Two treatment methods used by most water districts to remove contaminants before piping water to homes are coagulation and filtration. You will investigate both of these methods in this activity.

Coagulation (co-AGG-you-LAY-shun) involves using chemicals to attract contaminants into large clumps. These clumps then settle to the bottom of the water tank. **Filtration** (fil-TRAY-shun) traps and separates solid contaminants from the water by making the water flow through filters.

CHALLENGE → **How are coagulation and filtration used to clean water?**

MATERIALS

For each group of four students
- 1 SEPUP tray
- 1 cup of dirty water
- 1 cup of clean water
- 1 container of alum (aluminum sulfate)
- 1 filtration tube filled with gravel, sand, and charcoal
- 1 tube holder
- 2 small plastic spoons
- 1 graduated cup
- 1 graduated cylinder

For each pair of students
- 2 square-bottomed vials with caps, labeled A and B
- 1 dropper

For each student
- 1 pair of safety goggles

Coagulation and filtration remove contaminants from dirty water.

SAFETY

Wear safety goggles at all times during this lab. Do not allow the solutions to touch your skin or clothing. Clean up any spills immediately. If accidental contact occurs, inform your teacher, and rinse exposed areas.

Be careful when handling the tubes in Part B. The contents are messy and can ruin your clothes. Be sure to carefully clean up any spills.

PROCEDURE

Part A: Coagulation with Alum

Work in pairs to conduct Part A.

1. In your science notebook, prepare a data table like the one below.

Water Coagulation Observations		
	Vial A	Vial B
Water before treatment		
Water after Procedure Step 5		
Water after 2 minutes		
Water after 5 minutes		

2. Use your dropper to fill each vial about half full of dirty water.

3. In your data table, record your observations of the water in each vial.

4. Use a small spoon to add one level spoonful of alum to the water in Vial B.

5. Tightly cap both vials, hold the caps on with your thumbs, and shake them five times. Then set them on the table, and record your observations.

6. Record your observations again after two minutes and after five minutes.

7. Use your dropper to carefully remove the partially clean liquid layer from Vial B. Place the liquid into the graduated cup. The other pair in your group of four will add their partially clean liquid to this cup, too.

8. Answer Analysis Questions 1 and 2.

Part B: Filtration

Work in groups of four to conduct Part B.

9. In your science notebook, prepare a data table like the one below to record your results.

Water Filtration Observations

	Clean Water	Partially Clean Water from Part A
Before filtering		
After filtering		

10. Obtain a filtration tube filled with gravel, sand, and charcoal.

11. Place 10 mL of clean water in large Cup A of a clean SEPUP tray.

12. Place 10 mL of the partially clean water from Part A into large Cup E of the SEPUP tray.

13. Observe and record the color and appearance of each kind of water in the "Before filtering" column of your data table.

14. Place the filtration tube and holder over Cup B of the SEPUP tray. Use the graduated cylinder to measure 10 mL of clean water. Gently pour the water into the tube. Wait a few minutes until all of the water has dripped into Cup B.

15. When there is no more water dripping from the tube, move the tube and holder over to Cup D of the SEPUP tray.

16. Use the graduated cylinder to measure 10 mL of the partially cleaned water that you saved from Part A. Gently pour the water into the tube. Wait a few minutes until all of the water has dripped into Cup D.

17. Observe and record the color of each filtered water sample in the "After filtering" row of your data table.

ANALYSIS

1. What was the purpose of the water in Vial A?

2. How well did the coagulation steps in Part A work to remove contaminants from the water? Be sure to explain how your observations support your answer.

3. What was the purpose of filtering some clean water in Part B?

4. How well did coagulation followed by filtration work to remove contaminants from the water? Be sure to explain how your observations support your answer.

5. What more would you want to know about your coagulated and filtered water sample before you would be willing to drink it?

READING

About 90% of Americans get their drinking water from publicly-owned community water systems. The Safe Drinking Water Act that Congress passed in 1974 regulates these public water systems and gives the EPA the authority to set limits on contaminants in drinking water. The EPA and its state partners enforce the regulations.

The other 10% of the population gets its water from private wells that serve fewer than 25 people. These wells tap into groundwater and are not required to meet the federal standards. Some states, however, set standards for these wells. Health officials recommend that wells be tested yearly, but the owners are responsible for the safety of their own water.

CHALLENGE

How do community water districts ensure that the water they provide is safe?

A municipal water treatment plant treats millions of gallons of water each day.

READING

When reading, answer the Stopping to Think questions in your mind. They can help you find out whether you understand the main ideas.

Protecting Water at the Source

The source of water for public drinking systems is either surface water or groundwater. Surface-water sources include rivers, lakes, and reservoirs. Groundwater is usually obtained by digging wells, but it sometimes flows to the surface in natural springs.

Protecting drinking water begins by protecting the water source from direct contamination. That means it is important to protect the lake, reservoir, or well that is the source of drinking water. But it also means protecting the entire area of land that drains water into the source. This area of land is called a watershed. For example, a number of community water districts, such as the one in St. Louis, Missouri, obtain water from the Mississippi River. The Mississippi River has a huge watershed, shown on the map below. Contaminants that enter the river at any point upstream of where a public water district draws its water can be present in that district's water.

STOPPING TO THINK 1

What are the main sources of drinking water?

MISSISSIPPI WATERSHED
REGIONS

Cleaning the Water at a Water-Treatment Plant

Before delivering water to homes, community water districts treat it at a facility called a water-treatment plant to remove contaminants. When water leaves the water-treatment plant, it must meet all required health standards.

Each community water district selects the methods of water treatment it needs to treat the contaminants found in its water source. A typical water-treatment process is shown below. The most common treatment processes are coagulation, filtration, and disinfection. You investigated some of these in Activity 42, "Water Purification."

THE WATER TREATMENT PROCESS

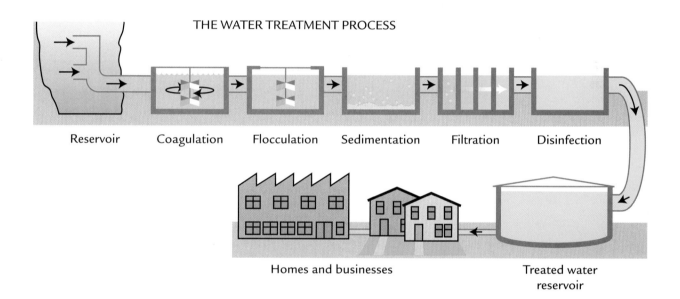

Reservoir   Coagulation   Flocculation   Sedimentation   Filtration   Disinfection

Homes and businesses

Treated water reservoir

Coagulation

Coagulation involves two steps: flocculation followed by sedimentation.

In **flocculation** (flock-you-LAY-shun) chemicals are put into the water to attract contaminants. Aluminum sulfate (alum) is one of several chemicals that are used for this purpose. The chemicals are stirred slowly into the water so that they will mix with and pull together the contaminants into large clumps.

Sedimentation involves letting the clumps formed by flocculation sink to the bottom of the water.

STOPPING TO THINK 2

a. Look back at Activity 42, "Water Purification." What steps of the activity corresponded to the flocculation process? Explain how these steps model flocculation.

b. What steps of the activity corresponded to the sedimentation process? Explain how these steps model sedimentation.

c. What word means the combination of flocculation and sedimentation?

Filtration

Filtration is a physical process that removes solid contaminants from the water. The filter can be made of any material that allows water to flow through it while it traps solids. In past activities, you have used paper filters. In water treatment plants, the filters are usually made of layers of sand, gravel, and charcoal. The solid contaminants are too large to pass through the spaces between the pieces of sand, gravel, or charcoal. A tank where water is filtered is shown in the diagram on the previous page. Some filtration systems use a form of charcoal called activated charcoal, which can attract and hold some contaminants on the surface of its particles.

STOPPING TO THINK 3

What steps of Activity 42, "Water Purification," corresponded to the filtration process?

Disinfection

In **disinfection** substances called disinfectants are added to the water to kill biological contaminants, like bacteria and viruses. The most common disinfectants are compounds that contain chlorine. When chlorine is the disinfectant, the process is called **chlorination**. As you learned in Activity 34, "Water Pollution," chlorination has almost wiped out several diseases, such as cholera and typhoid, that once killed thousands of people at a time. After disinfection, the chlorine level of the water is reduced to a lower level before the water is piped to customers. Chlorination is one of the major public health advances of the past one hundred years.

Fluoridation

After treating the water to remove contaminants, many public water plants add fluoride to water before delivering it to their customers. Fluoride is added because it greatly reduces tooth decay and prevents cavities.

Storing and Delivering the Water

The treated water is stored in closed tanks or reservoirs. Underground pipes carry the water to homes and businesses. Large water systems may contain thousands of miles of pipes and serve millions of people.

....

STOPPING TO THINK 4

    a. What is the purpose of adding fluoride to water?

    b. Why do you think water plants leave some chlorine in the water that they pipe to customers?

....

ANALYSIS

1. What do you know about the source of your community's drinking water?

2. Do you think there are other communities that might contribute contaminants to your water source or get their water from the same source?

3. Look at the map below, and find the Great Lakes. Why do you think the United States and Canada cooperate to keep the Great Lakes clean?

4. The reading describes two chemicals that are used to remove contaminants from drinking water. What are these chemicals, and what is the purpose of each one?

5. Which water source would you expect to be more likely to become contaminated by pesticides—surface water or groundwater? Explain why you think that.

6. **Reflection:** Based on what you have learned about the water cycle and your water source, what kinds of contaminants are you concerned about?

EXTENSION

Visit the *Issues and Physical Science* page of the SEPUP website for links to sites that will help you find out the source of your tap water, and investigate how the water is treated before it is delivered to your home.

Carla went to the Willow Grove Water District to find out about her town's drinking water supply. The water district gave her a copy of its most recent annual water quality report. She learned that the report covered both biological and chemical contaminants. As she read the report, Carla found she had many questions about the kinds of contaminants.

CHALLENGE

What does the town's water quality report say about the safety of Willow Grove's drinking water?

PROCEDURE

You will be recording information from this activity on Student Sheet 31.1, "KWL: Willow Grove's Water Quality," from Activity 31, "Willow Grove's Troubled Waters."

1. Review what you have written on your Student Sheet 31.1, "KWL: Willow Grove's Water Quality." Think about what you have learned about Willow Grove's water since you last wrote on the KWL. You may want to refer back to Activity 41, "Testing Water Quality," and review that information. Fill in what you think are the most important ideas to know from those activities in the Know column. Write down anything that you still want to know about Willow Grove's water in the Want to Know column.

2. Read the Willow Grove water quality report. As you read, think about the information and evidence in the report. After you read each section, discuss what you have learned with your group. Write down important points in the Learned column on your KWL.

3. Discuss the report and Analysis Questions 1 and 2 with your group.

4. Work on your own to write answers to Analysis Questions 3–6.

Willow Grove
Annual Water Quality Report

This report describes the drinking water sources and quality for Willow Grove during the past calendar year (January through December). It also includes background on major classes of water contamination.

Where does our drinking water come from?

Drinking water may come from surface water or groundwater. Surface water is open water in rivers, streams, lakes, ponds, and reservoirs. Groundwater is found below ground in the spaces between and within layers of rock. People access groundwater at natural springs or by digging wells. The Willow Grove Water District draws water from one surface water source: Willow Lake. Half of the homes in the Willow Grove area obtain their water from private wells that are not tested by the water district.

How does water get contaminated?

Water may become contaminated with either natural substances or substances that result from human activity. As it travels over the surface or through the porous layers of rock underground, water may dissolve natural minerals. It may also pick up substances produced by industry, agriculture, or household activities. These substances can be either biological or chemical contaminants.

What kinds of contaminants can be in water?

There are five major classes of contaminants that can be present in any source of water. These are described here in Table 1.

Table 1: Major Classes of Contaminants		
Type	**Definition**	**Where do they come from?**
Microbial	Tiny organisms such as bacteria, protozoa, and viruses	Human and animal waste
Inorganic chemicals	Metals or salts that may occur naturally in the land	Industry, oil and gas production, mining, farming, household activities, and illegal dumping of toxic wastes
Pesticides and herbicides	Synthetic chemicals that kill insects,weeds, and other pests	Farming, gardening, and other pest control activities
Organic chemicals	Carbon-containing chemicals such as gasoline, liquids. Includes volatile organic chemicals (VOCs),which evaporate easily and are often flammable	Industry (such as petroleum refineries), gas stations, storm runoff from parking lots, and illegal dumping of toxic wastes
Radioactive contamination	Substances that contain elements that decay into other elements	Natural radioactive deposits, mining activities, and oil and gas production

WILLOW GROVE WATER-TESTING RESULTS

After we treat Willow Lake water at our plant, we test for more than 90 possible water contaminants. We also test for turbidity. However, we only report on contaminants that were detected. The results from last year are presented in Table 2, "Water Quality Data for Detected Contaminants." Table 2 also includes the national standards in the MCL (maximum contaminant level allowed) column. You may be concerned about biological contaminants such as *Cryptosporidium* and *Giardia*, but they are not reported because they were not detected. Similarly, you may be concerned about a chemical contaminant such as mercury, but it also was not detected.

Water Quality Report, continued

Table 2: Water-Quality Data for Detected Contaminants

Regulated Contaminant	MCL	Average Level Found	Source
Inorganic compounds			
Copper	AL = 1.3 ppm	0.04 ppm	Industrial waste, corroding plumbing pipes
Iron	300 ppb	50 ppb	Naturally present in the environment; corrosion of iron plumbing pipes
Lead	AL = 15 ppb	6 ppb	Naturally present in the environment, corroding plumbing pipes
Nitrate	10 ppm	0.35 ppm	Fertilizer, industrial waste, human and animal waste
Sulfate	250 ppm	17 ppm	Naturally present in the environment
Organic compounds			
Atrazine (a herbicide)	3 ppb	0.25 ppb	Fertilizer
Microbes			
	% of positive samples permitted	**% of positive samples detected**	
Coliform (including *E. coli*)	5%	1%	Animal and human waste
Also tested:			
	Acceptable range	Level detected	
pH	6.5–8	8.4	Mining waste, industrial waste, fertilizer
Turbidity	< 1 NTU	0.78 NTU	Soil runoff

Terms used in this report
MCL—The maximum contaminant level allowed in drinking water.
AL—action level
NTU—nephalometric turbidity units for measuring cloudiness
ppm—parts per million, or mg/L-milligrams per liter
ppb—parts per billion, or μg/L-micrograms per liter
<—less than

ANALYSIS

1. Apply what you have learned about types and sources of biological and chemical contamination to classify each major type of contaminant in Table 1, "Major Classes of Contaminants," as biological or chemical contamination.

2. In the past year, were any of the contaminants above the maximum contaminant level?

3. Why are the MCLs and ALs reported in parts per million and parts per billion?

4. Looking at the water-quality report data, which regulated contaminants do you think would be particularly important for the city to pay attention to? Rank the top three, and explain why you think they should be watched.

5. Imagine you work for the Willow Grove Water District. Use the information you wrote on Student Sheet 31.1, "KWL: Willow Grove's Water Quality," to help you write—in seven or eight sentences—a statement to the public that summarizes the results of this report.

6. If you were Carla and you read this report, would you still be concerned about Willow Grove's drinking water? Explain your answer.

EXTENSION 1

Obtain the latest water quality report for your area. You can usually find this on the Internet by searching for your local water district or for your town or city's name and "water quality report." Or go to the *Issues and Physical Science* page of the SEPUP website for a link to this information.

- How does your local water report compare to the one for Willow Grove?
- Were any contaminants detected? Were any of them over the MCL?

EXTENSION 2

Choose two of the contaminants listed in Table 2, "Water Quality Data for Detected Contaminants," of the Willow Grove Water Quality Report, and convert the MCL/AL into percentages, fractions, and ratios.

LABORATORY

You learned in Activity 37, "What Dissolves?" that some substances dissolve easily, or are soluble, in water. Other substances do not dissolve, and are called insoluble. When solutes react, new substances can form. If the new substances are not soluble in water, they will form a solid. An insoluble solid that forms when two solutes interact is called a **precipitate.**

In this activity you will determine how much of a chemical works best to precipitate a copper contaminant.

CHALLENGE

How can you use a chemical reaction to remove a contaminant from a solution?

These two liquid substances react to form a yellow precipitate.

MATERIALS

For each group of four students

 1   dropper bottle of water
 1   dropper bottle of 5% sodium carbonate
 1   dropper bottle of copper chloride
 1   cup of water

For each pair of students

 1   SEPUP tray
 1   SEPUP filter funnel
 2   pieces of filter paper
 1   stir stick
 1   dropper
      paper towels

For each student

 1   Student Sheet 45.1, "A Precipitation Reaction"
 1   pair of safety goggles

SAFETY NOTE

Wear safety goggles at all times during this lab. Do not allow the solutions to touch your skin or clothing. Clean up any spills immediately. If accidental contact occurs, inform your teacher, and rinse exposed areas.

PROCEDURE

1. With your partner place a white sheet of paper under your SEPUP tray. This will help you see the colors of the solutions as you do the activity.

2. Inspect the data table provided for you on Student Sheet 45.1, "A Precipitation Reaction." At every step in the Procedure, you will fill in the appropriate part(s) of the table with data or observations for all of the tests done by your group.

3. Put five full droppers of water contaminated with copper chloride into large Cup A of your SEPUP tray. Record your observations of the copper chloride on your data table.

4. Use the dropper to put 20 drops of the copper chloride solution from Cup A into each of large Cups B and C.

5. With your group of four, decide which pair will collect data for tests 1 and 2 and which pair will collect data for tests 3 and 4 on Student Sheet 45.1, "A Precipitation Reaction." Look at the Student Sheet to determine the number of drops of water to add to Cups B and C based on the two tests you have been assigned.

6. Look at your Student Sheet 45.1, "A Precipitation Reaction," to determine the number of drops of 5% sodium carbonate to add to Cups B and C.

7. With your group of four, observe all four cups carefully. Record your observations before and after mixing the solution in each cup. Decide in which cup(s) you think all of the contaminant has reacted to become a precipitate. Record your inference and observations for each test on your data table.

8. Fold two filter papers, moisten them, and place them into two filter funnel openings. Place the filter funnels onto your SEPUP tray so that the openings are over Cups D and E.

9. Using the dropper, transfer as much as you can of the material from Cup B of your tray onto the filter over Cup D. Rinse the dropper in the cup of water. Do the same for Cup C, using the filter over Cup E of the tray.

10. While the mixtures are filtering, with your group of four think of a way you might test the filtrate from all four filters to confirm that most of the contaminant has been filtered out of the water. Hint: Think back to activities you have done that involved copper.

11. Once the mixtures have filtered, observe the appearance and quantity of the contents of the filter paper and the filtrate. Finish filling in the data table on your Student Sheet.

12. Test the filtrate in all four cups for the presence of the contaminant using the test you designed in Procedure Step 10. Record your observations on Student Sheet 45.1, "A Precipitation Reaction."

13. Dispose of the solutions in your SEPUP trays as directed by your teacher.

ANALYSIS

1. What was the contaminant in this activity?

2. What evidence indicates that a chemical reaction occurred when you mixed solutions of sodium carbonate and copper chloride?

3. a. You added sodium carbonate solution to the copper chloride solution. Where do you think the solid that appeared came from?

    b. Why does that substance get trapped by the filter paper?

    c. What property(ies) does (do) all solid precipitates that form and settle to the bottom when two solutions are mixed have?

4. Describe two ways the control in Test 1 helped you analyze the data.

5. a. Did precipitation work for removing the contaminant from the water? Explain, using evidence from the investigation.

    b. Did your procedure for testing the presence of contaminant in the filtrate work well? How did you know how well it worked?

    c. If your procedure did not work well, think of at least one way you could improve it.

6. How could the procedure in this investigation be useful for purifying wastewater?

7. Copper is a metal. Look at the Periodic Table of the Elements, and list two other elements that you think this procedure would work well for if they were contaminants.

LABORATORY

In Activity 41, "Testing Water Quality," you tested water from several sources in Willow Grove for chemical contaminants. In one of your tests you measured the pH of the water. Pure water has a pH of 7, which is **neutral.** That is, pure water is neither acidic nor basic. A solution with a pH less than 7 is acidic, and the chemical found in the water is called an **acid.** The higher the concentration of acid in a solution, the more **acidic** the solution is, and the lower the pH number. A solution of water with a pH greater than 7 is basic, and contains a substance called a **base.** The higher the concentration of base in a solution, the more **basic** the solution is, and the higher the pH.

In this activity, you will learn how to use an acid–base indicator to measure how acidic or basic a solution is. An **indicator** is a substance that shows whether another substance is present. Some indicators can also tell you how much of the substance is present.

CHALLENGE ⟶ **How can solutions be tested to identify them as acidic, basic, or neutral?**

Many common household liquids are acidic or basic solutions.

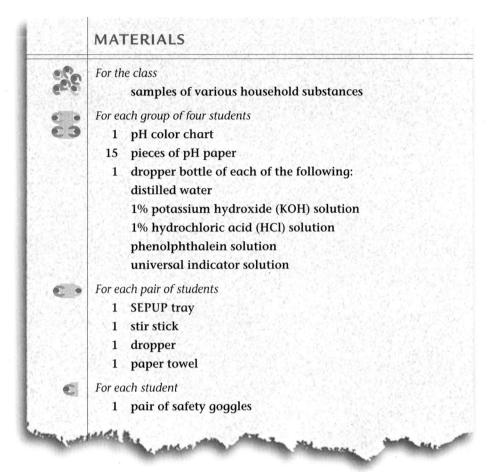

MATERIALS

For the class

samples of various household substances

For each group of four students

1 pH color chart

15 pieces of pH paper

1 dropper bottle of each of the following:

distilled water

1% potassium hydroxide (KOH) solution

1% hydrochloric acid (HCl) solution

phenolphthalein solution

universal indicator solution

For each pair of students

1 SEPUP tray

1 stir stick

1 dropper

1 paper towel

For each student

1 pair of safety goggles

SAFETY

Wear safety goggles at all times during this lab. Do not allow the solutions to touch your skin or clothing. Clean up any spills immediately. If accidental contact occurs, inform your teacher, and rinse exposed areas. Wash your hands after completing this activity.

PROCEDURE

Part A: Testing Solutions with Acid–Base Indicators

1. You will test at least nine liquids with the following three indicators: phenolphthalein (FEE-null-THAY-leen), universal indicator, and pH paper. Read through the Procedure Steps for Part A.

2. Within your group, discuss how you could use small Cups 1–9 of your SEPUP tray to test three liquids—water, an acid (HCl), and a base (KOH)—with the three indicators. Come up with a plan for which liquid and which indicator you will place in each small cup. Write your plan in your science notebook.

3. In your science notebook set up a data table for recording your observations from all the tests you will do.

4. Using your plan as a guide, put five-drop samples of the three solutions to be tested—water, hydrochloric acid, and potassium hydroxide—into Cups 1–9 of the SEPUP tray.

5. Test each solution with each of the three indicators.

   • For phenolphthalein and universal indicator, use 1 drop to test each solution.

   • For the pH paper, use a separate strip to test each solution.

6. On your data table, record the changes you observe. Rinse your tray with water, and then dry it.

7. Your teacher will provide various household liquids for testing. Choose three of those liquids for your first set of tests. Follow the same testing procedure that you used in Procedure Steps 3–6 to test each liquid with the three indicators.

8. Use Procedure Steps 3–6 to test another three household liquids.

9. Clean the tray, and wash your hands when you are finished.

Part B: Diluting an Acid or a Base

10. One pair of students in your group of four will prepare a serial dilution of the HCl solution while the other will prepare a serial dilution of the KOH solution. Decide together which pair will dilute which solution.

11. Make a data table in your science notebook similar to the one below.

Serial Dilution of a 1% _____ Solution

Cup	Concentration (as a fraction)	Concentration (ppm)	pH Paper Color	Universal Indicator Color	Estimated pH
1					
2					
3					
4					
5					
6					
7					

12. Put 10 drops of water in Cup 7 of your SEPUP tray.

13. Put 10 drops of the 1% HCl or KOH in Cup 1.

14. In Cups 2–6 perform a serial 1/10 dilution of the solution you are investigating. Rinse the dropper and stir stick with clean water between dilutions.

    Hint: If necessary, refer to Activity 40, "Parts Per Million," to review how to do the serial dilution.

15. Test the pH of the solution in each cup with pH paper. Record the results.

16. Test the pH of the solution in each cup with universal indicator. Record the results.

ANALYSIS

1. Group the nine substances you tested based on how they interacted with the indicators.

2. Which do you think is the most useful indicator? Explain your answer by considering the advantages of each indicator.

3. What happens to the pH of an acid or a base solution as you dilute it with water?

4. Do you think that dilution with water is a good method for treating industrial waste that contains an acid or a base? Explain the reasons for your answer.

5. **Reflection:** Think about your experiences tasting or touching everyday substances like vinegar, lemon juice, and detergents that you now know to be acidic or basic. What do the acidic substances seem to have in common? What do the basic substances seem to have in common?

Wherever chemical solutions are involved, pH matters. Some important chemical reactions, such as those involved in corrosion of iron or digestion of food, will only take place within a specific pH range. In agriculture, the soil's pH affects crop yields of fruits, vegetables, and grains, such as wheat, barley, and corn. The control of pH is also important within your body. For example, the pH of your blood is maintained at a slightly basic level of approximately 7.4. In your stomach an acidic pH between 2 and 4 helps you digest your food. The pH of water in the environment is also important because it affects the survival of fish and other organisms. Scientists measure pH when they study acid rain and when they work to maintain drinking water quality.

CHALLENGE ➔ **What is pH, and how does it affect the quality of water?**

Populations of brook trout have been drastically reduced by the effects of acid rain on freshwater lakes and streams in the northeastern United States.

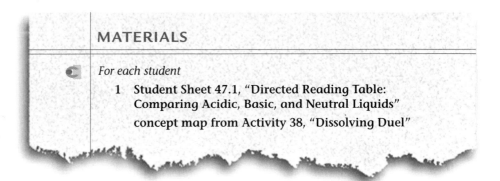

MATERIALS

For each student

1   Student Sheet 47.1, "Directed Reading Table:
    Comparing Acidic, Basic, and Neutral Liquids"
    concept map from Activity 38, "Dissolving Duel"

READING

Use Student Sheet 47.1, "Directed Reading Table: Comparing Acidic, Basic, and Neutral Liquids," to guide you through the following reading.

The pH scale

As you observed in the last activity, the pH of a solution is a number that expresses how acidic or basic it is. The **pH scale** ranges from 0 for very acidic to 14 for very basic. At the middle of the scale, 7, is a neutral liquid, such as distilled water. The scale is not linear with equal increments like a ruler or a thermometer. The pH scale is a lot like the Richter scale used to measure the strength of earthquakes. An 8.0 earthquake is 10 times stronger than a 7.0 earthquake, and a pH of 3 is 10 times more acidic than a pH of 4. For every increase or decrease in pH of 1.0 unit, the **acidity** or **basicity** of the solution changes tenfold.

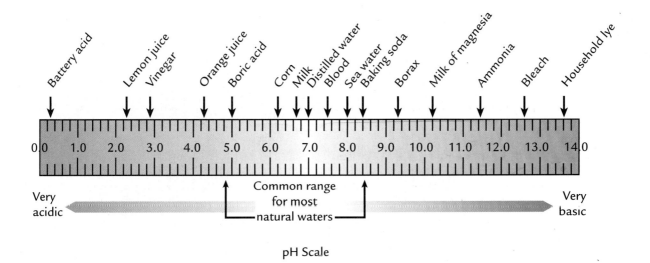

pH Scale

The color change of a pH indicator results from a chemical reaction between the indicator and the acid or base dissolved in water. An acidic solution contains acid and turns pH paper deep orange or red. A basic solution contains a base, and turns pH paper blue or violet. Acids are recognizable by their sour taste and because they can dissolve some metals. Bases—from soap to bleach to drain cleaner—have other properties. They tend not to react with metals and are bitter in taste. They are slippery to the touch because they react with your skin oils to form a substance a lot like soap. However, both acids and bases can be corrosive to human skin, if the pH is below 2 or above 12.

Acids, Bases, pH, and Industry

Controlling pH is important in the production of foods, paper products, and chemicals. The low pH of vinegar preserves foods, such as pickles, because it slows the growth of bacteria and other microbes. Because they are chemically reactive, acids and bases are also important in the manufacture of many products. For example, sulfuric acid is by far the largest single product of the chemical industry and is used to make fertilizer, refine petroleum, and clean and process metals. Nitric acid is used to make explosives and dyes. The bases sodium hydroxide and potassium hydroxide are used to make soaps. Sodium hydroxide is also the main ingredient in drain cleaners. Ammonia, a base that contains nitrogen, is used both as a fertilizer and to produce other fertilizers.

Orange juice and vinegar are two familiar liquids that contain acids.

Drain cleaner and household ammonia are two familiar liquids that contain bases.

pH and the Environment

If the pH of water in rivers, streams, and lakes becomes too high or too low, many animals and plants cannot survive. Wastes released by human activity may disturb the acid–base balance in bodies of water. Even a small change from the normal range can harm some aquatic life and cause changes in ecosystems that are hard to predict. Most organisms that live in freshwater are healthiest at pH values from 6 to 9. Variations in pH outside of this range reduce populations of organisms by decreasing survival of adults and reducing reproductive rates.

pH and Drinking Water

The federal government's standards for drinking water require a pH between 6.5 and 8.5. Acidic or basic tap water may react chemically with water pipes and release contaminants into the drinking water. The biggest hazard is that acid may dissolve lead out of the metal of some pipes into the water flowing through them. Lead can have serious health effects that vary with dosage and among different individuals. Young children are much more sensitive than adults, but adults can also be affected. Lead acts on the brain, nervous system, and other organs, causing effects from behavioral and learning problems to seizures and even death.

ANALYSIS

1. In what ways can the pH or acidity of water affect:

   a. living things, such as fish?

   b. people?

2. Fill in the blanks of the following sentences with the correct number.

   a. A solution with a pH of 5 is ___ times as acidic as a solution with a pH of 6.

   b. A solution with a pH of 4 is ___ times as acidic as a solution with a pH of 6.

3. Add the following words to your concept map from Activity 38, "Dissolving Duel."

   acid

   base

   neutral

   pH

4. Compare and contrast acids and bases by completing a Venn diagram. In your science notebook, make a larger version of the Venn diagram shown below. Compare acids and bases by recording common features in the space where the circles overlap. Contrast acids and bases by recording unique features of each kind of substance on the far side of each circle.

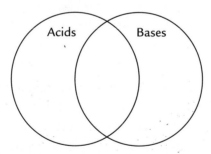

5. What do you predict will happen to pH when an acid and a base are mixed together? Explain your prediction.

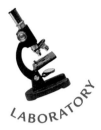

LABORATORY

*P*eople in Willow Grove are anxious because the Acme Metals Company is expanding. The company returns its wastewater to the Fenton River. People in Willow Grove boat and swim at the river and are considering using it as a drinking water source. Carla read the factory's web page on the Internet, where it said, "We treat the waste to make it safe before returning the water to the river. The acid waste will be diluted and neutralized before it is released. This neutral waste will have little or no impact on the diversity of wildlife in the river. It will not cause problems in Willow Grove's drinking water."

So far, you have seen that indicators change colors, depending on the pH of the solution. You've also learned that as acids and bases are diluted, they become more like water, that is, more neutral. However, dilution is often an impractical solution to the problem of chemical contamination, because it requires a very large volume of water. In this activity, you will explore another approach for treating wastewater that contains an acid or a base.

CHALLENGE ➡ **What happens when you mix an acid and a base?**

MATERIALS

For each group of four students

1 dropper bottle of each of the following:
1% hydrochloric acid (HCl) solution
1% potassium hydroxide (KOH) solution
distilled water
universal indicator solution

For each pair of students

1 SEPUP tray
1 stir stick
1 piece of white paper

For each pair of students

1 pair of safety goggles

SAFETY

Wear safety goggles at all times during this lab. Do not allow the solutions to touch your skin or clothing. Clean up any spills immediately. If accidental contact occurs, inform your teacher, and rinse exposed areas. Wash your hands after completing the activity.

PROCEDURE

Part A: Mixing an Acid and a Base: Qualitative Observations

1. Put 10 drops of HCl solution in small Cup 1 of your SEPUP tray. Add 1 drop of universal indicator.

2. Put 10 drops of water in small Cup 2 of the SEPUP tray. Add 1 drop of universal indicator to Cup 2.

3. Observe what happens when you gradually add KOH solution to the 10 drops of HCl solution in Cup 1. Add the KOH one drop at a time, and stir after each drop. Record your observations in your science notebook.

4. Discuss your results with the class.

Part B: Mixing an Acid and a Base:
Quantitative Observations

5. Plan and conduct an investigation to measure how many drops of KOH it takes to neutralize 10 drops of HCl. Record your results.

6. Predict how many drops of HCl it will take to neutralize 10 drops of KOH. Record your prediction in your science notebook.

7. Plan and conduct an investigation to measure how many drops of HCl it takes to neutralize 10 drops of KOH. Record your results.

8. On the transparency displayed by your teacher, record the numbers of drops you used for each part of the investigation.

ANALYSIS

1. What happens as you add an acid to a basic solution or add a base to an acidic solution?

2. Which solution seems more powerful in this investigation, the acidic or the basic? Explain your answer.

3. Based on what you know so far, which do you think is a better way of neutralizing an acid: diluting it with water, or adding a base? Explain your answer.

 4. Given two solutions, how might you determine:

   a. whether these solutions are acidic or basic?

   b. which is more acidic or basic?

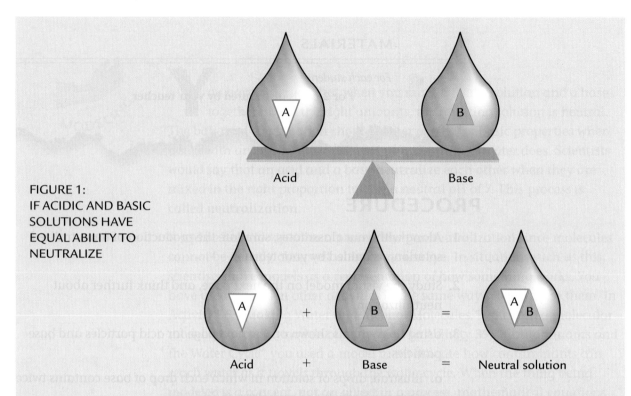

FIGURE 1:
IF ACIDIC AND BASIC
SOLUTIONS HAVE
EQUAL ABILITY TO
NEUTRALIZE

Acid

Acid + Base = Neutral solution

If, however, the acidic solution is twice as powerful as the basic solution, then each drop of acid has twice as many particles as each drop of base. Therefore, to neutralize the solution two drops of base are needed for every one drop of acid.

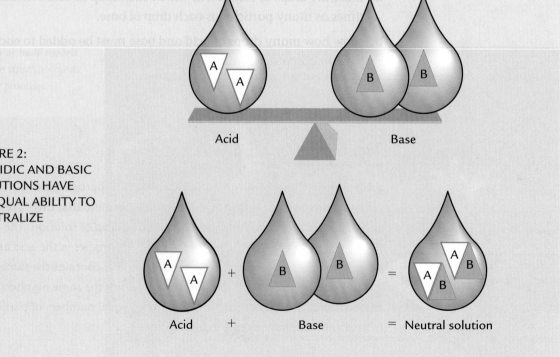

Acid   Base

FIGURE 2:
IF ACIDIC AND BASIC
SOLUTIONS HAVE
UNEQUAL ABILITY TO
NEUTRALIZE

Acid + Base = Neutral solution

ANALYSIS

 1. For the example in Procedure Step 1, how many drops of base would be needed to neutralize:

   a. 2 drops of acid? Explain, or draw a diagram to show your reasoning.

   b. 10 drops of acid? Explain, or draw a diagram to show your reasoning.

   c. 4 liters of acid? Explain your reasoning.

 2. In the example in Procedure Step 2, how many liters of base would be needed to neutralize:

   a. 1 liter of acid?

   b. 200 liters of acid?

 3. Based on the results from the class, are there more particles of acid in a drop of 1% hydrochloric acid (HCl) or more particles of base in a drop of 1% potassium hydroxide (KOH)? Explain how you figured out your answer.

 4. Draw a diagram to show the number of drops of 1% HCl and 1% KOH that would make a neutral solution. Illustrate the ratio of particles in the drops.

5. Given that the HCl and KOH solutions used in Activity 48, "Mixing an Acid and a Base," were 1% (each of them contains one gram of solute per 100 grams of solution), how could you explain that the ratio of particles per drop of the neutral solution is not 1:1?

In the last activity, "A Model for Acid–Base Neutralization," you learned that an acid and a base balance, or neutralize, each other to form a neutral solution when the number of acid particles and base particles are equal. In this activity, you will explore the chemical reaction that takes place when you mix an acid and a base. First, your teacher will conduct a demonstration. Then you will read about how scientists explain the chemistry of acids, bases, and neutralization.

CHALLENGE

What chemical reaction takes place when you neutralize an acid or a base?

This student is adding base to a solution containing acid and an indicator.

MATERIALS

For each student

concept map from Activity 38, "Dissolving Duel"

Venn diagram created for Activity 48, "Acids, Bases, and the pH Scale"

1   Student Sheet 50.1, "Testing Electrical Conductivity of Solutions"

1   Student Sheet 50.2, "Three-Level Reading Guide: Acids, Bases, and Neutralization"

NEUTRALIZATION: GATHERING MORE EVIDENCE

Before you read the text, observe the demonstration your teacher will conduct. Record the results of the demonstration on Student Sheet 50.1, "Electrical Conductivity of Solutions."

READING

Use Student Sheet 50.2, "Three-Level Reading Guide: Acids, Bases, and Neutralization," to guide you through the reading.

Two Kinds of Chemical Bonds: Ionic and Covalent

All atoms are neutral. They contain enough negatively charged electrons to balance the positive charges in the nucleus. In Activity 36, "Making Water and Alcohol Molecules," you connected the model atoms with white tubes that represented chemical bonds. To understand these bonds, it helps to think of the atom as a positively charged nucleus surrounded by negatively charged electrons. This is shown in the picture to the right.

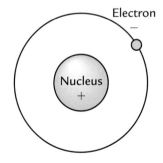

You probably know that opposite charges attract and like charges repel. Sometimes the positively charged nucleus attracts electrons from another atom. When the positively charged nuclei of two atoms attract negatively charged electrons from both atoms, they form a bond.

Water, alcohol, and table sugar are examples of compounds that are held together by covalent (koe-VAY-lunt) bonds. In **covalent bonds**, atoms share electrons. The diagram below illustrates a covalent bond. Covalent bonds hold atoms together to form molecules.

A COVALENT BOND

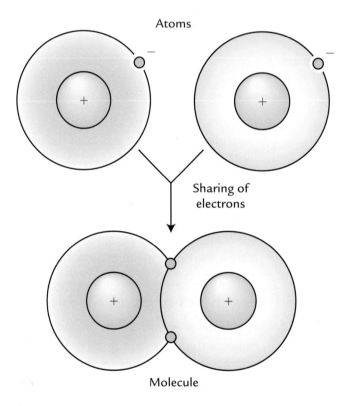

Atoms

Sharing of electrons

Molecule

In other compounds the atoms are held together by another type of bond, called an ionic (eye-ON-ick) bond. **Ionic bonds** form when electrons are transferred from one atom to another, as shown on the next page. The atom that loses one or more electrons is now positively charged and is called a positive ion. The atom that gains one or more electrons is now negatively charged and is called a negative ion. An **ion** is an atom or group of atoms that has gained or lost one or more electrons and is now either positively or negatively charged. The positively charged ion and negatively charged ion attract each other and form a bond, but they don't form a molecule. A compound that forms as a result of ionic bonding is called an ionic compound. Table salt, NaCl, is an example of an ionic compound.

AN IONIC BOND

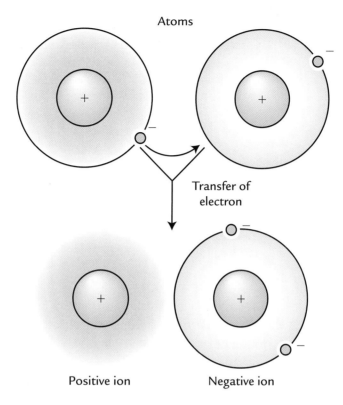

Atoms

Transfer of
electron

Positive ion   Negative ion

Dissolving Covalent and Ionic Compounds

When you dissolve some substances in water, the substance separates into
molecules. For example, when you dissolve sugar in water, individual
sugar molecules mix in among the water molecules.

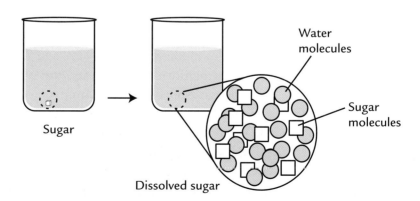

Sugar

Water
molecules

Sugar
molecules

Dissolved sugar

When other substances, such as acids, bases, and salts, are added to water, they release positive and negative ions that mix completely with the water molecules. For example, when table salt dissolves in water, it separates into separate Na^+ and Cl^- ions, as shown in the diagram below.

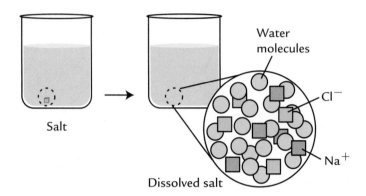

When hydrogen chloride (HCl, a covalent molecule) dissolves in water, it releases H^+ and Cl^- ions. Any substance that increases the concentration of H^+ ions when it dissolves in water is an acid. When a KOH molecule dissolves in water, it releases K^+ and OH^- ions. Any substance that increases the concentration of OH^- ions when it dissolves in water is a base. You have observed that substances that separate into ions when they dissolve conduct electricity. These substances are called electrolytes.

Reacting Acids and Bases

In Activity 49, "Modeling Acid–Base Neutralization," you used models to explain the neutralization of an acid with a base. Another way to represent the neutralization process is with a chemical equation. A **chemical equation** is another kind of model for a chemical reaction.

One way to write the equation for the reaction of hydrochloric acid (HCl) and the base potassium hydroxide (KOH) is in a word equation:

> **Hydrochloric acid + potassium hydroxide $\longrightarrow$ potassium chloride + water**

Another way to write the equation is to use the chemical formulas for each compound in the reaction:

> $HCl + KOH \longrightarrow KCl + H_2O$

Potassium chloride, like sodium chloride (NaCl) is classified in a group of chemicals called salts. A **salt** is an ionic compound that contains positive and negative ions. The general equation of an acid with a base is:

> **An acid + a base $\longrightarrow$ a salt + water**

This can be simplified to show only the neutralization of the acid and base as:

$$H^+ + OH^- \longrightarrow H_2O$$

This equation explains why the product of this reaction is neutral. The numbers of H^+ ions and OH^- ions are equal, and they react to form water. It also explains why the product of this reaction conducts electricity. The other product of the reaction is a salt with the formula KCl. When a salt dissolves it separates into charged ions that can conduct electricity. If you let the water evaporate from the solution, crystals of potassium chloride will form.

You may be surprised to learn that table salt is only one of many compounds classified as salts. Most of the salt in the ocean is sodium chloride, but some of it is potassium chloride and other salts. Potassium chloride is the substitute for table salt that people on low-sodium diets often use.

ANALYSIS

1. What is the difference between a covalent and an ionic bond?

2. Explain at the chemical level why a base can be used to neutralize an acid.

3. Copy the lists of words shown below.

List 1	List 2	List 3	List 4
bond	sugar	neutral	acid
covalent	covalent bonds	positive	base
water	salt	ion	sugar
ionic	molecules	negative	electrolyte
			salt

a. In each list, look for a relationship among the words or phrases. Cross out the word that does not belong.

b. In each list, circle the word or phrase that includes the others.

c. Explain how the word or phrase you circled is related to the other words on the list.

4. Add the following words to your concept map from Activity 38, "Dissolving Duel":

   H$^+$ ion
   OH$^-$ ion
   negative
   neutralize
   positive
   water

5. Alan says that adding a base to acid waste is a perfect way to treat the waste because it makes the waste disappear. Zack says that adding a base to neutralize an acid is an improvement, but not a perfect way to treat the waste. Based on what you learned in this activity:

   a. Who do you think is correct, Alan or Zack? Explain why.

   b. Explain your answer at the level of the chemical reaction between an acid and a base.

   c. Write the chemical equation that illustrates your answer to Analysis Question 5b.

LABORATORY

*T*he town of Willow Grove is booming. The newspaper has recently published an article about how the expansion of the Acme Metals Company is causing an increase in the number of people moving to and living in Willow Grove. Willow Grove Water District needs more water than Willow Lake can supply to support the growing drinking water needs of the town. The water board is considering adding Fenton River water to their supply. They have asked Acme Metals to verify the testing and treatment processes they use for their wastewater.

In previous activities you have been investigating the concepts of solubility, dilution, filtration, precipitation, and neutralization. Imagine that you are a scientific consultant to the Acme Metals Company who has been hired to help them evaluate their wastewater. First you must test the wastewater to determine if there are contaminants. If you find contaminants, you will design a treatment process to present to the Acme Metals board and compare it to their current treatment process. The company can then present to the Willow Grove Water District the best process for returning safe, low-contaminant, neutral wastewater to the Fenton River.

CHALLENGE ➡ **How will you test and treat the Acme Metals wastewater?**

MATERIALS

For each group of four students

1   dropper bottle each of:
   ammonia
   potassium thiocyanate
   universal indicator
   hydrochloric acid (HCl)
   sodium carbonate
   potassium hydroxide (KOH)
   Acme Metals wastewater
   water
1   container of nitrate indicator powder
1   graduated plastic tube with cap

For each pair of students

1   SEPUP tray
1   SEPUP filter funnel
1   stir stick
1   dropper
2–6   pieces of filter paper

For each student

1   pair of safety goggles
1   Literacy Student Sheet 1b, "Writing a Formal investigation Report"

SAFETY

Wear safety goggles at all times during this lab. Do not allow the solutions to touch your skin or clothing. Clean up any spills immediately. If accidental contact occurs, inform your teacher, and rinse exposed areas.

PROCEDURE

Part A: Testing the Acme Metals Wastewater

1. With your partner, look at all of the materials listed. Look back at all of the investigations you have done over the course of the unit. Discuss a wastewater testing procedure for the Acme Metals wastewater using the appropriate materials.

2. In your science notebook, write a purpose, hypothesis, materials list, and the steps of your procedure for testing the Acme Metals wastewater.

3. In your science notebook, draw an appropriate data table to record and organize your data.

Industries must follow safety guidelines when they discharge wastewater to the environment.

4. Take your procedure and data table to your teacher for approval.

5. Carry out your approved plan. Record all the data you collect.

Part B: Treating the Acme Metals Wastewater

6. Using the materials listed and the results of your testing in Part A, develop a treatment procedure that removes any contaminants that were found in the Acme Metals wastewater. If no contaminants were found, explain the evidence that led you to that conclusion. The ideal treatment:

   • results in a solution that is neutral and does not produce a precipitate when a drop of sodium carbonate is added.

   • does not add any more chemicals than necessary.

7. In your science notebook, write the purpose, materials list, and the steps of your treatment procedure.

8. In your science notebook, draw a data table to record and organize all the observations and measurements you plan to make.

9. Take your procedure and data table to your teacher for approval.

10. Carry out your approved plan. Record all the data that you collect.

ANALYSIS

1. Were any contaminants found in the Acme Metals wastewater? If so, which ones? Explain the evidence that supports your answer.

2. If treatment was required, was your plan successful? Explain how you know if it was successful or not.

3. Are there any changes you would make to your treatment plan based on the results?

4. Use Literacy Student Sheet 1b, "Writing a Formal Investigation Report" to write a final report to the Acme Metals corporate board and Willow Grove Water District on the testing and treatment of the Acme Metals wastewater. Include the following:

    title
    abstract
    data
    data analysis
    conclusion

5. At the end of your conclusion in your report, write a paragraph that summarizes your recommendation to the Acme Metals corporate board for the treatment and disposal of the Acme Metals wastewater. It should include a clear statement of the trade-offs involved with filtration, dilution, neutralization, and precipitation.

EXTENSION 1

Sample and test water from a local stream or lake.

EXTENSION 2

Visit a municipal wastewater treatment plant or an industrial site that treats its own wastewater.

The residents of the Shadow Hills neighborhood need to make a decision about which water source to use. Should they join Willow Grove Water District, or continue to get water from their wells? Carla and her family plan to attend a Homeowners' Association meeting to give their opinion. Whatever the outcome, they may decide to buy bottled water to drink. What would you do if you lived in Shadow Hills?

CHALLENGE ➡️ **What source of water should the Shadow Hills neighborhood and Carla's family use?**

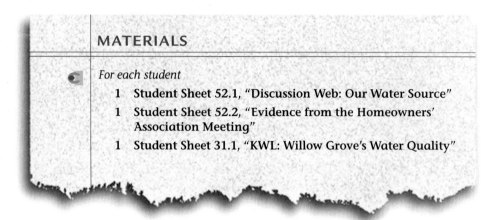

MATERIALS

For each student

1   Student Sheet 52.1, "Discussion Web: Our Water Source"
1   Student Sheet 52.2, "Evidence from the Homeowners' Association Meeting"
1   Student Sheet 31.1, "KWL: Willow Grove's Water Quality"

PROCEDURE

1. Work with your group to make these two decisions:

   • Should Shadow Hills residents join Willow Grove Water District, or continue to use water from their wells?

   • What are the best recommendations for improving water safety in Willow Grove?

2. Look back over all of the information you have gathered about Willow Grove's water and Carla's neighborhood. Include the information you recorded throughout the unit on Student Sheet 31.1, "KWL: Willow Grove's Water Quality." Also, recall the decision that the water board made during the voting at the end of the last activity about whether or not the water district should begin using Fenton River to supply water to the town.

3. With your group members, complete Student Sheet 52.1, "Discussion Web: Our Water Source." This will help you identify the advantages and disadvantages of joining the water district and of continuing to use well water.

   Remember to listen to and consider the ideas of the other members of your group. If you disagree with others in your group, explain why you disagree.

4. Work with your group to prepare a brief presentation that describes your thoughts about which water Shadow Hills should use, and any recommendations for improving water safety in Willow Grove.

5. Make your presentation to the class and listen to those of the other groups. As you listen to each presentation, record the information on Student Sheet 52.2, "Evidence from the Homeowners' Association Meeting."

6. When all presentations are complete, discuss within your group which presentation makes the most sense.

7. Participate in a class vote to decide which plan should be implemented.

ANALYSIS

1. If you were Carla, would you:

    a. want to join the Willow Grove Water District or continue to use well water? Be sure to explain the trade-offs involved and the advantages and disadvantages of each water source based on information you gathered over the course of the unit.

    b. drink water from the tap or buy bottled water for drinking?

2. **Reflection:** In the last activity and this one, you looked at the water issue in Willow Grove from several perspectives: that of the water district, a consulting scientist, Acme Metals Company, Shadow Hills Homeowners' Association, and Carla as an individual. People, businesses, agencies, and organizations that are involved in a decision about an issue are called stakeholders.

    a. Why is it important to look at an issue from many perspectives in order to make a decision about it?

    b. Do you personally identify with one perspective over others? What information leads you to identify with that perspective?

Energy

D

Energy

Van watched Diego take a strange palm-sized device out of his backpack. "Hey Diego, what is that?"

"It's my solar charger. My cell phone is dead and I need to recharge it."

As Diego unfolded a small plastic case with black panels inside it, Van said, "*That* can charge a phone? Wow, that's cool. How does it work?"

"Well, these solar panels absorb the Sun's energy and make electricity out of it," explained Diego as he connected the charger to his cell phone. "It's great because I don't have to plug the phone into the wall. I can charge it outside."

"Looks expensive," said Van. "How'd you get it?"

"It didn't cost that much so I bought it with my allowance. I found it on-line one day when I was supposed to be doing my homework. Compared with plugging the phone into the wall, it cost money to start. But soon it saved more money than I paid and from now on it won't cost anything to charge my phone. The sun gives free energy! My parents like that they don't pay to charge my phone on their electric bill."

"Does it run on batteries?" ask ed Van.

"No, it runs on sunlight," said Diego. "It works pretty well and is better for the environment."

Van wasn't exactly sure what Diego meant when he said that the solar panels were better for the environment. He wondered why it made a difference where the electricity came from. He wondered how the energy supplied by the sun was the same or different than the energy supplied by a battery.

• • •

In this unit, you will learn about the transfer and transformation of energy in our everyday lives. By exploring how energy can be used more efficiently at home, you will learn the answers to some puzzling questions: Where does all the energy around us come from? Are there different types? Does it ever run out? How does it get from one place to another?

INVESTIGATION

Yasmin and her mother examined the form that came with their new water heater. "Look," said Yasmin, "We can get a huge rebate!"

Her mother looked more carefully at the paper. "You're right, our water heater qualifies because it is more energy efficient than our old one."

As Yasmin's mother sat down and started to fill out the form, Yasmin read over the accompanying flyer. Something caught her attention again. "Mom, did you know that there is a free service that will come here and tell us how to save even more energy?"

"Oh that would be great," said Yasmin's mother. "Last winter we had a pretty high electricity bill. I don't want to waste my hard-earned money if I don't have to."

CHALLENGE ⟹ **What does it take to reduce energy use in a home?**

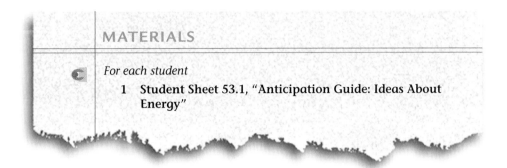

MATERIALS

For each student

1 **Student Sheet 53.1, "Anticipation Guide: Ideas About Energy"**

PROCEDURE

1. In your group, brainstorm a list of typical household activities where you see energy in use.

2. Put your list in order, from the most to least energy used in a typical home during one year.

3. Look at the table on the next page related to two homes that are similar in size but located in different parts of the country.

4. For each of the home features, explain as best you can how that feature is related to the energy consumption in the home.

5. Compare the data for Home A and Home B on the next page. For each home feature, decide which house you think consumes less energy. Record your ideas for each home in your science notebook.

Local utility companies charge residents monthly for electricity and other energy uses.

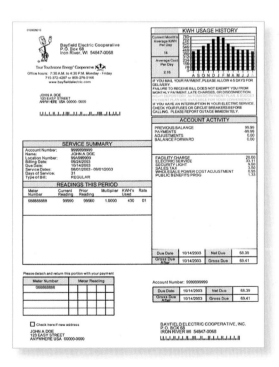

Comparing Energy Use in Two Similar Homes

Home Feature	Home A, Texas	Home B, New York
Heating source	Oil	Natural gas
Cooling source	Electricity	Electricity
Insulation	Ceiling	Exterior walls, ceiling
Window type	10 single pane	5 single pane, 3 double pane
Window treatment	Reflective film	No treatment
Hot water heater	Electric	Natural gas
Air conditioning	Central	1 high-efficiency window unit
Appliances	3 high efficiency, 3 not high efficiency	5 high efficiency
Lightbulbs	10 incandescent	3 incandescent, 8 compact fluorescent
Nearby vegetation	Grass	Tall shrubbery, maple trees

Home A, Texas

Home B, New York

ANALYSIS

1. How do the climates of the two home locations influence the energy used in the homes?

2. In the context of this activity, what does the term "energy efficient" mean? Explain, and give an example from this activity.

3. If the people who live in homes A and B have similar lifestyles, which home do you think uses less energy in a year? Use data from the table to support your choice.

4. What could be done to reduce the energy needs of:

   a. Home A?

   b. Home B?

5. **Reflection:** What steps have you and your family taken to reduce energy use in your home?

LABORATORY

*Y*asmin spent part of the morning helping her mother install weather strip-ping at the bottom of the doors to the outside of their house. When they finished, they started talking about energy. Yasmin knew from school that **energy can cause objects to change, move, or work.** Yasmin's mom was thinking about how energy moved through the house. She told Yasmin that energy is observable when it moves from one place or object to another. "Like when the oil in the fur-nace is burned and energy is released. Or when I swing this hammer," she said. "The energy from my hand is transferred to the hammer and then to the nail."

Energy appears in many ways. **Potential energy** is stored energy that has not yet been used, such as energy stored in the oil in the furnace, the built-up elec-tron charge on your clothes, or a rubber band that is fully stretched. When potential energy is due to an object's position above the earth, such as how high a hamme r is held, it is called **gravitational potential energy.** When an object is moving, it has **kinetic energy.** For example, a faster-moving hammer has more kinetic energy when it hits a nail than a slower one.

CHALLENGE

How does the height and mass of an object affect its gravitational potential energy?

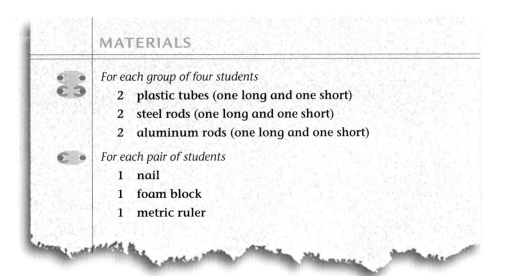

MATERIALS

For each group of four students
2 plastic tubes (one long and one short)
2 steel rods (one long and one short)
2 aluminum rods (one long and one short)

For each pair of students
1 nail
1 foam block
1 metric ruler

SAFETY

Nails are sharp and can cause injury if misused. Follow the safety precautions your teacher demonstrates.

PROCEDURE

1. Look at the metal rods. Record the similarities and differences between them in your science notebook. Be as specific as you can about each rod.

2. Look at the plastic tubes. Record the similarities and differences between them in your science notebook. Be as specific as you can about each tube.

3. Design an experiment that will determine which combination of plastic tubes (long, short) and metal rods (long, short) transfers the *most* and the *least* energy to the nail.

   When designing your experiment, think about these questions:

   What is the purpose of your experiment?

   What variable are you testing?

   What is your hypothesis?

   What variables will you keep the same?

   What is your control?

   How many trials will you conduct?

   Will you collect qualitative or quantitative data or both? How will the data help you form a conclusion?

   How will you record the data?

4. Record your hypothesis and your planned experimental procedure in your science notebook.

5. Make a data table that has space for all the data you need to record during the experiment.

6. Obtain your teacher's approval of your experiment.

7. Conduct your experiment, and record your results.

ANALYSIS

1. Which combination of tube height and rod mass transferred the most and least energy to the nail? Explain the evidence you gathered to make this conclusion.

2. Where was the rod located when there was the most:

   a. gravitational potential energy?

   b. kinetic energy?

3. Do you think that all the energy from the rod transferred to the nail? Describe any evidence that showed it did or did not.

4. How do the following variables affect how much energy is transferred to the nail?

   a. Mass of the rod

   b. Height of the rod

   c. Shape of the rod

5. In the situation shown below, how much gravitational potential and kinetic energy does the block have at each position?

a. When released from rest:
   Potential energy = 100 J
   Kinetic energy   = _____

b. Halfway down:
   Potential energy = _____
   Kinetic energy   = _____

c. Just before it hits:
   Potential energy = 0
   Kinetic energy   = _____

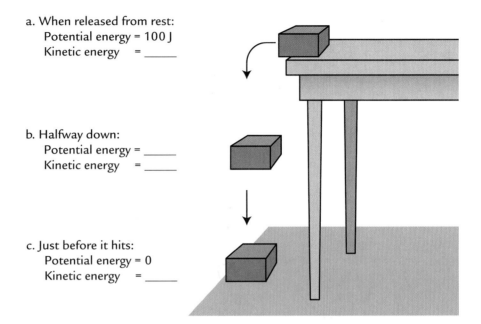

ROLE PLAY

Energy is **transferred** when it moves from one place to another, as in the last activity when the energy from the rod was transferred to the nail. Energy is **transformed** when it changes from one type to another. In the last activity, the gravitational potential of the rod when held up high was transformed into kinetic energy just before it hit the nail. In this activity, you will further explore the transformation of gravitational potential energy into kinetic energy.

The next day, Yasmin and her Uncle Raymond spent the day at the amusement park. They went there often because her uncle worked for the park. Of all the rides, Yasmin loved the roller coaster the most. That got her thinking. "Uncle Raymond," she said, "this roller coaster is kind of like the hammer and the nail. At the top of the hill there is a lot of potential energy in the cars and the passengers."

"That is right, Yasmin," Uncle Raymond said. "And as we move down the hill, the gravitational potential energy is transformed into kinetic energy. We move the fastest at the bottom where there is the most kinetic energy."

"Geeeez, there is energy everywhere," Yasmin said. Then she had an idea. "Uncle Raymond, would you be willing to come to school and talk to my class about energy and roller coasters?"

CHALLENGE ➡ **How is energy transformed on a roller coaster?**

MATERIALS

For each student

1 Student Sheet 53.1, "Anticipation Guide: Energy Ideas," from Activity 53, "Home Energy Use"

1 Student Sheet 55.1, "Talking Drawing: Roller Coaster Energy"

PROCEDURE

Use Student Sheet 55.1, "Talking Drawing: Roller Coaster Energy," to prepare yourself for the role play.

1. Assign one of the four roles to each person in your group.
   • *Mateo Masoni, interviewer for the Student Science Hour*
   • *Raymond Li, engineer for Coasters Inc.*
   • *Dr. Sara Low, physics professor*
   • *Niki Jackson, amusement park director*

2. Read the following role-play aloud as a group.

It's a Thrill! Roller Coaster Energy

Mateo: Welcome to the Student Science Hour. Today we have brought together a panel of experts who will help us explore the science behind roller coasters. What is responsible for the thrilling ride down a coaster? Energy!

Panelists, please introduce yourselves, and describe your backgrounds.

Dr. Low: Hello, my name is Sara Low. I am a physics professor at State University. Specifically, I study how energy transforms from one type to another.

Ms. Jackson: My name is Niki Jackson. I am in charge of the amusement park. One of my responsibilities is to make sure the guests are safe while they are having a good time. I use my science and business background to help decide what types of coasters we should have in the park.

Mr. Li: And I'm Raymond Li. I'm an engineer for a company that designs and builds roller coasters. My expertise is in classic wooden coasters that are still in use and need to be maintained.

Mateo: I'm glad that you could take the time to join us today. Now let's talk about park rides. Ms. Jackson, I understand that some riders worry that roller coasters are dangerous. I mean, hanging hundreds of feet in the air cannot possibly be safe, right?

Ms. Jackson: Although roller coasters are designed to frighten passengers, they are statistically the safest ride in the park. Not to mention one of the most popular. A person has a one in one-and-a-half billion chance of being killed on a roller coaster. That mortality rate is lower than for children's wagons, chewing gum, golf, and folding lawn chairs.

Mr. Li: The safety of the riders is a very serious matter for roller coaster designers and engineers. Safety factors are built into every aspect of the coaster. Coasters are built much stronger than they need to be. We also duplicate the safety factors in case of failure. The majority of incidents at amusement parks result from unsafe behavior by the guests' or operators rather than the park's equipment. Although it rarely happens, people have died on a coaster due to a heart ailment they didn't know they had.

Ms. Jackson: Every day, safety experts go over every centimeter of track and examine each portion for wear and tear, or anything that could indicate a problem.

Mateo: Dr. Low, can you describe the energy transformations that are involved in a roller coaster?

Dr. Low: The cars, hooked together to form the train, are pulled up the first hill, known as the lift hill, by a cable or chain. The energy that runs the cable comes from traditional energy sources such as electricity. That energy is transformed into the motion that lifts the train and passengers. As the train travels up the lift hill, it gains gravitational potential energy. The higher it goes and the more massive the train and people in it, the more gravitational potential energy it will have at the top.

Mr. Li: I'd like to add that once the train reaches the peak of the first hill, the train is disengaged from the chain and no more energy is put into the train system until it reaches the end of the ride. Tall coasters give more exciting rides because they start with more gravitational potential energy.

Dr. Low: It's true that when the park compares roller coaster designs, the lift hill height is an important consideration.

Mateo: But energy must be involved after the first peak.

Dr. Low: Oh yes. Energy is transformed throughout the ride. The gravitational potential energy of the train and passengers at the top of the hill becomes transformed into kinetic energy as it rolls down the first hill. At the bottom, the kinetic energy is the greatest and the train is moving the fastest.

The Kingda Ka roller coaster in New Jersey is one of the tallest in the world. The first hill is 139 meters (456 feet) tall and its top speed is 57 meters/second (128 miles per hour).

Mateo: Then the coaster climbs the next hill. Mr. Li says energy is not added to the train, so how does it get up the next hill?

Dr. Low: The kinetic energy at the bottom of the hill sends it up the next hill. As it climbs the hill, the kinetic energy of the train is transformed back into gravitational potential energy. At the top of the next hill, most of the energy has been transformed into potential energy and the process starts over again. Coasters are a result of continuous energy transformations between gravitational potential energy and kinetic energy.

Mateo: I have noticed that on a roller coaster, the first hill is taller than all the others. Why is that?

Mr. Li: That is a good observation, Mateo. In fact, each hill the coaster travels up is smaller than the previous one. That is because every time gravitational potential energy is transformed into kinetic energy, some of it is also transformed into other types of energy. Some of the transformed energy heats up the wheels and tracks. Some more of the transformed energy results in the sound of the train riding on the track.

Mateo: I get it. If the next hill is too high, the train won't make it to the top because it has lost some energy.

Dr. Low: Well, yes. But to be accurate, the energy isn't lost. It is still there, but it is no longer kinetic or gravitational potential energy. It has been transformed into different types of energy during the process.

Mr. Li: A properly designed roller coaster has enough energy to complete the entire course without additional outside energy despite the reduction of available kinetic energy as it travels. At the end of the ride, brakes bring the train to a complete stop, and it is pulled back into the station by a cable.

Mateo: I have one last question for each of you. What is your favorite kind of roller coaster ride?

Mr. Li: I like wooden roller coasters. Although corkscrews and loops are much more difficult to build in wooden coasters, the wooden ones give a rougher ride, and, I think, a great sensation of being airborne. There is a lot of debate about which is better, wooden or steel coasters, but I definitely think the wooden ones have more character and provide the best ride.

Ms. Jackson: Our park has an inverted roller coaster where the train runs under the track instead of on top of it. That type is my favorite because your legs are exposed instead of your arms, which makes it feel really scary.

Dr. Low: I like coasters that are tall. By tall, I mean a tall lift hill. There is even one that that is over 120 meters, which is about 400 feet. All that energy means it hits 225 km/hr, or 140 mph, at the bottom of the first hill. It is a short ride, just two hills, but very thrilling.

Mateo: Unfortunately we have run out of time for the Student Science Hour. Thank you all for joining us today.

The first hill of a roller coaster is always the tallest and the following hills decline in height.

ANALYSIS

1. Look at the diagram of a roller coaster below. At which point does a train on this roller coaster:

   a. have the most gravitational potential energy? Explain your choice.

   b. have the most kinetic energy? Explain your choice.

   c. have both kinetic and gravitational potential energy? Explain your choice.

2. Kinetic energy is related to the speed of an object. In which place, Point E or Point F, is the train moving faster? Explain in terms of kinetic energy.

3. As the train travels on the track, the energy of the train changes back and forth from gravitational potential to kinetic. What other energy transformations occur as the train travels the track? Explain.

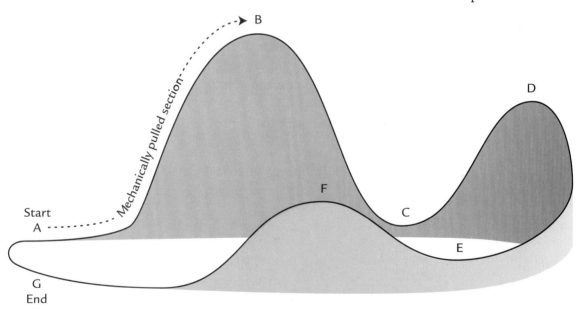

4. Why can't a roller coaster go up a hill that is higher than the hill it just came down?

EXTENSION

Learn more about roller coasters by visiting the *Issues and Physical Science* page of the SEPUP website.

In the last activity, some of the kinetic energy of the train was transformed into thermal energy during the roller coaster ride. In this activity, you will explore a similar transformation. You will investigate the transformation of kinetic energy—in this case, moving metal pellets, or shot, in a vial—into heat. **Heat** is the movement of thermal energy from hot to cold. An object does not "have" heat. Rather, heat is the process of energy movement from a higher-temperature object to a lower-temperature object because of the temperature difference. **Temperature** is a measure of the average energy *per molecule* of a substance. Although related, temperature and heat are not the same thing. For example, a spoonful of water and a large pot of water both boil at the same temperature. However, the pot of boiling water has more total energy and releases more energy during cooling than the spoonful of water.

Although temperature and heat are not the same thing, they are related because temperature measurements are used to determine heating. In this activity, you will measure a change in temperature to indicate the transformation of energy. The change is due to friction, which heats up objects when they rub against each other.

CHALLENGE ⟶ **How can kinetic energy be transformed into another energy type?**

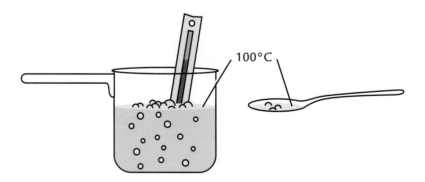

100°C

Boiling water in a pot and spoon are at the same temperature, but have different amounts of thermal energy.

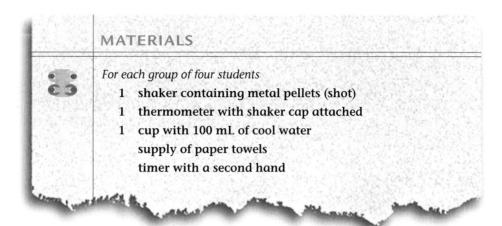

MATERIALS

For each group of four students
1   shaker containing metal pellets (shot)
1   thermometer with shaker cap attached
1   cup with 100 mL of cool water
    supply of paper towels
    timer with a second hand

SAFETY

Handle the thermometers carefully. Do not forcefully push the thermometer into the shaker. If accidental breakage occurs, inform your teacher immediately.

PROCEDURE

1. Prepare a data table similar to the one below.

2. Take the room temperature with the thermometer, and record it in your science notebook.

Shot Shaker Data

Time (sec)	Trial	Initial Temperature (°Celsius)	Final Temperature (°Celsius)	Temperature Change (°Celsius)	Average Temperature Change (°Celsius)
10	1				
10	2				
10	3				
20	1				
20	2				
20	3				
30	1				
30	2				
30	3				

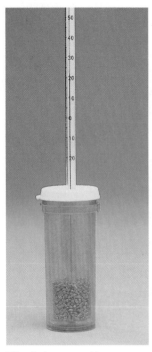

The shaker assembly

3. Take the regular cap off the shaker and replace it with the one with the thermometer attached, making sure the thermometer bulb is surrounded by the pellets as shown to the left.

4. Observe the initial temperature of the pellets. If the initial temperature is more than 2°C above room temperature, remove the inner vial containing the pellets and immerse it in cool water until the temperature is within 2°C of room temperature. Dry it off, and place it back inside the larger vial.

5. In your data table record the initial temperature of the pellets.

6. Exchange caps, and make sure the regular cap snaps tightly onto the shaker. Then, while holding the cap on with your thumb, shake the vial as fast as you can for 10 seconds.

7. Turn shaker onto its side, remove regular cap and *gently* insert the thermometer with shaker cap attached. When the cap is secured, turn the shaker upright.

8. Wait until the alcohol in the thermometer stops moving and record the temperature.

   Hint: The thermometer reading rises slowly, so you may need to be patient to get an accurate reading.

9. Find the temperature change by subtracting the initial temperature from the final temperature. Record the temperature change in the data table.

10. Repeat Steps 4–9 for Trials 2 and 3.

11. Calculate the average temperature changes for the three trials, and record them in the table.

12. Repeat Steps 4–11, this time shaking the vial for 20 seconds.

13. Repeat Steps 4–11, this time shaking the vial for 30 seconds.

ANALYSIS

1. For each time interval, why did you perform three trials and then average the temperatures?

2. Describe any possible sources of error in your experiment, and explain how each may have affected your results.

3. Use evidence gathered in this investigation to describe the relationship between:

   a. shaking time and temperature change.

   b. shaking time and energy transfer.

4. Of the two descriptions below which, a or b, correctly describes the transformation of energy shown in the diagrams below? Explain your choice.

    a. potential energy ⟶ temperature

    b. kinetic energy ⟶ thermal energy

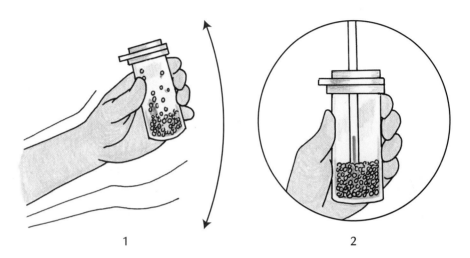

1   2

LABORATORY

Many devices that we use every day transform electrical energy to other forms of energy, such as sound, light, and thermal energy. One common device is the electric motor, in which electricity and magnetism make a wire coil spin. In this activity, you will build a simple electric motor and investigate some of the factors that affect how it spins. You will also use a motor as a generator to light an LED bulb.

Electric motors run many devices, both large and small.

CHALLENGE ⟶ **How can you make a motor spin faster?**

MATERIALS

For the class

   1   set of neodymium magnets

For each group of four students

   3   battery holders with batteries
   2   bar magnets
   2   wire leads with clips
   1   pair of copper support strips
   1   motor mount
   1   wire coil
   1   electric motor
   1   compass
   1   LED bulb

PROCEDURE

Part A: Investigating electric motors

1. In your group, make a simple electric motor by setting up the equipment shown in the diagram below. Put the magnet close to the coil, but do not connect the wire leads to the battery yet.

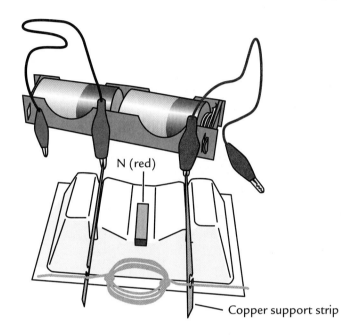

2. Spin the coil of wire with your fingers. Check that the coil stays centered between the copper support strips and that it does not hit the magnet.

3. Connect the wire leads to the battery, and record your observations.

   Hint: If the coil doesn't move, try giving it a small push with your finger to start it. If it still doesn't move, let your teacher know.

4. Disconnect the wire leads from the battery.

5. Design an investigation to test the variables that influence how fast the motor spins.

   When designing your experiment, think about the following questions:

   What is the purpose of your experiment?

   What is your hypothesis?

   What variable are you testing?

   What variables will you keep the same?

   What data will you record?

6. Record your hypothesis and your planned experimental procedure in your science notebook.

7. Conduct your investigation, and record your results in your science notebook.

Part B: Investigating electric generators

8. Hold the small electric motor about 1 cm from a compass, and move it around the compass. Record your observations.

9. With the two wire leads attach the motor to the battery holder as shown below. Unclip one of the leads from the battery. Record your observations in your science notebook.

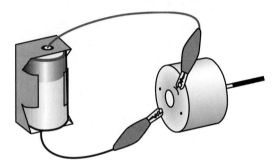

10. Reclip the wire leads so that their positions are switched from the way that they were in Step 9. Observe and record any similarities and differences between these observations and those you made in Step 9. Unclip one of the wire leads from the battery.

11. Repeat Steps 9 and 10 but replace the motor with the LED bulb. Record your observations in your science notebook.

12. Repeat Steps 9 and 10, but this time use the wires to attach the motor to the LED bulb instead of to the battery holder, as shown below.

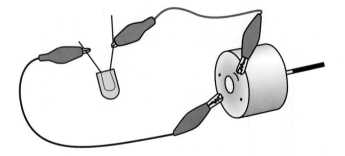

13. Hold the body of the motor in one hand, and grasp the rotor of the motor between the thumb and forefinger of your other hand. Spin the rotor as fast as you can. Do this several times, and record your observations in your science notebook.

14. Repeat Step 13, but this time spin the motor in the other direction.

ANALYSIS

1. Electromagnetism refers to the magnetism that occurs when electric charges are in motion. What evidence did you observe for the existence of electromagnetism in this activity?

2. What does an electric motor need in order to work?

3. What does an electric generator need in order to work?

 4. Using evidence from your investigation, describe the variables that influence how fast a motor spins.

5. Predict the variables that would affect the amount of electricity a generator generates. Explain the reasoning behind your prediction.

EXTENSION

Design an experiment to investigate how changes to the coil affect how fast a motor spins.

Energy is involved in everything that happens. We are aware of energy when it is released or absorbed. Examining the changes of energy in action has led to one of the most important scientific ideas central to all science disciplines.

CHALLENGE **What is the guiding principle behind the behavior of energy?**

Energy, light, and sound are released when fireworks explode.

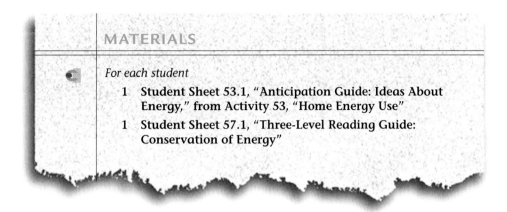

MATERIALS

For each student

1   **Student Sheet 53.1, "Anticipation Guide: Ideas About Energy," from Activity 53, "Home Energy Use"**

1   **Student Sheet 57.1, "Three-Level Reading Guide: Conservation of Energy"**

READING

Use Student Sheet 57.1, "Three-Level Reading Guide: Conservation of Energy" to guide you through the following reading.

ENERGY ACTION

Releasing Energy, Absorbing Energy

From our everyday experiences, energy seems to us like it is something that people consume. It often appears that energy is "used up" when, actually,

Oil was formed over millions of years deep inside the earth from decayed plants and animals. The plants and animals absorbed energy from other sources such as food and sunlight.

it has not disappeared. Instead, energy is transferred and/or transformed into another energy type. For example, the energy in the food we eat food provides thermal energy for our bodies. Or the chemical energy in gasoline is released and transformed into the motion of the car. Everyday energy "consumptions" are really energy transformations in which energy is released.

Following energy as it is transferred and transformed shows us a chain of interactions that both release and absorb energy. Take oil, for example. Oil formed in the ground over millions of years from the decay of dead plants and small animals. The energy in the plants originally came from sunlight, which the plants transformed into chemical energy through the process of photosynthesis. The energy in the animals came from the food they ate. When oil in a furnace burns, the chemical potential energy in the oil is released as thermal energy which we feel as warmth.

The Law of Conservation of Energy

If you compared the amount of chemical potential energy of the oil in the furnace before it was burned to the amount of thermal energy coming out of the furnace, you would find they were different. There is less energy released from burning oil than there was chemical potential energy stored in it. What happened to the other energy? Not all of the chemical energy in the oil is transformed into thermal energy during the burning. Some was transformed into an energy type that's easy to overlook. In the case of the burner, a small amount of the chemical potential energy in the oil was transformed into light and some into sound, and some remained in the ash and was not released. Sometimes the "missing" energy from a process is called "lost energy." This lost energy has turned into another energy type that is not recognized or used. Sound and light may not be energy useful for heating in this example, but it must be considered part of the total energy released by the burning oil.

The total amount of energy in a system is the same before and after a transformation. Energy can be transferred or transformed, but cannot be lost or destroyed. This idea is known as the **Law of Conservation of Energy**. This means that the total amount of energy before something happens must be equal to the amount afterward, regardless of the process or energy types involved. The Law of Conservation of Energy doesn't say which kind of energy must be present before and after an event, just that the total energy doesn't change.

The Law of Conservation of Energy is one of the central principles in science and applies to many disciplines. For example, a biologist can apply this law when examining a food web. Biologists have tracked the amount of chemical energy in a producer, such as grass, through several consumers, such as a cow and a person. It appears that some of the chemical potential energy in all of the grass eaten by the cow is "lost" before the person drinks milk from the cow. However, a closer look reveals that this chemical energy was transformed into a variety of energy types, including the mechanical energy used by the cow to move around and the energy released by the cow's metabolism.

The Process of Heating

Thermal energy is almost always released during an energy transformation. For example, a lightbulb transforms electrical energy into light, but the system loses energy by heating. A hot lightbulb is evidence of this. When you drive a nail into a block, the nail becomes warm, indicating that some of the mechanical energy hitting the nail was turned into thermal energy. The process of heating, although useful in many situations and critical to life, is not always desirable. With the lightbulb, usually the desirable energy type is light, not thermal energy.

The interior of a motor.

Large generators at a hydroelectric power plant.

A combustion engine is assembled.

Thermal energy that is released during a transformation is not lost or destroyed but is dissipated, or spread out, which makes it hard to harness. Therefore, transforming thermal energy into other types of energy is more difficult than many other transformations. Even with the most innovative technology, only about 40% of thermal energy can be converted into useful mechanical energy. Similarly, it is difficult to convert thermal energy into chemical or electrical energy. Although many transformations release thermal energy, it can be a challenge to capture and use it.

Energy Efficiency

No energy transformations result in 100% useful energy, and people who are concerned with energy evaluate energy transformations by efficiency. **Efficiency** is the ratio of useful energy that is released to the total energy absorbed by the process. For example, a car's engine transforms the chemical potential energy of gasoline into other types of energy. About 74% of the energy in the gasoline is released by heating, but only the remaining 26% is transformed into motion from the engine. Although no energy is created or destroyed, the engine's efficiency is only 26%, or the portion of useful energy that was released. Interestingly enough, since the engine has to overcome air, road, and transmission resistance, it turns out that only about 3% of the original chemical potential energy actually moves the car.

Appliances and other devices are rated by the government for their energy efficiency. When a certain model of an appliance is described as "energy efficient," it usually means that it uses less energy than comparable models that produce the same result. For example, a newer refrigerator that has an "Energy Star" consumes less energy than older models of refrigerators consume to cool the same volume of food at the same temperature. By consuming less energy to do the same work, an Energy Star appliance increases efficiency.

New appliances come with a tag that provides an energy efficiency rating.

An important idea that is related to efficiency is the term conservation. **Energy conservation** (not to be confused with the Law of Conservation of Energy) means to reduce, or "save," the total energy transformed in the first place. For example, someone who turns out lights when not using them is conserving energy. Keeping a lightbulb off when not in use is related to conservation because it will use less energy, or conserve energy. Another way to conserve energy is to use an energy-efficient device that uses less energy when it is on. Using energy efficiently saves energy resources, reduces environmental pollutants, and reduces cost. For these reasons, learning how to convert energy more efficiently is a major goal of technology and engineering.

ANALYSIS

1. Which of the following diagrams accurately applies the Law of Conservation of Energy to a toaster in use? Explain your choice.

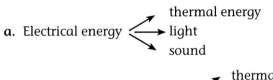
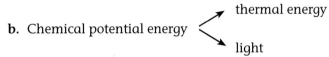

   a. Electrical energy ⟶ thermal energy / light / sound

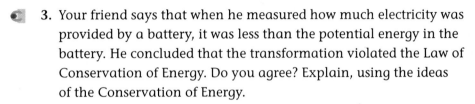

   b. Chemical potential energy ⟶ thermal energy / light

 2. Your friend tells you that a "generator makes electricity." Do you agree or disagree with her statement? Explain why in terms of the Law of Conservation of Energy.

 3. Your friend says that when he measured how much electricity was provided by a battery, it was less than the potential energy in the battery. He concluded that the transformation violated the Law of Conservation of Energy. Do you agree? Explain, using the ideas of the Conservation of Energy.

4. Which energy is often called the "graveyard of kinetic energy" and why?

5. What is the efficiency of an engine that gives off 70% thermal energy?

Since energy is never created or destroyed, it is possible to follow energy transfer through many transformations. If you follow energy transformations far enough, you will find something interesting: most of the energy here on earth can be traced all the way back to the Sun. The Sun emits electromagnetic energy, or light, which is produced from nuclear reactions occurring in its center. When the Sun's energy reaches us here on Earth, it is transformed into many types of energy that sustain life.

CHALLENGE ➡ **Can you follow the transforming energy?**

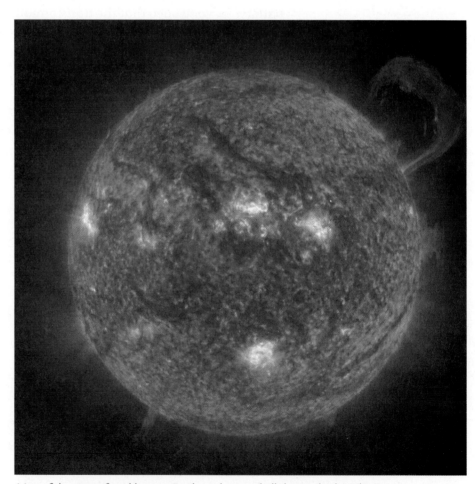

Most of the energy found here on Earth can be traced all the way back to the Sun.

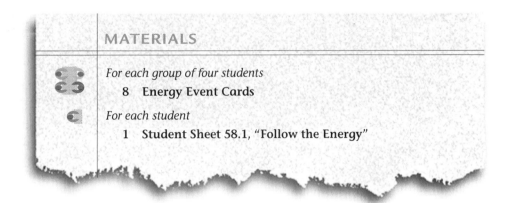

MATERIALS

For each group of four students
8 **Energy Event Cards**

For each student
1 **Student Sheet 58.1, "Follow the Energy"**

PROCEDURE

1. Look at the table "A Summary of Energy Types" on the next page that describes different types of energy found in nature or human inventions.

2. With your group, examine the eight Energy Event Cards, and compare them to the table.

3. Chose an Energy Event Card, and identify all the energy types involved in the transformation shown. Use Student Sheet 58.1, "Follow the Energy," to record the energy types before and after the transformation.

4. In the last column on Student Sheet 58.1, "Follow the Energy," write a complete sentence or two that describes the energy transformation shown on the Energy Event Card. Include all the energy types you listed.

5. Repeat Steps 3–4 for the other seven Energy Event Cards.

ANALYSIS

1. Copy the lists of words shown below.

List 1:	List 2:	List 3:
kinetic energy	chemical energy	fossil fuels
potential energy	potential energy	stored energy
light	nuclear energy	chemical energy
sound	thermal energy	absorb energy
		release energy

   a. Look for a relationship among the words in each list. Cross out the word in each list that does not belong with the others.

   b. Circle the word in each list that is a category that includes the others.

   c. Explain how the word you circled relates to the other words in the list, and how the word you crossed out does not fit in the list.

A Summary of Energy Types

Energy Type	Name	Depends on	Description	Example
Potential Energy	Chemical	Type of substance	Energy stored in the bonds of atoms	Energy stored in fossil fuels and food
	Elastic	Springiness of object	Energy stored by stretching or compressing	Energy stored in a stretched rubber band or compressed foam
	Electric (static)	Electron-charge buildup	Energy stored by the buildup of charges (electrons or ions)	Charge building up on person walking on a rug or combing fine hair
	Gravitational	Height and mass	Energy stored due to an object's mass and height	Energy stored due to the mass and position of a train on the top of a roller coaster or water at the top of a waterfall
	Nuclear	Stability of atom	Energy that is stored in the nucleus of atoms	Energy stored in uranium-238 atoms, energy stored in the nucleus of hydrogen atoms in the center of the Sun
Kinetic Energy	Electric (current)	Charge, conductivity	Movement of charge and energy from one place to another	Lightning, electricity through wires
	Light	Intensity and frequency	Energy transferred by the rapid movement of electromagnetic fields	Sunlight or X rays
	Motion (kinetic)	Mass, speed	Movement of an object from one place to another	Wind or a moving train
	Sound	Loudness	Energy transferred by the vibration of an object	Music in air or voices under water
	Thermal	Mass, material, and temperature	Energy transferred in transit from a hot to a cold object	Hot plate heating up water, or hot water cooling to room temperature

2. The diagram below shows the transfer of energy from the Sun all the way to a student using a computer. Using the table on the previous page, decide on the type of energy at each of the situations. There may be more than one energy type at each place.

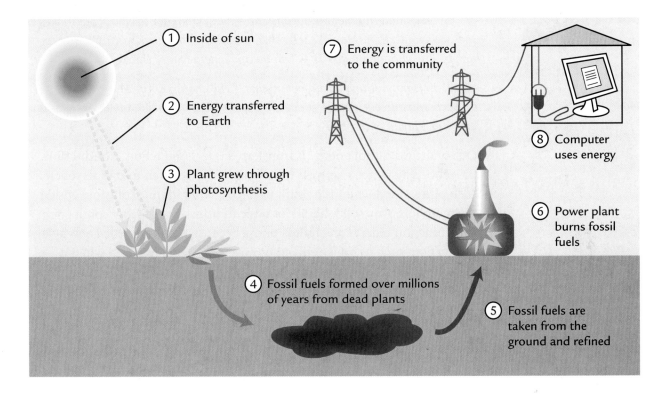

① Inside of sun

② Energy transferred to Earth

③ Plant grew through photosynthesis

④ Fossil fuels formed over millions of years from dead plants

⑤ Fossil fuels are taken from the ground and refined

⑥ Power plant burns fossil fuels

⑦ Energy is transferred to the community

⑧ Computer uses energy

LABORATORY

Mom, there is one thing I don't get about heat," said Yasmin. " I under-stand that heat is a transfer of energy from hot to cold. That makes sense when two things touch each other, like when a hot pack warms up my hands. But what about air? How can thermal energy move through nothing?"

"Well, air is not nothing," said her mother. "The energy is transferred when molecules bump into each other. It doesn't matter if the molecules are in a gas, like air, or in a liquid or a solid."

One of the ways that energy is transferred is by conduction. **Conduction** is the process by which energy is transferred directly when materials touch each other. Conduction is a result of electron and atomic collisions inside the materials. Any solid, liquid, or gas can transfer energy by conduction. Sometimes an object can change phase because it has absorbed energy by conduction, such as an ice cube that turns from solid to liquid when it melts in a drink. Materials that have a structure that easily allows energy transfer are called **conductors**. Examples of good conductors are copper and aluminum.

CHALLENGE ➡ **How can you increase the energy transferred to an ice cube?**

CONDUCTION IN A GAS

The diagram shows the collision of a single hot atom (red) and cool atom (pink). As a result of the collision, some of the thermal energy from the hot atom is transferred to the cool one.

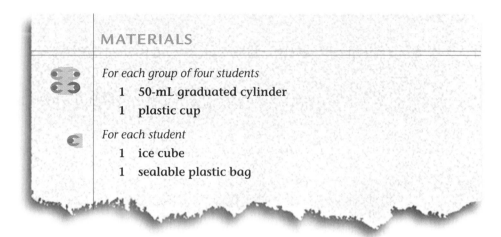

MATERIALS

For each group of four students

1   50-mL graduated cylinder

1   plastic cup

For each student

1   ice cube

1   sealable plastic bag

SAFETY

Do not put the ice or the bag in your mouth.

PROCEDURE

1. Review the Ice-Melting Rules shown below.

2. With your group, discuss the things you could do to melt as much of the ice cube as possible in the set timeframe. Record your ice-melting plan in your science notebook.

3. Your teacher will instruct you on how to get your ice cube. Then melt as much of it as you can in the time allowed.

4. When the contest is over, carefully pour the water from your plastic bag into the graduated cylinder, and record the volume of the water in your science notebook. Each member of your group will do this separately.

5. Record the volume of water your teacher obtained in the control bag.

Ice-Melting Rules

• Keep the ice cube in the plastic bag until the end of the contest.

• You may not put the ice or the bag in your mouth.

• Handle your bags carefully. A broken bag will disqualify you.

• Keep all water in the plastic bag. Water that spills or leaks out of the bag will not be measured.

• Watch carefully for your teacher's start and stop signals.

• As soon as the contest time is up, remove the remaining ice from the plastic bag, place it in the cup provided, and set it aside.

ANALYSIS

1. What volume of water did you collect? Compare your results with the control and with other students' results.

2. What did you do to maximize the rate at which your ice melted? Describe the techniques you used.

3. When melting the ice, how did you use:
   a. conduction?
   b. energy transformation(s)?

4. Which of your classmates' techniques seemed to transfer:
   a. the most energy?
   b. the least energy?

5. List all of the variables that affected how fast the ice melted. Choose one of these variables, and design an investigation to test if changing this variable would affect the melting speed.

LABORATORY

asmin wanted to know what her mother was doing. It was a beautiful fall day, but instead of heading outside as usual, she was pulling out hammers, nails, masks, and a big roll of thick, cloth-like material. Uncle Raymond was on his way over, too. "Mom, what's going on?" Yasmin asked.

"I am going to insulate the house today," her mother said. "I want to reduce our energy bill by making the house more energy efficient."

Yasmin looked over the items on the floor. She loved to build things. "Can I help, Mom?"

"Sure you can. Just make sure to put on long sleeves and a mask so you won't inhale fibers from the insulation."

Sometimes we need to minimize the transfer of energy. Materials that are poor conductors and, therefore, slow down the rate of energy movement are called **insulators**. Examples of insulators are wood, wool, and paper. In houses, insulating materials help to keep energy from transferring outdoors in the winter and from moving inside in the summer.

CHALLENGE How can you insulate an ice cube?

This fiberglass insulation minimizes the heat transfer through the wall.

MATERIALS

For each group of four students

1   50-mL graduated cylinder
1   plastic cup

For each pair of students

1   ice cube
1   sealable plastic bag
1   empty 1.89-L (1/2-gal.) milk carton
    materials from home for preserving your ice cube

SAFETY

Do not put the ice or the bag in your mouth.

PROCEDURE

1. Review the Ice-Melting Rules in Activity 59, "Ice-Melting Contest," and "Additional Contest Rules" shown here.

2. Discuss with the class how to set up a control for this contest.

3. Work with your partner to design an insulating container for your ice cube. Discuss how you think your design will prevent energy transfer. Decide what materials you will need, and sketch your design in your science notebook.

4. With your teacher's permission, build the insulating container.

5. Your teacher will instruct you on how to get your ice cube. Then preserve as much ice as you can in the time allowed.

6. As your ice cube sits in its insulating container, read the article on the next page. Answer the questions with your partner.

7. When the contest is over, carefully pour the water from your plastic bag into the graduated cylinder, and record the volume of water in your science notebook. Each member of your group will do this separately.

8. Record the volume of water your teacher obtained in the control bag.

9. With your partner, present your design to another pair of students. Get their feedback on what could improve your insulating container. Then switch roles, and provide ideas on how to improve the other pair's design.

10. With the feedback from the previous step, redesign the insulating container to improve it.

ADDITIONAL CONTEST RULES

• Keep the ice and bag on the table until directed to start the contest.

• No commercial coolers or thermoses allowed.

ANALYSIS

 1. What volume of water did you collect? Compare your results with the control and with other pairs' devices.

 2. What did you do to decrease the rate at which your ice melted? Describe the materials and techniques you and your partner used.

3. Which among your and your classmates' techniques seemed to transfer:

   a. the most energy?

   b. the least energy?

4. Look carefully at the pictures of buildings below. In your science notebook, write a short description of each picture. Be sure to include:

   a. what material you think the house is made of.

   b. how well you think that material insulates from thermal energy transfer.

EXTENSION

Research the materials that are shown in the houses below, and use the information to rank the houses from the best to the worst insulated.

A

B

C

D

READING

Keeping Cool

It's the hottest day of the summer. Your friend comes to visit, and the two of you decide to get cold drinks from the refrigerator. Once you have them, you alternate between sipping the cool drink and holding it against your hot forehead. Because of conduction, some of the energy from your body transfers to the cool drink when it touches your forehead. It may feel like the cold is moving into your body, but in actuality, what you feel is the loss of the thermal energy that transfers to the drink. The drink gets warmer while your head gets cooler. The energy transfer cools your body, and it feels great.

Before the refrigerator was invented, people used iceboxes to transfer energy from food to ice. Iceboxes were usually made of wood and were lined with such insulating materials as cork, sawdust, and seaweed. Large blocks of ice placed in the icebox absorbed energy from the food that people put in the icebox. As more and more energy was transferred to the block of ice, it melted. A drip pan collected the melted water, and emptying it daily was a common kitchen chore. The ice had to be replaced every few days, creating business for companies that cut ice in the winter from northern lakes and rivers, and stored and delivered it. Eventually, commercial freezers made artificial ice for iceboxes.

The first iceboxes were developed in the mid 1700s but did not have widespread use until the 1900s. At the start of the 20th century, about half of homes in the United States had an icebox, and half had no cooled storage

Men cut large blocks of ice from a lake, 1942

Iceboxes required new ice every few days.

at all. Modern refrigerators started appearing in homes around 1915, and by 1944, 85% of American homes had one. Today, virtually all homes in the developed world have refrigerators. The invention of the refrigerator has allowed the modern family to preserve food products for much longer periods of time than was previously possible.

In a closed icebox, the ice is warmed as energy is transferred to it from the food. In a modern refrigerator, the air in the refrigerator absorbs the energy from the food. Then a special gas absorbs energy from the air in the refrigerator. That gas, known as a refrigerant, expands as it absorbs the energy. In order for the refrigerant to expand, however, it had to have been compressed in the first place. The initial compression of the refrigerant takes energy. The energy is usually provided through a motor. (This explains why refrigerators consume energy even though there is less energy in the inside air of the refrigerator than outside.) The energy from the refrigerant is transferred to the air immediately outside the refrigerator with fans. A simplified version of the refrigeration cycle is shown on next page.

It is important to note that the diagram shows the refrigerant circulating in this cycle and not the air inside the refrigerator. The refrigerant is a special gas that is housed in the machinery behind the refrigerator compartment. The gas never touches the food or the air in the compartment as it circulates. Only thermal energy is transferred from the food compartment to the refrigerant.

REFRIGERATION CYCLE

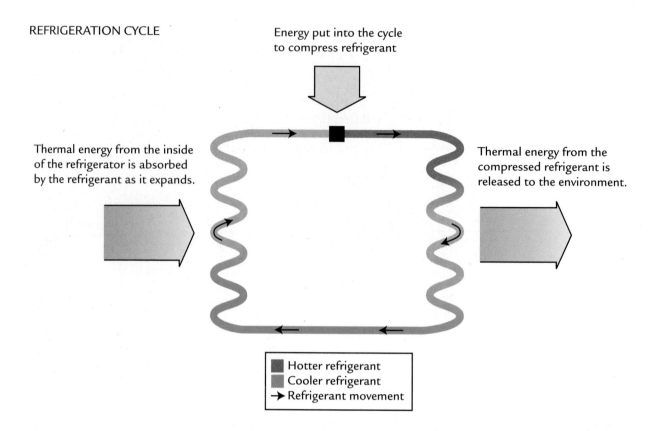

Air conditioners and refrigerators work on similar principles. In fact, air conditioning was developed in the early 1900s around the same time as refrigerators. Early air conditioners were made to improve industrial processes that need stable humidity and temperature, like printing, rather than for use in people's home. These days, air conditioning is commonplace in the United States in cars, houses, apartments, and commercial buildings to keep people comfortable.

Window-mounted room air conditioners, like refrigerators, have refrigerant flowing in the back of the device. In central air-conditioning systems the refrigerant equipment is usually located in an outdoor box next to the house or on the roof of the building. Fans in the air conditioner blow hot air away from the air conditioner and the cooled air toward the rooms to be cooled.

Both air conditioners and refrigerators work most efficiently when the volume of air they are trying to cool is well insulated. This prevents energy from moving into the space being cooled. For example, a refrigerator needs to be lined with insulating materials and have a good seal on the door. Air conditioners in a house should be in a well-sealed space that doesn't allow much energy to transfer through doors, walls, and windows.

The scientific understanding of energy transfer led inventors to develop solutions to the problems of controlling temperature. The development of the refrigerator and air conditioner has improved the quality of life and the way people live their everyday lives.

THINKING IT OVER

1. Which statement is scientifically accurate?

   a. "Don't let the cold energy out of the fridge!"

   b. "Don't let the energy into the fridge!"

   Explain your choice in terms of energy transfer.

2. Why is the air immediately around a refrigerator warm?

3. What happens if an air conditioner is used in a house that is not well insulated and not well sealed? Explain in terms of energy transfer.

LABORATORY

Yasmin, her mom, and Uncle Raymond were at a restaurant having break-fast. Uncle Raymond complained that his coffee had cooled off. He asked the waiter for a "touch up" of hot coffee. The waiter filled Raymond's half-full cup of cool coffee with steaming hot coffee. Raymond knew that Yasmin was studying energy. He looked over at his niece. "Now, Yasmin," he asked, "Is my coffee too hot to drink?"

CHALLENGE ⟹ **What happens to the energy when hot and cool water are mixed?**

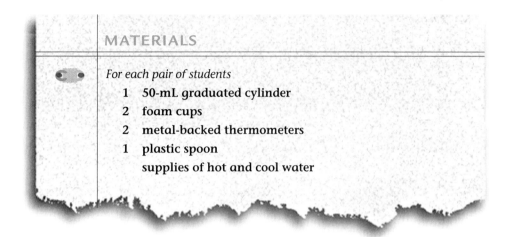

MATERIALS

For each pair of students

1 50-mL graduated cylinder
2 foam cups
2 metal-backed thermometers
1 plastic spoon
   supplies of hot and cool water

PROCEDURE

1. With your partner, consider what will happen if you mix each of the following:

Experiment 1: 60 mL of hot water (60°C) with 60 mL of cool water (20°C)

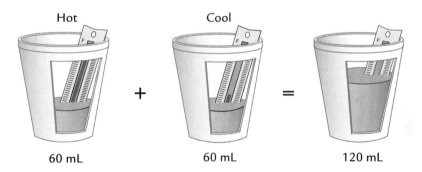

Hot	Cool	
60 mL	60 mL	120 mL

Experiment 2: 60 mL of hot water (60°C) with 30 mL of cool water (20°C)

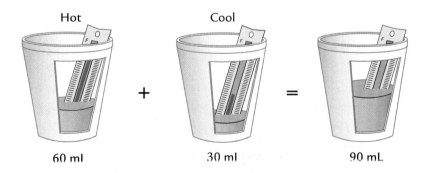

Hot	Cool	
60 ml	30 ml	90 mL

Experiment 3: 30 mL of hot water (60°C) with 60 mL of cool water (20°C)

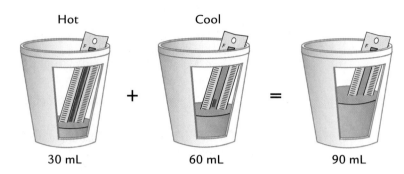

Hot   Cool

30 mL   60 mL   90 mL

2. Discuss what you think will happen to the energy and the temperature for each experiment. Record your predictions in your science notebook.

3. Make a table similar to the one below in your science notebook.

Mixing Water Data

Experiment	Water	Volume (mL)	Starting Temperature (°C)	Final Temperature (°C)	Temperature Change (°C)
1	Hot	60			
	Cool	60			
2	Hot	60			
	Cool	30			
3	Hot	30			
	Cool	60			

4. With your partner, follow your teacher's instructions for obtaining 60 mL of cool water and 60 mL of hot water in each of your foam cups.

5. Measure the starting temperature of the cool and hot water. Record the temperatures in the table.

6. Quickly add the cool water to the hot water. Stir gently with a spoon until the temperature of the mixture remains steady. Record the final temperature in the data table.

7. Calculate the temperature change for the mixture. Record the change in the table.

8. Empty the cups and repeat Procedure Steps 4–7, but use the volumes for Experiment 2 and Experiment 3.

ANALYSIS

1. Were the results what you expected? Compare your and your partner's predictions to the actual results.

2. When you mixed equal volumes of hot and cool water, how did the final temperature compare to the starting temperatures?

3. When you mixed **un**equal volumes of hot and cool water, how did the final temperature compare to the starting temperatures?

4. For all the experiments, explain what happened to the thermal energy in the water when the hot and cool water were mixed.

5. In any of the experiments, would it have been possible for the final temperature to be greater than the initial temperature?

6. Did any energy leave the cup-and-water system? Describe the evidence that supports your answer.

EXTENSION

Design an experiment to measure the temperature changes of hot and cool water that are not directly mixed, but instead are held next to each other. Use a plastic cup to separate the water, as shown in the diagram below. Before conducting the experiment, predict the temperature of the hot and cold water after a certain amount of time.

INVESTIGATION

When hot water melts an ice cube, some of the thermal energy of the liquid water is transferred to the ice through heating. This energy overcomes the forces between molecules in the ice. When enough energy has been transferred to the ice to create a phase change, the ice melts. The amount of thermal energy the ice absorbed while melting is equal to the thermal energy that the water released. This energy can be quantified by measuring the temperature change of the water and then using it to calculate the energy the water lost.

CHALLENGE ⟹ **How much energy does it take to melt an ice cube?**

The ice cubes absorb thermal energy, which causes them to melt.

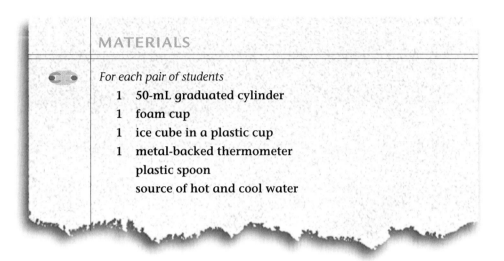

MATERIALS

For each pair of students

1 50-mL graduated cylinder
1 foam cup
1 ice cube in a plastic cup
1 metal-backed thermometer
   plastic spoon
   source of hot and cool water

SAFETY

Use caution when working with the hot water. If you spill any on your hand, hold your hand under cool water for five minutes.

PROCEDURE

1. Follow your teacher's directions for obtaining an ice cube and some hot water.

2. Put 100 mL of hot water into the foam cup.

3. Record the starting temperature of the hot water in your science notebook.

4. Immediately shake any water off of the ice cube, and place it in the hot water.

5. Gently stir until the ice is completely melted. Observe the cup carefully since it can be difficult to see the moment at which all the ice has melted.

6. As soon as the ice has melted, measure and record the final temperature of the water.

7. Calculate the change in the water temperature, and record it in your science notebook.

8. Calculate the amount of thermal energy lost by the water by using the formula below:

$$\text{energy released (°C g)} = \frac{\text{temperature change}}{\text{of water (°C)}} \times \frac{\text{mass of}}{\text{water (g)}}$$

Hint: 1 mL of water weighs 1 gram.

9. Record the energy lost by the water in your science notebook.

ANALYSIS

1. If the energy absorbed by the ice is exactly equal to the energy lost by the water, what was the amount of energy needed to melt the ice? Show your calculation.

2. Do you think *all* of the energy lost by the hot water was transferred to the ice? Explain.

3. Do you think that stirring the mixture had an effect on the melting of the ice? Explain why or why not.

4. Based on your answers to Analysis Questions 2 and 3, do you think your calculation of the heat energy absorbed by the ice is likely to be too high or too low? Explain.

5. How is the energy transfer in this experiment similar to the energy transfer that occurs in a house? Explain, and provide an example.

LABORATORY

Scientists use a device called a **calorimeter**, as shown below, to measure the amount of chemical potential energy there is in all sorts of materials. To determine the chemical energy of a material, scientists first measure the mass of a sample of the material. Then they place the sample in a sealed container called a bomb. They put the bomb in a well-insulated container filled with a known volume of water. An electrical spark from inside the bomb starts the sample burning. The water in the container absorbs the energy released by the burned sample. A thermometer measures the change in the temperature of the water. The potential energy of the original material is equal to the thermal energy transferred to the water.

In this activity, you will use a simple calorimeter to measure the amount of stored energy in a nut. When you eat a nut, or any other food, the potential chemical energy in it is released and used by your body. A calorimeter can determine the amount of stored energy in the nut, measured in calories. A **calorie** is the energy unit you explored in Activity 62, "Quantifying Energy"—it is the energy required to raise the temperature of one gram of water by 1°C. When describing the energy available in food, such as with the nut, the unit Calorie is used. A **Calorie**, with a capital C, is 1,000 calories.

CHALLENGE ➡ **How many Calories are in a nut?**

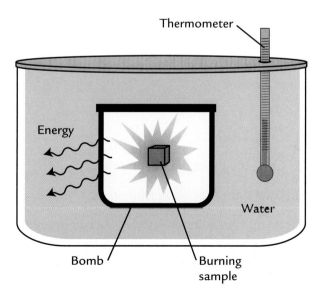

A CALORIMETER

Thermometer

Energy

Water

Bomb

Burning sample

MATERIALS

For each group of four students

1   wire coat hanger, wrapped with aluminum foil

1   aluminum beverage can

1   nut

1   SEPUP fuel holder

1   50-mL graduated container

1   glass thermometer

    wooden matches or lighter

1   cup of water

    tongs or potholder

For each student

1   pair of safety goggles

1   Student Sheet 53.1, "Anticipation Guide: Ideas About Energy," from Activity 53, "Home Energy Use"

SAFETY

Be sure to wear safety goggles during this investigation. Long hair must be tied back, and loose sleeves rolled up. If anything besides the nut starts to burn, inform your teacher immediately. **Be especially careful not to get clothing or your hair near the flame.** Make sure to keep a cup of water close by the experiment as a fire-safety precaution.

Notify your teacher if you are allergic to nuts.

The can may become quite hot. Carefully follow all instructions from your teacher.

PROCEDURE

1. Carefully place the nut on the fuel holder.

2. Pour 100 mL of water into the can.

3. Set up your calorimeter with the can hanging from the bent coat hangar as shown on the next page. Position the bottom of the can so it will be in the flame of the burning nut, but not so low that it will put out the flame.

THE CALORIMETER
APPARATUS.

4. Just before lighting the nut, record the starting temperature of the water.

5. Light the nut. When it begins to burn, slide it under the can, and let it burn completely. If you think the nut stopped burning before all its energy was transformed, ask your teacher for advice on relighting it.

6. As soon as the nut stops burning, use the thermometer to stir the water gently inside the can, and record its final temperature.

7. Calculate the change in the water temperature, and record it in your science notebook.

8. Calculate, in calories, the amount of heat energy the water gained, by using this formula:

$$\textbf{energy released (calories)} = \frac{\textbf{temperature change}}{\textbf{of water (°C)}} \times \frac{\textbf{mass of}}{\textbf{water (g)}}$$

Hint: 1 mL of water weighs 1 gram.

9. There are 1,000 calories in 1 Calorie. Determine how many Calories were in the nut, and record it in your science notebook.

ANALYSIS

1. How many Calories were in your nut? Show your calculation.

2. Explain, in terms of energy transfer and transformation, what caused the temperature of the water to change.

3. Was all of the energy from the burning nut transferred to the water? If not, explain what happened to the energy that was not transferred to the water.

4. How would you improve the design of this calorimeter so that it would work better?

   a. Draw a detailed, labeled diagram of your improved calorimeter. Be sure that you could build it yourself, if you had the materials.

   b. Explain why your design is better than the one you used.

5. If you burned a puffed cheese snack of the same size as the nut, would you get the same result? Why or why not?

6. A curious student wanted to know if the calorimeter would work with different amounts of water. The table below shows the results from her burning three nuts of the same type and mass, but using varied amounts of water in the can. Explain from the table below whether the calorimeter measured the energy in the nut properly when used with each amount of water.

EXTENSION

With your teacher's permission, measure the temperature change caused by burning a marshmallow or a puffed cheese snack.

Nut Experiment Data		
Experiment	Mass of Water (g)	Temperature Change (°C)
Nut 1	200	19
Nut 2	100	39
Nut 3	50	77

Food nutrition labels are required to show information about the energy in the food, measured in Calories.

Nutrition Facts

Serving Size 1 cup (228g)
Servings Per Container 2

Amount Per Serving

Calories 250   Calories from Fat 110

	% Daily Value*
Total Fat 12g	18%
Saturated Fat 3g	15%
Trans Fat 3g	
Cholesterol 30mg	10%
Sodium 470mg	20%
Potassium 700mg	20%
Total Carbohydrate 31g	10%
Dietary Fiber 0g	0%
Sugars 5g	
Protein 5g	

Vitamin A	4%
Vitamin C	2%
Calcium	20%
Iron	4%

* Percent Daily Values are based on a 2,000 calorie diet. Your Daily Values may be higher or lower depending on your calorie needs.

	Calories:	2,000	2,500
Total Fat	Less than	65g	80g
Sat Fat	Less than	20g	25g
Cholesterol	Less than	300mg	300mg
Sodium	Less than	2,400mg	2,400mg
Total Carbohydrate		300g	375g
Dietary Fiber		25g	30g

Now that Yasmin understood that energy can be measured, she started paying more attention to amounts of energy in her daily life. For example, she noticed that in addition to paying for heating the house with natural gas, her parents get a bill every month for the amount of electricity the family uses. When Yasmin took a household energy survey, she found that electricity was in almost constant use. She wondered where all that electrical energy came from.

Electrical energy used in the home and elsewhere comes from transforming natural resources of one kind or another. Some of those natural resources are renewable, and some are nonrenewable. A **renewable resource** is one that has a continuing supply, such as sunlight, water, wind, and biomass. To be considered renewable, a resource must be supplied faster than it is used up. A **nonrenewable resource**, such as coal, natural gas, and petroleum, is one that has a limited supply; once it is used up there is no more of it.

CHALLENGE

What are the advantages and disadvantages of the different sources of energy that produce electricity in the United States?

Electricity is brought to communities from power plants through transmission lines.

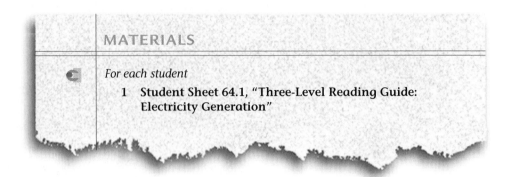

MATERIALS

For each student
1   **Student Sheet 64.1, "Three-Level Reading Guide: Electricity Generation"**

READING

Use Student Sheet 64.1, "Three-Level Reading Guide: Electricity Generation," to help you complete the following reading.

Where Does Electricity Come From?

Electrical energy is a convenient and important kind of energy. For over 100 years, people have put it to work in almost every area of human life. Americans use about 3.9 million *million* kilowatt-hours of electricity every year. (One kilowatt-hour is equal to the energy needed to light a 100-watt lightbulb for 10 hours.)

The term **electricity generation** refers to any one of several types of energy that is transformed into electricity. The transformation is usually done at a centralized **power plant**, which then distributes the electricity to the area around the plant. The first power plants burned coal to generate electricity. As well as coal, today's power plants run on other fossil fuels, the force of water, and nuclear energy. The newest ways of generating electricity— often called alternative energy—include solar power, tidal harnesses, wind generators, biomass, and geothermal resources. In fossil fuel, biomass, geothermal, or nuclear power plants, heat is released that boils water. High-pressure steam from the water turns the blades of a turbine. A **turbine** is like a large fan that uses mechanical energy to turn the blades. Then a **generator** transforms the rotating energy of the turbine into electricity.

Electrical power comes mainly from regional power plants. Those power plants are themselves fueled by various energy sources. In the United States, the major sources are coal, nuclear power, and natural gas. The chart on the next page shows the types of electricity generation we use in the United States and in what amounts. The map on the next page shows what parts of the country use what kinds of fuel.

U.S. ELECTRICAL SOURCES IN 2010

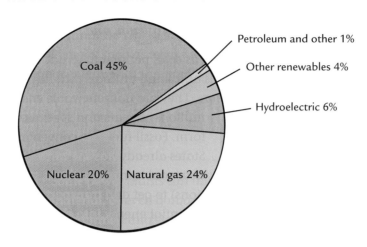

MAJOR POWER PLANTS IN THE CONTINENTAL UNITED STATES, BY TYPE

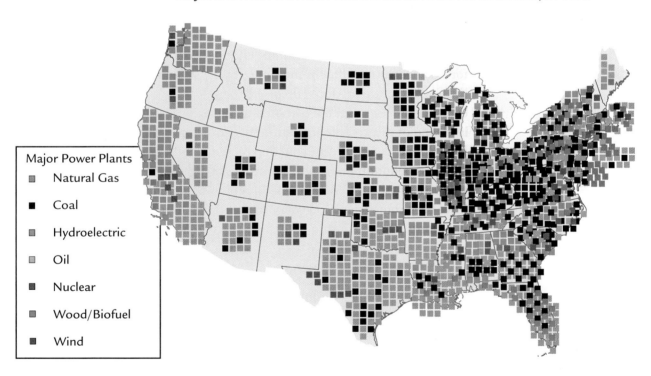

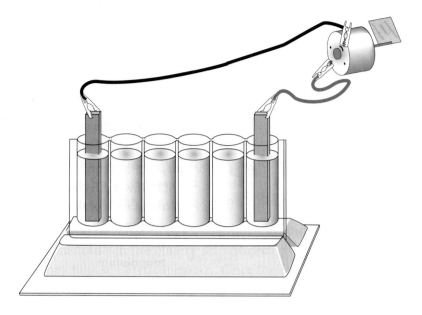

4. Lower the copper and magnesium strips into the outside slots of the SEPUP wet cell as shown. **There should be a small amount of metal sticking out of the cells.**

5. Observe the motor spinning.

   Hint: If the motor doesn't spin, try giving the flag a small push with your finger to start it. If it still does not spin, let your teacher know.

6. Once the motor spins, disconnect the wire leads. Remove the two metal pieces. Dry them, and then shine them with a piece of sandpaper. It is extremely important to completely dry the metals on a paper towel and clean both sides with the sandpaper!

Part B: The Effects of Different Metals

7. You just tested two metals, copper and magnesium, that, along with the electrolyte, transformed chemical energy into electrical energy. The motor transformed the electrical energy into the mechanical energy that caused the shaft to turn. Design an investigation to test other combinations of metals. While you're designing the investigation, think about the following questions:

   What is the purpose of your investigation?

   What will you observe or test?

   What materials will you need to conduct your investigation?

   How will you record your observations?

   How will you use the results to make a conclusion?

8. Obtain your teacher's approval for your investigation.

9. Conduct your investigation, and record the results in your science notebook.

Part C: Other Effects

10. Investigate what happens when you place the metals closer together. Use two strips that caused the motor to turn slowly. Place them in the slots at opposite ends of the SEPUP wet cell. In steps, move one strip from slot to slot so that it gets closer to the other strip. Observe what happens to the motor during each step. Make a table in your science notebook to record the results.

11. Investigate what happens to the direction the shaft turns when you reverse the connections. Use the zinc and copper combination of metals to explore this. Record your observations in your science notebook.

12. Investigate what happens to the motor as you gradually remove both of the metal strips from the electrolyte. Use a combination that caused the motor to spin rapidly to explore this. Record your observation in your science notebook.

ANALYSIS

1. Was there a chemical change when you inserted the strips into the electrolyte? Describe any evidence that supports your answer.

2. Use your results from Part B to rank the metal combinations from 1 to 6, with 1 as the highest-releasing electrical energy rate, and 6 as the least. Describe any evidence that determined the ranking.

   Magnesium/copper

   Magnesium/iron

   Zinc/copper

   Zinc/magnesium

   Zinc/iron

   Copper/iron

3. Look at the table below that describes the reactivity of the metals used in this activity. Compare the table to your response in Analysis Question 2.

   Based on the comparison:

   a. Does reactivity alone indicate what combinations of metals will release the most energy?

   b. What patterns do you see that could indicate why the most and least energy combinations occurred?

   c. Gold is the least reactive metal known and tends not to give up electrons. Which metal from the table would you pair it with to make a strong battery? Explain your choice.

 4. Make a table that summarizes your investigation in Part C. It should identify each effect, summarize the results, and include a brief explanation of why you think each result happened.

Reactivity of Common Metals		
Metal	**Reactivity**	**Tendency to Give Up Electrons**
Magnesium	Most	Most
Zinc	↓	↓
Iron		
Copper	Least	Least

5. From the materials in this activity, draw and label a battery that would produce the most energy.

EXTENSION

Design and conduct an investigation that tests the effect of changing the concentration of the electrolyte.

65A

Energy and Magnetic Fields

LABORATORY

In Activity 56A, "Motors and Generators," you generated electricity by transforming the kinetic energy of a spinning coil and the potential energy associated with a magnet. You also made a motor spin by applying an electric current to a coil of wire positioned close to a magnet. In neither case did the magnet touch the rest of the motor or generator. How then was the magnet able to affect the motor and generator?

The answer is that there is a magnetic field around the magnet. The field cannot be seen by the human eye but can be detected by the effect that it has on other magnetic objects. In this activity you will map magnetic fields with a compass. You will also read about fields and electromagnets.

CHALLENGE → **What are the properties of magnetic fields?**

A representation of the Earth's magnetic field

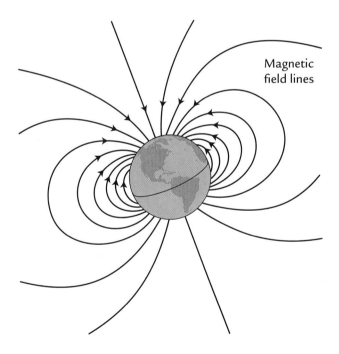

Magnetic field lines

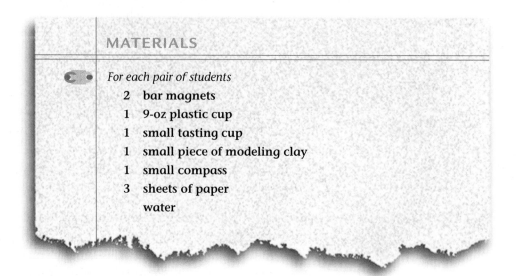

MATERIALS

For each pair of students

2   bar magnets
1   9-oz plastic cup
1   small tasting cup
1   small piece of modeling clay
1   small compass
3   sheets of paper
    water

PROCEDURE

Part A: Investigating magnetic fields

1. With a partner, take a small piece of modeling clay and fix one of the bar magnets flat inside the bottom of a tasting cup.

2. Fill the large plastic cup about two-thirds full of water. Make sure that the plastic cup is far from other magnets and from anything that contains iron.

3. Float the tasting cup on the water. If the tasting cup tilts to one side adjust the position of the magnet so that it is better centered.

4. Observe the movement of the tasting cup and the direction that the bar magnet is pointing. Record your observations in your science notebook.

5. Remove the magnet from the tasting cup, and place it end to end with a second magnet in the center of a sheet of paper. Position the magnets on the paper so that the ends with the red dots are pointing north.

6. Sketch the outline of the magnets on the paper. Mark the end with the red dot with the letter N and the other end with a letter S.

7. Place the compass close to the corner of one end of the magnets.

8. With a pencil make a dot on the paper to mark the position of the needle of the compass pointing away from the magnets.

9. Move the compass a small distance away from the magnets so that the other end of the needle is touching the dot you made in Step 8.

10. With a pencil make a dot on the paper to mark the position of the needle of the compass pointing away from the magnets as shown top right.

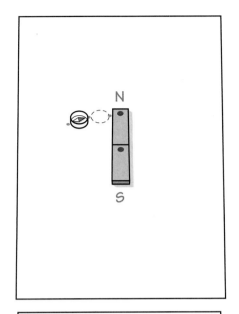

11. Repeat Steps 9–10 until the dots go off the page or return to the magnets.

12. Draw a smooth line through the dots you have made. Add an arrow to the center of the line pointing from the N end of the magnet to the S end.

13. Position the compass at another spot next to the magnets. Repeat Steps 8–12.

14. Repeat Step 13 at a minimum of eight positions around the magnets.

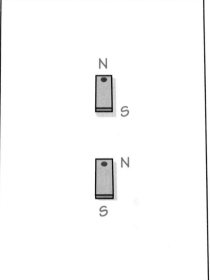

15. Place the two magnets about 5 cm apart in the center of a fresh sheet of paper. Arrange the magnets so that the N end (red dot) of one magnet is facing the S end of the other as shown center right.

16. Follow Steps 6–14 to plot the magnetic field between the two magnets.

17. Repeat Steps 15 and 16 with the two magnets arranged in the center of a fresh sheet of paper so that the N ends of the two magnets face each other as shown bottom right.

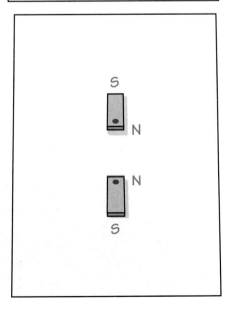

PART B: READING
Magnetism and Electromagnetism
Force Fields

When you pull a door open or push a drawer closed, you are applying a force directly to the door or drawer. It isn't always necessary, however, to make physical contact to apply a force provided a field is present. A field is a way of describing how two objects can interact with one another without touching. You will have experienced three types of fields—gravitational, magnetic, and electric. Gravitational fields affect anything with mass. Magnetic fields affect anything that is magnetic. Electric fields affect anything with charge. For each of these fields, work must be done to move against the field. For example, to move a mass away from the surface of the Earth requires work to be done, as when you lift a rock. As work is done the mass gains potential energy. When the mass is released it falls back to the Earth's surface and transforms the potential energy into other forms of energy, such as kinetic energy.

There are many similarities between gravitational, magnetic, and electric fields, but there are some important differences. Electric and magnetic fields can be made to cause both attraction and repulsion. When your clothes stick to your body on a dry day, it may be due to attraction between opposite charges on your body and clothes. When the north poles of two magnets are close together, they will repel one another. Gravitational fields, on the other hand, only cause attraction and never repulsion. Electric and gravitational fields are similar in that they only need a single mass or charge to form a field. Magnetic fields always involve pairs of north and south poles.

The Earth's magnetic field provides protection from the Sun's solar wind. (Illustration not to scale.)

We spend our entire lives in the Earth's magnetic field. Humans are not usually sensitive to magnetic fields, but birds and some mammals detect them. Some animals, such as migrating sea turtles, even rely on the Earth's magnetic field to navigate great distances. The Earth's magnetic field stretches into space and protects the surface of the Earth from charged particles from the sun (called the "solar wind").

Electromagnetism

The bar magnets that you used in the activity contained iron. Metals such as iron, cobalt, and nickel can behave as magnets. However, magnetic fields are also be produced by the flow of electricity. This is called electromagnetism. Unlike a regular bar magnet, an electromagnet can be controlled by varying the electric current. It becomes stronger when more current is applied and will stop being a magnet when the current is switched off. To make electromagnets even stronger, the electrical wires are often wound in coils around an iron core. Some electromagnets are tiny and are used to control switches in circuits as shown at left. They may also be big and powerful, such as those used to move cars and other metal objects in scrap yards, as shown below.

A reed switch is a tiny electromagnet found in some electronic devices.

ANALYSIS

1. What made the floating magnet move in Procedure Step 4?

2. What is a compass needle? Explain by using evidence from this activity.

3. State which kind of field causes the effect described in each of the following situations. Give reasons for your answers.

   a. An anchor sinks to the bottom of a lake.

   b. Your hair sticks to a comb.

   c. Two paper clips attract each other.

4. Describe the energy transformations in each of the following situations. Give reasons for your answers.

   a. A hot-air balloon takes passengers on a ride.

   b. An electromagnet is used to move a car to the top of a pile of junk.

Junkyards use large electromagnets to move iron and steel.

The batteries in the previous activity were part of an electrical circuit. A **circuit** is any path along which electrical energy can transfer. A circuit has to be a continuous loop made of electrically conducting material, such as copper. A circuit will work only if all the conductors in the loop are connected. For example, a light switch breaks a circuit when turned off and completes the circuit when turned on.

There are many kinds of circuits that range from simple to complex. With batteries a simple **series circuit** is one where all the components in the circuit are connected in succession with a battery. There is only one path for the electrical energy in the circuit. In a **parallel circuit**, the components are set up in the circuit so that the electrical energy has more than one conducting path from the battery.

CHALLENGE ⟶ **How is energy transferred and transformed in an electrical circuit?**

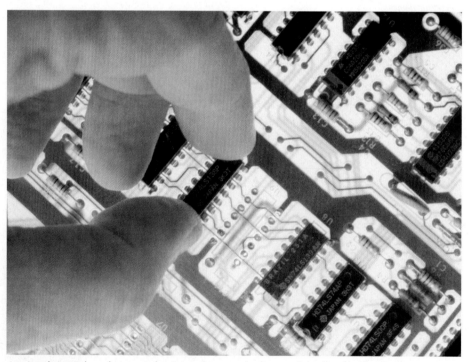

A printed circuit board uses conductive pathways etched onto a board to connect components.

MATERIALS

For each group of four students

1 buzzer
1 motor
1 strip each of:
   aluminum
   copper
   iron
   zinc
   magnesium
   polystyrene plastic
1 small carbon rod
1 glass rod
1 ceramic tile
1 block of wood
1 piece of granite
1 lightbulb in socket
2 wire leads with clips

For each pair of students

2 wire leads with clips
1 D (1.5 V) battery
1 battery holder
1 lightbulb in socket

PROCEDURE

ELECTRICITY SYMBOLS

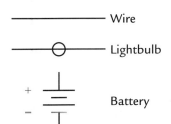

Part A: Conductors in a Circuit

1. With your partner, use the equipment to make one of the bulbs light up. In your notebook, draw a diagram of the circuit.

2. Replace the bulb and the socket with the motor. Observe and record what happens when the motor is part of the circuit.

3. Replace the motor in the circuit with the buzzer. Observe and record what happens when the buzzer is part of the circuit.

4. Design an investigation to determine what items from the materials list conduct electricity when placed in the circuit. Describe your design in your science notebook. Be sure to include:

The purpose of your investigation.

What you will observe or test.

What materials you will need for conducting your investigation.

What materials you predict will be good conductors.

How you will record your observations.

How you will use the results to make a conclusion.

5. Obtain your teacher's approval of your investigation.

6. Conduct your investigation, and record your results.

Part B: Series and Parallel Circuits

7. In your group of four, combine all your materials. Connect two batteries, four wire leads, and three lightbulbs in series. Use the diagram below to help you build the series circuit.

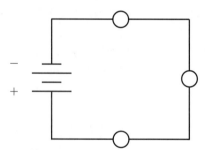

8. Unscrew one of the bulbs from the socket and observe what happens. Secure the lightbulb back into the socket, and record your observations in your science notebook.

9. Remove one of the bulbs and one wire from the circuit, and observe the circuit. Record your observations in your science notebook.

10. Remove another bulb and wire from the circuit, and observe the circuit carefully. Record your observations in your notebook. Make sure to comment on the differences between the 3-, 2-, and single-bulb combinations in series.

11. Disconnect the circuit.

12. Now build a parallel circuit using two batteries, six wire leads, and three lightbulbs. Use the diagram below to help you make the parallel circuit.

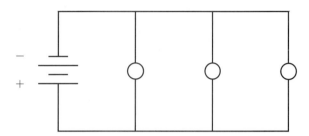

13. Remove one of the bulbs from its socket, and observe what happens. Return the lightbulb to the socket, and record your observations in your science notebook.

14. Replace one of the bulbs with the motor, and observe what happens.

15. Replace the motor with the buzzer, and observe what happens.

16. Remove the motor, and observe the circuit with two bulbs. Record your observations in your science notebook.

17. Remove another bulb and a wire from the circuit, and observe the circuit carefully. Record your observations in your science notebook. Make sure to comment on the differences between the 3-, 2-, and single-bulb combinations in parallel.

ANALYSIS

 1. Which materials were the best conductors? Explain how you know these materials conducted electricity better than other materials.

2. Describe the transfer and transformation of energy involved in a battery that lights up a bulb and runs a motor in a circuit.

3. Create a larger version of the Venn diagram shown below. Record the similarities of series and parallel circuits in the space that overlaps. In the labeled spaces that do not overlap, record differences between the circuits.

 4. Holiday lights are light-bulbs that are wired in a parallel circuit. Why is this a better idea than putting them in series?

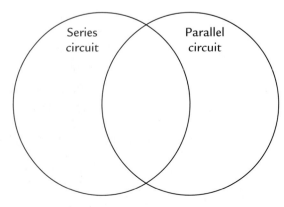

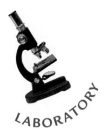

LABORATORY

Yasmin knew the lights in her room transformed electrical energy into light energy as part of an electrical circuit in the house. One time, she accidentally touched a lightbulb of a lamp she had just turned off, and it was quite hot. That means that some of the electrical energy was transformed into heat instead of light. She wondered how much of the bulb's energy was "lost" or given off as heat.

CHALLENGE → **What is the efficiency of a lightbulb?**

MATERIALS

For each group of four students

1   9-volt battery
1   battery harness and leads
1   foam cap with flashlight bulb and socket
1   foam cap
2   hot bulb trays
1   graduated cylinder
2   metal-backed thermometers
1   timer

For each student

1   Student Sheet 53.1, "Anticipation Guide: Ideas About
    Energy," from Activity 53, "Home Energy Use"

SAFETY

**Do not try this investigation with any other kind of battery or electrical
energy source without consulting your teacher. Never, under any
circumstances, place plugged-in electrical appliances in or near water.**

PROCEDURE

Part A: Collecting Data

1. Using the graduated cylinder, carefully measure 12 mL of water into the
   circular cup of one of the hot bulb trays.

2. Carefully place the foam cap with the bulb over Cup A and insert the
   thermometer, as shown on the next page.

3. Make a data table in your science notebook like the one on the next page.

4. Measure and record in the table the initial temperature of the water.

5. Prepare a control for this experiment in the second hot bulb tray. Decide
   in your group what to place in the control cup and what measurements
   to take.

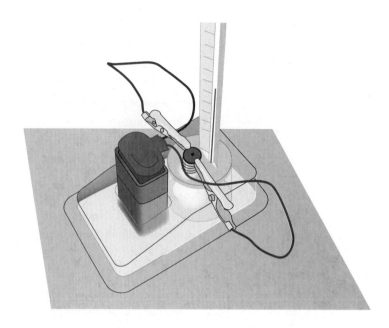

6. Clip one wire to one of the prongs on the brass socket. Clip the other wire to the other prong.

7. Connect the battery to the harness so that the bulb lights, as shown above. Keep the lighted bulb in the water for exactly 3 min. Time this as precisely as you can.

8. After 3 minutes, disconnect the battery from the bulb. Measure and record the temperature of the water.

9. Calculate the temperature changes of the water in the experimental and control cups. Record the results in your data table.

Lightbulb Data

Cup	Volume of Water (mL)	Time (minutes)	Initial Temperature (°C)	Final Temperature (°C)	Temperature Change (°C)
Experiment					
Control					

Part B: Calculating Efficiency

10. Make a table in your science notebook like the one below. Show your work and the calculations done in Procedure Steps 11–14 in this table.

Lightbulb Calculations

Cup	Thermal Energy Released (calories)	Electrical Energy Absorbed (calories)	Thermal Energy Output (%)	Light Efficiency (%)
Experiment				
Control				

11. Calculate the thermal energy released from the flashlight bulb using the equation:

energy released (calories) = temperature change (°C) × mass of water (mL)

Hint: 1 mL of water weighs 1 gram.

12. If the flashlight bulb uses about 27 calories of electrical energy for each minute it is lit, calculate the electrical energy input using the equation:

$$\textbf{electrical energy absorbed (calories)} = \frac{\textbf{time bulb is lit (minutes)}}{} \times \textbf{27 calories per minute}$$

13. Calculate the percent of thermal energy produced by the bulb using the equation:

$$\textbf{thermal energy output (\%)} = \frac{\textbf{thermal energy released}}{\textbf{electrical energy absorbed}} \times \textbf{100\%}$$

14. Calculate the light efficiency of the bulb using the equation:

Light efficiency (%) = 100% − thermal energy output (%)

ANALYSIS

1. Answer the following questions about the control in Cup E:

   a. Why should you use a control in an experiment?

   b. What did you place in the control cup? Explain why.

   c. What measurements did you take? Explain why.

   d. What did the results of your control tell you?

2. A typical lightbulb is about 5% efficient at producing light energy. Does your calculation agree with this? Explain why you think your calculation is or is not the same.

3. Are lightbulbs better at producing light or heat? Explain, using results from this experiment.

4. Do you think you would be more concerned about inefficient bulbs in a home that is in a warm climate or a colder one? Explain.

An incandescent, compact fluorescent, and halogen lightbulb.

5. The bulb used in this activity is an incandescent lightbulb. Look at the table below that compares an incandescent lightbulb to other kinds of bulbs that are about the same brightness. Answer the following questions:

   a. Which is the best lightbulb? Using the table, explain the evidence that helped you decide.

   b. Why do you think people buy more incandescent lightbulbs than any other bulb?

Comparisons for Equally Bright Lightbulbs

Characteristics	Incandescent	Compact Fluorescent	Halogen
Efficiency	5%	20%	9%
Rate of energy use	100 watts	23 watts	60 watts
Average lifetime	1,000 hours	12,000 hours	2,000 hours
Cost of one bulb	$0.75	$8.50	$6.00
Cost of electricity over lifetime of bulb	$12.00	$33.50	$14.00
Total cost per hour	$1.28	$0.35	$1.00

A light-emitting diode (LED) is an expensive but efficient kind of lightbulb. Although not typically used in homes, they are often used in car headlights, bicycle lights, traffic lights, and other road signs.

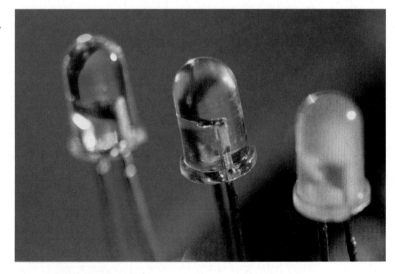

LABORATORY

asmin and her family were interested in renewable energy sources. After doing a little research, she began to focus on solar energy. She wondered if solar energy has enough advantages to justify installing it where she lives. Compared to other parts of the country, the climate Yasmin lives in tends to be cloudy and cold, particularly in winter.

While sunlight supplies only a small portion of the electricity used in the United States today, this amount is increasing. The Sun's energy is becoming a popular source of energy as more and more people view solar cells as a technology that can contribute to a sustainable energy supply. Solar **photovoltaic** (fo-toe-vol-TAY-ick) cells, also known simply as solar cells, transform sunlight directly into electricity. Often a group of photovoltaic cells are connected together, usually in series.

CHALLENGE ⟹ **How can you use solar cells to produce the most energy possible?**

Photovoltaic cells on the rooftops of homes provide electrical energy.

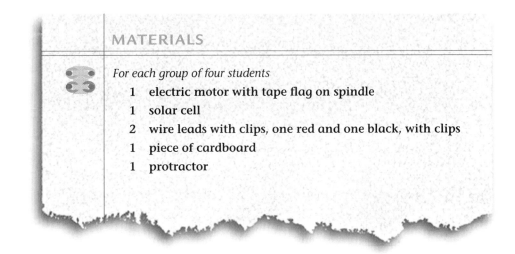

MATERIALS

For each group of four students

1	electric motor with tape flag on spindle
1	solar cell
2	wire leads with clips, one red and one black, with clips
1	piece of cardboard
1	protractor

PROCEDURE

Part A: Making a One-cell Circuit

1. With your group, set up a circuit that uses the photovoltaic cell to run the motor, as shown in the diagram below.

   • Decide on a method to measure how fast the motor spins.

   • Design an experiment to test how the angle of the Sun on the cell affects the rate at which the motor spins. While you're designing the investigation, think about the following questions:

   • What is the purpose of your investigation?

   • What will you observe or test?

   • What materials will you need for your investigation?

   • How will you record your observations?

   • How will you use the results to make a conclusion?

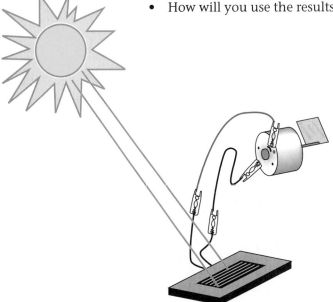

2. Obtain your teacher's approval for your investigation.

3. Conduct your investigation, and record the results in your science notebook.

Part B: More Effects

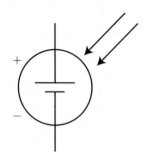

The schematic diagram
for a photovoltaic cell

4. Design a second investigation similar to the one in Procedure Step 3. Investigate how the amount of sunlight that falls on the solar cell affects the speed of the motor. Simulate the effects of a cloudy day by blocking portions of the cell with the cardboard.

5. Join with another group to connect two solar cells in series to drive the motor. Measure the speed of the motor, and record it in your science notebook. Compare it to the speed of a single cell.

ANALYSIS

1. For the solar single-cell setup that made the motor spin the fastest:

   a. Sketch and describe the setup, including the position of the solar cell relative to the Sun.

   b. Explain why you think this setup worked the best.

2. For the two-cell setup:

   a. Sketch and describe the setup.

   b. Compare and explain the effect of having two solar cells in series to having one.

3. In most of the United States, why don't solar cells provide enough electricity to run a house through a full day or a full year? Use evidence from this investigation to explain.

EXTENSION

Build a circuit where two solar cells are combined in parallel to run the motor. Measure the speed of the motor, and compare it to the speed when the cells are combined in series.

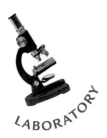

LABORATORY

Most of the energy types on Earth can be traced back to energy radiating from the Sun. As important as the Sun is to us, only a small fraction of its total radiant energy reaches Earth. Of the energy that does reach Earth, we can use only some of it to directly heat such things as houses, pools, office buildings, and food. In the last activity, you explored how solar energy can be transformed into electricity. In this activity, you will determine how efficient it is to transform the Sun's radiant energy into thermal energy.

CHALLENGE **What is the efficiency of a solar energy collector?**

MATERIALS

For each group of four students

1 water pump, with clear tubing and connector
1 piece of black plastic tubing
1 white plastic tubing holder
1 D-cell (1.5 V) battery
1 battery holder
2 wire leads with clips: one red, one black
2 metal-backed thermometers
1 50-mL graduated cylinder
1 foam cup
1 plastic cup

SAFETY

Do not try this investigation with any other kind of battery without consulting your teacher. Never, under any circumstances, place plugged-in electrical appliances in or near water. Be careful not to break the thermometers. Be aware that the metal on the thermometers may become quite hot in the sunlight.

PROCEDURE

Part A: Gathering the Data

1. With your group, use the diagram of the completed setup shown on the next page to guide you through the procedure.

2. Adjust the angle of the plastic holder so that it faces the Sun.

3. Attach one end of the black tubing to the pump by pushing it into the cylindrical opening on the side of the pump's base. The pump transports the heated water to and from the cup through the tubing.

4. Attach the red wire to the positive terminal of the pump (look for the small +). Connect the black wire to the negative terminal of the pump (look for the small –).

5. Place the pump upright in the foam cup. Avoid pinching the tubing.

6. Place the other end of the black tubing in the cup. This end of the tube returns the water to the cup. Make sure it is positioned so that it does not pour water onto the pump.

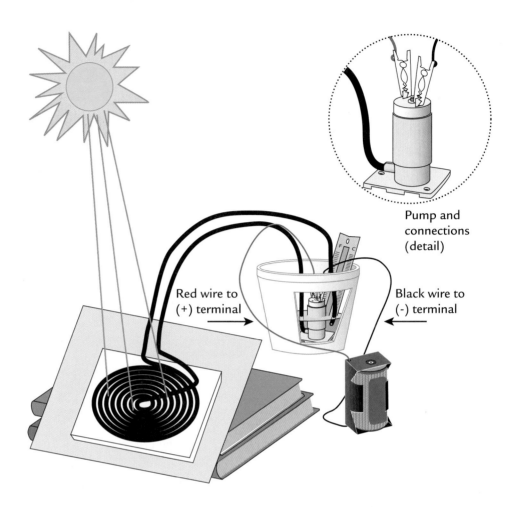

Pump and
connections
(detail)

Red wire to
(+) terminal

Black wire to
(-) terminal

7. Place the battery in the holder so that its tip (positive end) faces the side of the holder that has the red connector. Attach the red wire from the pump to the red wire from the battery.

   Note: Do not attach the black wire at this time!

8. Measure 100 mL of water into the plastic cup. Carefully pour just enough water from the plastic cup into the foam cup, which contains the pump, to cover the base of the pump.

   Note: Do not completely submerge the pump in water.

9. Place a thermometer in the foam cup with the pump. Take the temperature of the water in that cup. Leave the thermometer inside the cup.

10. Make a data table of your own design to record the temperature of the water every minute for 15 minutes. Remember to include a place to record the temperature of the class control.

11. To start the water pump, connect the black wire to the negative terminal of the battery. Begin timing. As water goes from the cup into the tubing, slowly add the rest of your 100 mL water. Do not allow the water level in the cup to rise more than 1 cm above the base of the pump.

12. Allow the pump to run for 15 minutes with direct sunlight on the tubing. Measure the temperature of the water every minute. Record this data in your table.

Note: Check the pump every few minutes to make sure it is still sitting in the water. The pump will be damaged if it runs without water.

13. After 15 minutes, disconnect the wires from the pump. Record the final temperatures of the water in the pump cup and the class control data. Calculate the change in temperatures, and record it in your table.

Part B: Calculating Efficiency

14. Make a table like the one below in your science notebook. Show the calculations for Procedure Steps 15–18, and record them in your table.

Calculating Energy Efficiency	
Energy transferred to water (calories)	
Area of solar heater (cm²)	
Energy transferred to the tubing (calories)	
Efficiency of heating system (%)	

15. You put 100 mL of water in the cup. Calculate how many calories of energy were transferred to the water.

Hint: Look back at Activity 67, "Hot Bulbs," to remember how to calculate the calories transferred to the water.

16. The tubing holder is approximately 20 cm wide.

a. With your group, decide what method you should use to determine the area of the solar heater.

b. Estimate the surface area of the solar heater in centimeters. Explain how you came up with this number.

17. If the Sun supplies 1.5 calories of energy per square centimeter per minute to the Earth, calculate how many calories were supplied to your tubing in 15 minutes.

18. Calculate the efficiency of the solar heating system using the following equation:

$$\text{Efficiency (\%)} = \frac{\text{calories transferred to the water}}{\text{calories supplied to the tubing}} \times 100\%$$

Part C: Improve the Design

19. With a partner from your group, brainstorm ways to improve the solar heating system.

20. Present your design to the other pair in your group. Get their feedback on what might improve your insulating container. Then switch roles, and provide feedback on their ideas.

21. As a group of four, choose the best ideas from the brainstorming, and redesign the solar heating system.

22. Retest the collector as described in Part A of the Procedure.

23. Recalculate the efficiency of the solar heating system as described in Part B of the Procedure.

ANALYSIS

1. The efficiency of a photovoltaic cell is about 11%. How does the efficiency of your solar heater compare?

2. How could you improve the design of your collector to increase its efficiency?

EXTENSIONS

Run the pump for the solar water-heater system using electricity from two solar cells placed in series rather than the battery. Investigate whether one solar cell will run the pump or if it takes more. Investigate ways to control the speed of the pump using the solar cells.

A woman in China uses a solar collector at her home to warm a tea kettle.

MODELING

When solar energy hits an object, the light can do several things. The light can be **absorbed**, or captured, by the object and transformed into heat. The light might also be **transmitted**, or travel through, the object and remain unaffected. Or, the light could be **reflected**, or bounced off, the surface of the object. In many cases, the light does some of each of these three. An example is when light hits glass: most of the light is transmitted through (since you can see through it), some is reflected (since you can see your own image), and a small amount is absorbed (since the glass heats up). Every object transmits, reflects, and absorbs some amount of solar energy depending on its individual properties.

CHALLENGE

Can you control the solar energy in a model house?

Light hitting this glass is reflected, transmitted, and absorbed.

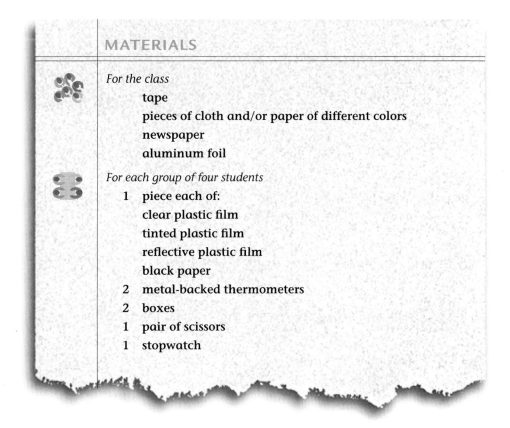

MATERIALS

For the class
> tape
> pieces of cloth and/or paper of different colors
> newspaper
> aluminum foil

For each group of four students
> 1 piece each of:
> clear plastic film
> tinted plastic film
> reflective plastic film
> black paper
> 2 metal-backed thermometers
> 2 boxes
> 1 pair of scissors
> 1 stopwatch

PROCEDURE

Part A: Build Your Model Houses

1. With your group, and using the materials provided for the class, modify one of your boxes (model house) so that it will absorb as much solar energy that can be transformed into heat as possible. Do not cut into or change the volume of the box.

2. Place one of the metal-backed thermometers in the center of your house.

3. Using the class materials, modify the other box so that it will absorb as little energy as possible. Do not cut into or change the volume of the box.

4. Place the second metal-backed thermometer in the center of your second house.

5. In your science notebook, draw a diagram of the two houses, and explain the choices you made in building it. Label the houses, "Warm House" and "Cool House."

Reflective windows are commonly used on commercial buildings to help control the solar energy going through the windows.

Part B: Testing Your Model Houses

6. Making sure your houses are NOT in sunlight, measure the temperature inside each house, and record it in your science notebook.

7. Place your houses in the sunlight for the time allowed by your teacher.

8. Record the final temperature inside your houses.

9. Calculate the temperature change in each house, and record it in your science notebook.

ANALYSIS

1. What was the change in temperature of each of the two houses you designed? If the changes were different, explain why. In your explanation use the words *absorb*, *reflect*, and *transmit*.

 2. Compare your designs to those of your classmates. What materials tended to:

   a. absorb solar energy? Explain.

   b. reflect solar energy? Explain.

   c. transmit solar energy? Explain.

 3. Imagine you are living in Texas during the summer. What type of window film would you want on your home's windows? Explain your choice, using evidence from this activity.

   a. clear

   b. tinted grey

   c. reflective

 4. Imagine you are living in New York during the winter. What type of window film would you want on your home's windows? Explain your choice, using evidence from this activity.

   a. clear

   b. tinted grey

   c. reflective

READING

It would be simple to design an energy-efficient home if the temperature was always 21°C (70°F), and people did not use appliances. Most people, however, live in areas where the temperature varies a lot, and they depend on their refrigerators, furnaces, air conditioners, televisions, computers, and other appliances and electronic devices. In this activity, you will read about the major factors that determine how much energy is used in a home. You will also read about some actions people can take to use energy more efficiently.

CHALLENGE

How can features in a home affect the energy efficiency of a home?

Use the "Listen, Stop, and Write" strategy to help you with this reading. Listen as your teacher reads aloud. When he or she stops reading, close your book. Write down the main ideas you just heard.

READING

Energy Use in the Home

Every year, the United States consumes more energy than any other country in the world. As shown in the diagram below, about 22% of that energy is used in residential homes. The diagram also shows how residential energy is generally used.

Most people can reduce their costs and consumption of nonrenewable energy by focusing on their transportation and their homes. Just by driving

U.S. ENERGY USE IN 2005

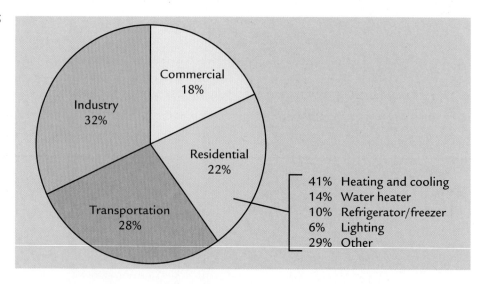

Industry 32%

Commercial 18%

Residential 22%

Transportation 28%

41% Heating and cooling
14% Water heater
10% Refrigerator/freezer
6% Lighting
29% Other

a gas-efficient car and driving less, for example, a person will buy less gasoline. Reducing energy use in the home, however, can be a little more challenging, especially for those who live in extreme climates where heating or air conditioning can be essential. Increasing efficiency in the home, however, is an important way to reduce energy use.

How much energy a home uses is affected by the size of the home, the number of people living in it, its location, the climate, and the type of energy available. In any case, however, better energy efficiency costs less and is less harmful for the environment.

Insulation

The biggest energy cost in a home is from maintaining a comfortable temperature. Since energy moves from a warmer to a cooler area, it can be difficult to keep warm air inside the building when it is cold outside and to keep hot air outside when it is very warm outside. The less energy it takes to accomplish that, the more energy-efficient the building. One way of slowing the movement of energy is to use insulating materials, such as concrete brick, and to insulate the walls of the building. In the summer insulation keeps a home cooler, and in the winter it keeps a home warmer. Insulation that is placed between walls and between floors and ceilings is made of various materials and comes in many forms, such as rolls or blankets of fibers, sprayed-in foam, or rigid sheets. It can be anywhere from three to 75 centimeters (1–30 inches) thick. How much insulation a building should have depends on its design, the climate, local energy costs, and the homeowner's budget. While most buildings have insulation in the walls, an energy-efficient home usually has insulation under the floors and above the ceilings as well.

Windows

Windows are a major source of energy transfer in a building. While most windows still have single panes of glass, high-performance windows have dual panes or even triple panes. This means there are two or three pieces of glass with a layer of air or some other gas, such as argon, in between them. That layer of air or gas acts as an insulator, preventing energy transfer. Additionally, high performance windows may have glazes that are similar to the films that you worked with in the last activity. These prevent energy transfer and also protect furniture from sun damage. High-performance windows have frames made of wood or fiberglass that also insulate. The windows are sealed tightly in their frames so air cannot leak in or out. No matter how efficient the window is, however, it does not block energy transfer as well as a solid wall does. Therefore, the more window space a home has, the less energy-efficient it will be overall.

Heating and Cooling Equipment

Heating systems are a significant factor in the total amount of energy used in a home—nearly half of a family's energy bill is spent on heating and

cooling it. Most of the time, a home's location determines what type of energy is available for heating and cooling. For example, natural gas is the cleanest-burning fossil fuel, but in many areas of the United States, it is not available. People in those areas must depend on electric heaters, oil, or propane gas for heat. Although renewable sources such as wind, solar, and geothermal energy are environmentally friendly, they are not available in many areas. Even if they are available, the cost to install them can be very high.

Many heating systems are built around a central furnace that burns a fossil fuel. A duct system or radiator system

Heating and cooling are important not only in homes, but also in large buildings. The heating, ventilation, and air conditioning (HVAC) systems in commercial buildings are designed to maintain a safe and healthy climate.

then distributes hot air or hot water around the house. The most common sources of energy for this type of heat are natural gas, propane, and oil. Sometimes a heater or furnace is located in one room only and energy is not distributed through the home; you might see this is in an old country house with a wood stove or in an apartment with a fireplace or a wall heater in the living room. Houses that do not have some kind of furnace often have baseboard heaters that run on electricity. The electricity comes from a utility company or from a renewable source such as solar.

Buildings can be cooled in several ways, too. A cooling system that includes air conditioning is one way, but passive-energy designs can also be effective. A passive-energy design doesn't depend on external energy to run it, as an air conditioner does. Instead it involves building the house in a way that the physical structure of the house and its outdoor surroundings control the temperature. One effective passive design for keeping a house cool is to plant trees and vegetation close to the house to provide shade, especially by the windows. Overhangs, such as wide roofs and window awnings that block the sunlight, are effective as well. Windows that block or reflect sunlight help keep energy out of a building. Another way to keep a house cool is to take advantage of natural ventilation. Architects often design houses with windows and doors placed in ways that allow air to circulate when

By changing the amount of solar energy coming into the building, the adjustable blinds on this building use a passive-energy design that controls the inside temperature.

there are breezes. Fans—whether ceiling fans, portable fans, or whole house fans—are less expensive to operate than an air-conditioning system. Unfortunately, some climates are too hot for houses to stay cool with these methods only—especially in summer. Many house in hot climates need both passive-energy designs and air conditioning.

Water Heaters

Most water heaters that supply hot water to bathrooms and kitchens consist of a large tank of water and a source of energy, such as gas, fuel oil, electricity, or even solar panels. Cold water runs into the tank at the bottom, and then as it heats up, a pipe takes it from the top of the water heater and through pipes to your faucets. Once the water is heated, it must stay warm and ready for use, and so energy-efficient water heaters are well insulated. Traditional hot water heaters use a significant amount of energy to keep the water in the tank warm so it is ready all the time. Newer water heaters, called "tankless" heaters, heat the water on demand instead of continually warming a tank that experiences energy loss. A tankless water heater system can supply a whole house or just a couple of faucets, such as in a bathroom. Tankless heaters are much more energy-efficient than traditional tank heaters, but sometimes they involve running water for a long time at the tap before hot water comes out.

Lighting and Appliances

Compact fluorescent lightbulbs use about one-third of the energy of typical incandescent bulbs. Additionally, because they do not get as hot, they are safer than other bulbs, especially halogen bulbs. As you discovered in a previous activity, compact fluorescent bulbs cost more to buy initially but save energy over time.

The energy efficiency of household appliances varies greatly. Older appliances, such as gas stoves where pilots for burners and the oven are always burning, tend to be much less energy-efficient than new ones. Even how appliances are used can make a difference in the amount of energy they consume. For example, leaving air space around a refrigerator's coils and keeping them clean makes a refrigerator more efficient. Opening the refrigerator door as little as possible and running a dishwasher on the shortest cycle or without the dry cycle improves energy efficiency. For washing clothes, using a low-water, front-loading machine and cold water save energy.

New appliances have two tags on them. One states the cost of the appliance; the other states how much it costs to operate the appliance for a year. This is called the energy rating because it gives a measure of the appliance's energy usage. Energy Star appliances have a high energy rating because they use energy more efficiently than standard appliances. However, Energy Star appliances are generally more expensive to buy. Like lightbulbs, often the least expensive appliance costs more money to operate.

Making Choices

When home dwellers select the things that make up their homes, such as construction materials, insulators, heaters, air conditioners, windows, and appliances, they are often faced with hard economic choices. On one hand, it takes less money to buy less efficient equipment. The payoff from a fluorescent lightbulb, an Energy Star appliance, or a new kind of water heater is not immediate. Over a few years, however, the extra up-front cost for an energy efficient item pays off, and the consumer starts saving money.

Many state and federal programs help home dwellers get the cash they need to buy more efficient equipment through rebates, tax incentives, and loans. Often, it makes the most sense to improve many things at once. For example, getting a more efficient furnace is not nearly as effective as getting the furnace and then keeping the heat in the home with new windows and insulation. Making an energy efficient home involves planning ahead, spending some money, and then having bit of patience for the savings to start.

This homeowner in Oregon took advantage of a tax incentive to outfit her home with a solar panel hot water system.

ANALYSIS

1. What are three things that people who live in older houses can do to make their houses more energy efficient? Explain why those actions would succeed.

2. Your community is building a new school on a tight budget. The town planners do not want to buy energy-efficient equipment for the school because it will cost more. Do you agree with this idea? Explain why or why not.

3. **Reflection:** What energy-efficient features described in the reading do you have, or could you have, in your own home?

EXTENSION

Find out more about making a home energy-efficient by going to the *Issues and Physical Science* page of the SEPUP website. Then use all the information you have to make an energy-improvement plan specifically for your home.

INVESTIGATION

The winter after Yasmin helped her mom insulate their house was very cold. When the energy bill came, they looked at it together to see the effect of the new insulation. "It is $320 lower than last winter!" said Yasmin triumphantly.

"Yes," said her mom, "But remember, it cost $400 to buy the insulation."

Her mom's remark upset Yasmin. She said, "Well, then why did we do it? We just lost money!"

"Because," her mother explained, "the savings are not a one-time event. We will continue to save every winter from now on. So next year, the insulation cost will be recovered. Every year after that, the money saved goes into our pocket."

"I see," said Yasmin thoughtfully, "It is better to look at energy use over a long time."

In this activity, you are part of a team of energy experts that works with families to reduce energy costs in the home. Your job is to improve energy efficiency and reduce the use of nonrenewable resources. The families each have a budget of $5,000 that they can spend now, and they will have another $5,000 in a few years for more improvements. Some families have also thought about borrowing money now or saving their current funds until later so they can make more improvements at one time.

CHALLENGE ➡ **Can you help a family decide what energy improvements they should invest in?**

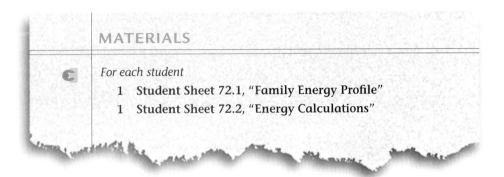

MATERIALS

For each student
1 Student Sheet 72.1, "Family Energy Profile"
1 Student Sheet 72.2, "Energy Calculations"

PROCEDURE

1. With your group, review the table of Energy Improvements shown below. Discuss what each improvement means. In your science notebook, explain how energy is conserved by each improvement.

Energy Improvements	
Energy Use in Home	**Ways to Improve Efficiency**
Heating and cooling	Install a programmable thermostat Add insulation Replace windows Seal windows, doors, ducts Replace source or burner Replace AC system
Water heater	Change type or use more efficient model
Refrigerator/freezer	Buy efficient model such as Energy Star
Lights	Use compact fluorescent
Other	Buy efficient appliances and electronics Add passive-energy devices

2. With the class, review the family profile on the next page.

Family Energy Profile: Buffalo, New York

ANNUAL ENERGY COST: $8,700

Buffalo

Average summer temperature: High: 27°C (80°F) Low: 18°C (63°F)

Average winter temperature: High: 0°C (32°F) Low: –7°C (19°F)

Yasmin, her brother Joe, and their mother live in a small house. Last summer, Yasmin helped her mom insulate the house, for which they got a rebate from the state. They think there must be more ways to save energy in their house. They use electric baseboard heat. They have a very old electric water heater and appliances, including the refrigerator that just broke. The windows are original to the house that was built in the 1960s, but the house has good ventilation and is shaded by trees. Yasmin's mom plans to do a lot of improvement work herself, except for large installations such as furnaces or solar panels.

Approximate Improvement Costs & Savings

Improvement	Cost of Materials (dollars)	Cost to Install (dollars)	Annual Energy Savings (dollars)
Programmable thermostat	50	50	300
Dual-pane windows (throughout house)	1,000	1,000	400
Seal windows, doors, ducts	100	50	300
Solar panels (at home)	10,000 (including rebates)	Included	2,200
Wind power (at home)	10,000 (including rebates)	Included	1,900
High-efficiency electric heat pump	1,300	200	1,300
Energy Star gas furnace	2,000	200	3,000
High-efficiency oil furnace	2,000	200	2,500
High-efficiency central air conditioning	3,000	1,000	20
Energy Star single-room air conditioner	200	20	10
Energy Star electric water heater, tankless	1,000	200	1,800
Energy Star gas water heater	500	200	850
Compact fluorescent lightbulbs	400	20	110
Energy Star refrigerator/freezer	1,500	50	20
Energy Star washing machine	500	50	100
Energy Star dryer, electric	500	50	50
Energy Star dishwasher	500	50	30
Deciduous trees and other shade vegetation	400	100	50

3. Your teacher will assign you a family that is profiled on Student Sheet 72.1, "Family Energy Profile." Read the profile carefully.

4. Consider the following for your family:

   • Needs based on the average high and low temperatures in the location

   • Immediate cost of the improvement versus the cost over a longer time

   • Major environmental impact of improvements

   • Other recommendations that are not included in the table of Energy Improvements

5. Use Student Sheet 72.2, "Energy Calculations," to help you calculate the long-term benefits of the improvements.

6. Use your ideas and your "Family Energy Profile" Student Sheet to decide what improvements your family should implement. As you work:

   • Listen to and consider explanations and ideas of other members of your team.

   • If you disagree with your team members about what features to include, explain why you disagree.

ANALYSIS

1. Write a report that gives your energy-improvement recommendation for your family within the budget given. In the report, explain why you recommend the improvement(s). Include a discussion of the trade-offs involved in the choices you made.

2. Would the recommendations you made work for families in other locations? Explain why or why not.

3. If money were not a limiting factor, what else would you recommend for your family?

4. How does reducing energy costs help the environment?

EXTENSION 1

Go to the *Issues and Physical Science* page of the SEPUP website, and investigate what energy saving measures you and your family can take where you live.

EXTENSION 2

Research the electricity costs in your area and compare them to the cities in the table below.

Electricity Costs in Five Cities*			
	Cost of Electricity (kWh)	Cost of Heating: Electric Heat per year (dollars)	Cost of Cooling: Central Air Conditioning per year (dollars)
Boise	.06	1,900	80
Buffalo	.15	5,400	90
Chicago	.08	2,900	100
Houston	.10	860	470
Palm Springs	.12	830	1,200

* The costs are for homes of a similar size and the same number of people living in each home.

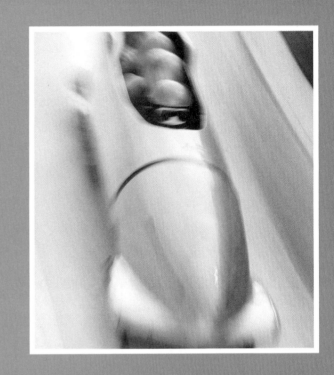

Force and Motion

E

Force and Motion

I can't wait until school is over," Jack said to his friend Uma. "My favorite relative, Aunt Tillie, is visiting. She drives a tour bus and today she is going to pick me up from school in it!"

When Tillie arrived, Jack climbed on board the bus, and sat up front so he could see everything. As Aunt Tillie turned onto a two-lane highway entrance, Jack noticed that there was a car right next to them. The car quickly accelerated past them and got on the highway. This got Jack thinking about how things move.

"Aunt Tillie," he asked, "Why can that car get up to highway speed faster than us? The engine on this bus is so much bigger."

"But that car is a lot smaller than this bus," she answered.

"So, why should that matter?"

"Well, it's physics, Jack," said Aunt Tillie. "It's hard to increase the speed of something big, like this bus. It needs a really big engine to create enough force."

"But the engine of the bus is big. It creates a lot more force than that little car's engine."

"Yes, but since the car is small, it doesn't need as much force to get it up to speed. Its smaller engine can create enough force to make it go faster than the bus."

• • •

How are forces related to motion? How does the size of something affect how it moves?

In this unit, you will learn how forces affect the motion of an object. By examining car collisions, you will also learn how an understanding of motion can improve safety on the road.

TALKING IT OVER

Last week, as Noah's dad was driving him to school, they were in a traffic accident. Although no one was hurt, the car is too damaged to drive and it has to be replaced. Noah's parents want to make sure that the next vehicle they buy is very safe. They've narrowed down the choice to two different vehicles that cost about the same. Even though Noah isn't old enough to drive yet, his parents want his opinion and they show him short advertisements for each one:

Vehicle 1

Rugged! Strong!
Now with more horsepower than any other vehicle in its class. You can safely take five people and all their gear anywhere you want to go. Yes, anywhere!

Vehicle 2

Quick! Responsive!
This high-performance sports sedan gives you quick acceleration and precision handling. And it's so roomy that a family of five can travel safely across town or across the country!

CHALLENGE ➡ **Which vehicle do you think is safer?**

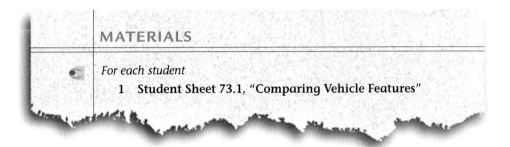

MATERIALS

For each student
1   Student Sheet 73.1, "Comparing Vehicle Features"

PROCEDURE

Part A: Prioritizing Vehicle Features

1. Discuss with your partner what you consider to be important features in a family vehicle.

2. In your science notebook:

   a. List the five features that are most important to you.

   b. List the five features that most affect a vehicle's safety.

   c. Circle any features that appear on both lists.

3. Ask your teacher for a copy of Student Sheet 73.1, "Comparing Vehicle Features." On it:

   a. Draw a star to the left of the names of the five features that are *most* important to you.

   b. Draw an "X" to the left of the names of the five features that are *least* important to you.

4. Answer Analysis Questions 1–2.

Part B: Analyzing Vehicle Features for Safety

5. For each feature listed on Student Sheet 73.1, use the "Effect on Safety" column to explain how you think that feature makes the vehicle more or less safe. If you don't think the feature has any effect, explain why not.

6. For each feature listed, compare the data for Vehicles 1 and 2. Circle the number of the vehicle which the data indicates would be safer.

7. Answer Analysis Questions 3–6.

ANALYSIS

1. Compare the features you listed in Step 2 to the features listed on Student Sheet 73.1. How are they:

   a. similar?

   b. different?

2. For each feature on Student Sheet 73.1 that you drew an "X" next to, explain why you decided it was less important.

 3. What factors other than safety do people consider when buying a car?

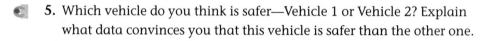 4. Do you think car features can:

   a. reduce damage, injuries, and fatalities in car accidents? Explain.

   b. prevent accidents? Explain.

 5. Which vehicle do you think is safer—Vehicle 1 or Vehicle 2? Explain what data convinces you that this vehicle is safer than the other one.

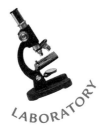

LABORATORY

Although many factors contribute to car accidents, speeding is the most common kind of risky driving. Unsafe speed is involved in about 20% of fatal car accidents in the United States.

Speed is the distance an object travels in a certain amount of time. For example, a car that travels a distance of 80 kilometers in one hour has a speed of 80 kilometers per hour. Any object's speed can be calculated by dividing the distance traveled by the time taken, as shown in the equation:

$$\text{speed} = \frac{\text{distance}}{\text{time}}$$

People use many different units to describe speed. These include miles per hour (MPH), kilometers per hour (kph or km/h), and meters per second (m/s).

CHALLENGE

How can you measure the speed of a moving cart?

This car speedometer shows speed in miles per hour and in kilometers per hour. Kilometers per hour is the speed unit commonly used in other countries.

INVESTIGATION

In the previous activity, you calculated the speed of a cart during its trip on a track. Sometimes, however, the speed of an object changes during a trip. For example, the driver of a car often changes the speed of the car because of traffic or road conditions. When the speed of an object changes over the course of a trip, a motion graph is useful because it shows the speed during all parts of the trip.

Teasha and Josh live next door to each other at the end of a long straight road that goes directly to their school. They live four miles from the school, and their parents drive them there in the mornings.

CHALLENGE

How can you use a graph to describe motion?

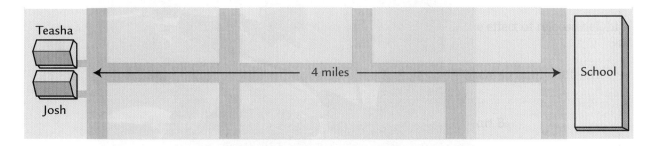

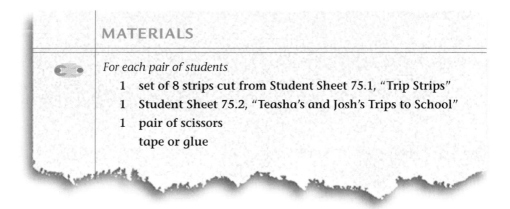

MATERIALS

For each pair of students

1 set of 8 strips cut from Student Sheet 75.1, "Trip Strips"

1 Student Sheet 75.2, "Teasha's and Josh's Trips to School"

1 pair of scissors

tape or glue

PROCEDURE

1. Cut apart the 8 trip strips along the dotted lines.

2. Read the trip strips. Each strip represents a story or one or more pieces of a story for two stories mixed together. Some of the strips describe Teasha's trip to school. The others describe Josh's trip.

3. With your partner, identify the strip that matches each segment of the two motion graphs shown on Student Sheet 75.2, "Teasha's and Josh's Trips to School."

4. Glue or tape each strip onto the segment of the graph that it describes.

5. Explain your choices in your science notebook.

ANALYSIS

1. Identify a place on each graph where the slope of the line changes. What does a change in the slope of a motion graph indicate?

2. Which student—Teasha or Josh—started out faster? Explain how you know this.

3. How far into the trip did Josh turn around? Describe what the graph looks like at this point in the trip.

4. Look at the motion graphs shown below. Match the descriptions here to the correct graphs:

   a. A car moving at a constant speed stops and then moves in the opposite direction at the same speed.

   b. A car moving at a constant speed stops and then moves faster in the same direction.

   c. A car moving at a constant speed changes to a higher constant speed.

   d. A car moving at a constant speed changes to a lower constant speed.

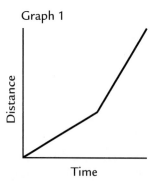

Graph 1

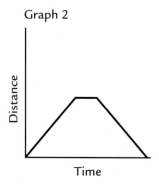

Graph 2

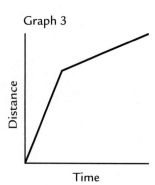

Graph 3

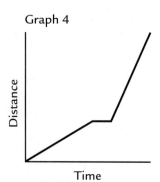

Graph 4

5. A car that accelerates (ak-SELL-ur-ates) is one that changes speed and/
or direction. Which graph below shows a car continually accelerating?
Explain how the shape of the graph shows this.

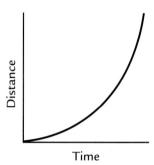 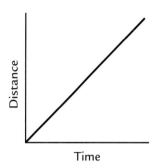

EXTENSION

Create one or more new character(s) also riding in cars for the scenario of
this activity. For each character, make up another set of trip strips and a
motion graph to go with them.

LABORATORY

In a car accident, both the speed of the car and the speed of the object it hits are likely to change. These changes happen because of forces that occur when any moving object collides (kuh-LYDZ) with another object. A force is a push or pull, and it is what changes the motion of an object. The change in an object's motion depends on two factors: the size of the force and the length of time the force is applied. In many car crashes, the length of time of the actual collision is very short.

CHALLENGE ⟹ **Does vehicle speed affect the forces involved in a collision?**

The force with which these cars hit is large, but the time it took to collide was short.

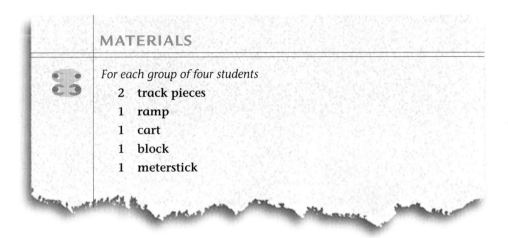

MATERIALS

For each group of four students
2   track pieces
1   ramp
1   cart
1   block
1   meterstick

PROCEDURE

1. In your science notebook, make a table like the one below.

Effect of Speed on Block Motion

Speed of Cart (Notch)	Distance Block Moves (cm)					Average Distance (cm)
	Trial 1	Trial 2	Trial 3	Trial 4	Trial 5	
Fast (A)						
Medium (B)						
Slow (C)						

2. Set up the ramp and track as you did in Activity 74, "Measuring Speed" but without the 100 cm marking.

3. Mark the track 5 cm from the bottom edge of the ramp, and place the block there, as shown below.

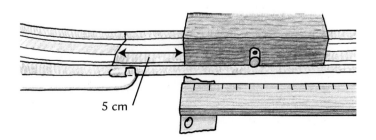

5 cm

4. Predict what will happen to the block and cart as a result of the collision. Record your prediction in your science notebook.

5. Hold the cart so that its rear axle is at Notch A on the ramp. As you learned in Activity 74, releasing the cart from Notch A results in the fastest cart speed.

6. Release the cart, and observe what happens. Measure the distance that the block moved down the track. Record the data as Trial 1 in your table.

7. Repeat Steps 3–5 four more times, and record the data as Trials 2–5.

8. Calculate the average distance the block moved and record this in your data table.

9. Predict what you think will happen to the block if the cart starts from Notch B. Remember that releasing the cart from Notch B results in a medium cart speed. Record your prediction in your science notebook.

10. Hold the cart so the rear axle of the vehicle is at Notch B on the ramp instead of Notch A, and repeat Steps 3–7.

11. Predict what you think will happen to the block if the cart starts from Notch C. Remember that releasing the cart from Notch C results in the slowest cart speed. Record your prediction in your science notebook.

12. Hold the cart so the rear axle of the cart is at Notch C on the ramp, and repeat Steps 3–7.

ANALYSIS

1. How does the speed of the cart affect how far the block moves?

2. Why do you think release height has this effect?

3. What part(s) of the experiment's design:

   a. increase your confidence in the data?

   b. decrease your confidence in the data?

4. When a car crashes, do you think its speed can make a difference in the amount of damage done? Explain, using evidence from this investigation.

LABORATORY

In the previous activity you investigated how the speed of the cart affects a collision. In this activity, you will investigate whether the mass of the cart affects the force it can apply during a collision. Mass describes the amount of matter in an object. For example, a small car has less mass than a big truck.

CHALLENGE   **Does the mass of an object affect the force it applies during a collision?**

What are the properties of this hammer that give it the potential to apply a lot of force?

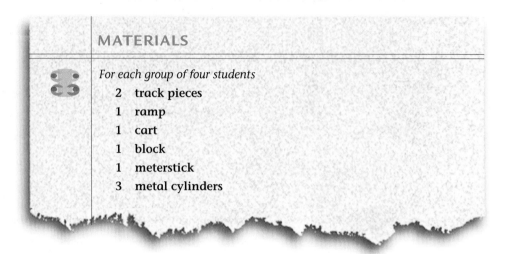

MATERIALS

For each group of four students

2   track pieces
1   ramp
1   cart
1   block
1   meterstick
3   metal cylinders

PROCEDURE

1. Write down your prediction of how changing the mass of the cart will affect a collision between the cart and a wooden block.

2. Write out a materials list and procedure for an experiment to test your prediction.

3. Prepare a data table for recording your measurements.

4. Show your plans to your teacher and get the necessary equipment.

5. Carry out your experiment and record your data.

ANALYSIS

1. Did the mass of the cart affect the collision? Explain how you know this.

2. Why do you think mass did or did not have the effect you predicted?

3. What part(s) of the experimental design:

   a. increase your confidence in the data?

   b. decrease your confidence in the data?

4. If your car were in a collision, would you rather be hit by Vehicle 1 (2,027 kg) or Vehicle 2 (1,415 kg) from Activity 73? Explain.

In the previous activities, you learned about force, mass, and changes in motion. In this activity, you will investigate the precise relationship between the mass of an object, the force applied to it, and the object's acceleration.

You also learned earlier that scientists measure speed in m/s (meters per second), and they measure mass in kg (kilograms). In this activity, you will need to know the standard international (SI) units used to measure force and acceleration. Acceleration is the change in speed (measured in meters per second) divided by time (measured in seconds), and so the unit for acceleration is meters per second per second (m/s·s or m/s^2). Force is measured in newtons (N). This unit is named after Sir Isaac Newton, a scientist who studied forces and motion.

CHALLENGE  **What is the mathematical relationship between force, acceleration, and mass?**

The golf ball in the photo far right will have a greater change in motion because it is hit with a greater force.

MATERIALS

For each student
graph paper

PROCEDURE

Part A: Graphing the Variables

1. The table below shows precise measurements from an experiment in which a force is applied to pull a block along a frictionless track.

Experiment 1		
Force (N)	Mass of Block (kg)	Acceleration of Block (m/sec^2)
4.0	2.0	2.0
2.0	2.0	1.0
20.0	2.0	10.0
10.0	2.0	5.0

2. Use the Experiment 1 data to make a graph of the relationship between acceleration and force. Title the graph, "Acceleration vs. Force." Label the graphed line "Experiment 1."

    Hint: Put the data for force on the x-axis and the data for acceleration on the y-axis.

3. Answer Analysis Question 1.

Part B: Finding the Equation

4. Use the Experiment 1 data to determine a mathematical equation that shows the exact relationship between mass (m), force (F), and acceleration (a). Record the relationship in your science notebook.

    Hint: Try adding, subtracting, multiplying, and dividing two of the measurements to see if you get the third.

Part C: Double-checking the Equation

5. The data table below shows measurements from Experiment 2. See whether your equation works for this set of data.

   • If it does, go on to Step 6.

   • If it doesn't, find a different equation that does work for both experiments.

Experiment 2		
Force (N)	Mass of Block (kg)	Acceleration of Block (m/sec^2)
4.0	4.0	1.0
2.0	4.0	0.5
20.0	4.0	5.0
10.0	4.0	2.5

6. Using the same graph you made in Step 2, plot the Experiment 2 data. Label the second line "Experiment 2."

ANALYSIS

1. Look at your graphed line for Experiment 1. Explain why it does or does not indicate that there is a relationship between force and acceleration.

2. Compare the two lines, "Experiment 1" and "Experiment 2" on your graph. Identify and explain:

   a. any similarities.

   b. any differences.

How does the acceleration of the dogs affect the force on the sled?

3. In your science notebook, make a table like the one below. Use your equation for force, mass, and acceleration to find the missing values.

Experiment 3

Force (N)	Mass of Block (kg)	Acceleration of Block (m/sec^2)
	5	5
	2	10
10		2
50	10	
100		25
1,000	40	

4. In the first activity, Vehicle 2 has a greater acceleration than Vehicle 1, but has a less forceful engine. How can this be? Explain in terms of your equation.

 5. One Newton of force is the same as 1 kg m/s^2. Explain how this unit of measurement is appropriate for your equation.

LABORATORY

It takes more force, and often more time and distance, for a heavier car to stop or swerve to avoid an accident. A heavier car has more inertia than a lighter car. **Inertia** (in-UR-sha) is the resistance of an object to changes in its motion. In other words, inertia describes the tendency of an object to continue moving at the same speed and in the same direction, such as a train traveling in a straight line at 60 MPH. Continuing at the "same speed" may mean a speed of 0 m/s, or continuing to not move.

The more mass an object has, the more inertia it has, and the greater the force it takes to change its motion. Understanding inertia helps us understand and predict what a vehicle will do when forces are applied or removed.

CHALLENGE How does inertia affect how an object moves?

The bigger ship has more inertia than the small boat.

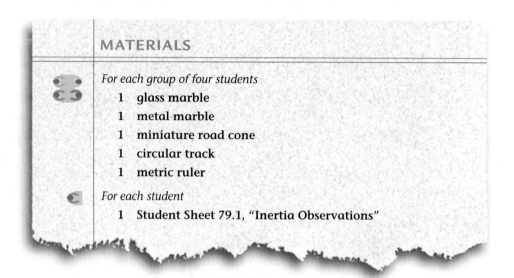

MATERIALS

For each group of four students

1   glass marble
1   metal marble
1   miniature road cone
1   circular track
1   metric ruler

For each student

1   Student Sheet 79.1, "Inertia Observations"

PROCEDURE

Part A: High Mass Marble

1. Set up the circular track as shown below, and make sure it is placed where everyone in your group can easily view it.

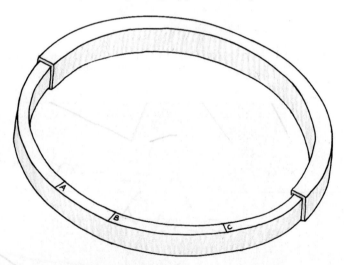

2. Practice sending the metal marble counterclockwise around the inside of the circular track with enough speed to make it go around two or three times before stopping.

   Hint: You may need to hold the track still while the marble is traveling around the track.

3. Set the opening to "A."

4. Discuss with your group where you predict the metal marble will roll once it has gone around the circular track and travels out through the opening.

5. Place the miniature road cone on the table to mark the position of your prediction from Step 4.

6. On Student Sheet 79.1, "Inertia Observations," show the path you predicted by drawing a series of three "x"s, each about 1 cm apart in the "Position A" diagram.

7. Using the same speed you practiced in Step 2, send the metal marble around the inside of the circular track and observe the path it takes after it travels out through the opening.

8. Repeat step 7 several times until the members of your group agree on the most common path of the marble.

9. Draw a solid line on the "Position A" diagram to record the most common path of the marble.

10. Discuss with your group why the marble took that path. Record your ideas next to the diagram.

11. Repeat Steps 3–10 for the Position B and C openings in the circular track.

Part B: Low Mass Marble

12. Repeat Steps 1–11 with the glass marble instead of the metal marble.

In which direction does the passengers' inertia carry them?

ANALYSIS

1. Describe the changes in direction and speed of the marbles when they traveled:

   a   inside the circular track.

   b. outside the circular track.

2. Describe any changes in the path of the marble that occurred when you changed:

   a. the opening position of the circular track.

   b. the mass of the marble.

3. Imagine that a car is approaching a curve in the road when it suddenly loses its steering and brakes. The area is flat and there is no guardrail on the road.

   a. Copy the diagram below in your science notebook. Then draw a line showing the car's path when it loses its steering and brakes.

   b. Explain why the car will take that path.

   c. How would your answer change if the car had more mass? Explain.

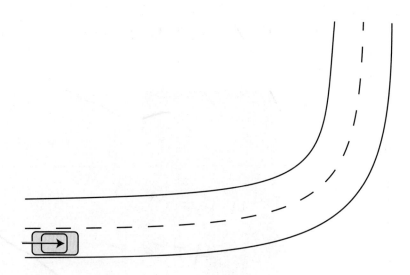

READING

Isaac Newton was a British scientist whose accomplishments included important discoveries about light, motion, and gravity. You may have heard the legend about how he "discovered" gravity when he was sitting under an apple tree and an apple fell on his head. He didn't really discover gravity, but he did realize that there is a gravitational force that constantly pulls objects toward the center of Earth. This force makes objects fall toward Earth if no other force is there to hold them up.

CHALLENGE

What relationships between force and motion did Newton discover?

MATERIALS

For each student

1 **Student Sheet 80.1, "Anticipation Guide: Newton's Laws of Motion"**

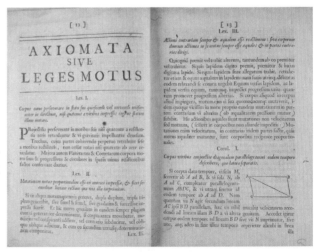

This image of Isaac Newton, above left, appears in one of his books, published in the 1600s. Newton wrote Laws of Motion *in Latin. The original book, above right, is in the collection of the Library of Congress in Washington, D.C.*

READING

Use Student Sheet 80.1, "Anticipation Guide: Newton's Laws of Motion," to prepare you for the following reading.

Force and Motion

People have probably always observed objects in motion and have made objects move around. For many centuries, scientists thought they knew everything about this. However, the Italian scientist Galileo Galilei, who lived from 1564 to 1642, began to think about motion in a new way. Isaac Newton, who was born the year Galileo died, built upon his discoveries and developed three laws. Newton's laws were revolutionary, as they seemed to go against everyday experience and observation. Today, parts of Newton's three laws are still the basis for understanding motion.

Newton's First Law: The Law of Inertia

Newton's first law, also known as the Law of Inertia, can be difficult to fully understand. It describes an object's resistance to changing its motion and its tendency to keep doing whatever it is doing. A change in motion can be a change in an object's speed, direction, or both. For example, a car that speeds up to pass another car, or that turns a corner is changing its motion. Newton's first law states that an object's motion cannot change unless a force acts on the object. In other words, it takes a force to overcome an object's inertia and to make the object go faster, slower, or change direction.

STOPPING TO THINK 1

Which has more inertia: a heavy ball or a light ball rolling at the same speed in the same direction? Think about which one is more resistant to a change in motion.

Since you may already know that it takes a force to change motion, you might be wondering, "What's so hard to understand about Newton's first law?" The difficulty is that this law also says that no force is needed to keep something moving. According to Newton's first law, if something is moving at a certain speed, it will keep on moving at that speed forever. It will not slow down and stop unless something pulls or pushes on it. The idea also applies to an object that is not moving. It will remain motionless until a force acts on it.

Newton's first law seems to contradict everyday experience. You've seen for yourself that when you kick, throw, or bat a ball along the ground it eventually stops by itself. And when you ride a sled or a scooter down a hill, you don't keep going forever; you slow down and stop. How can Newton's first law be correct?

Friction

What is not stated in Newton's first law, but plays an important role in motion, is the idea of **friction** (FRICK-shun). Friction is a force that exists at the boundary between any two pieces of matter that are in contact with each other. Friction is a force that opposes the motion of an object. For example, the friction between a rolling ball and the ground causes the ball to slow down and stop rolling. Friction between a sliding sled and snow causes the sled to slow down and stop sliding. Here on the earth, where there is friction everywhere, a force must be applied to an object in order to keep it moving.

If there were no friction, the inertia of a moving object would keep it moving the same way forever or until a force changes its motion. In outer space, which has no ground, water, or air to create friction, an object would keep moving forever at the same speed and in the same direction. This explains why the moons and the planets and other space objects have been moving for billions of years and will keep moving for billions more!

There is less friction between the puck and the ice (left) than there is between the ball and the rougher grass (right).

STOPPING TO THINK 2

What would happen to a baseball if you could throw it in outer space? Explain in terms of inertia and friction.

To keep a car moving, its engine has to keep pushing it to overcome the friction in several places, such as the road and the tires, and the windshield and the air. Many features on vehicles are designed to reduce friction as much as possible. Shapes are streamlined to reduce air friction, and oil and grease reduce friction between moving parts. If there is less friction to overcome, the engine doesn't need to apply as much force. Other vehicle features are designed to increase friction. Tires need to have friction so that they can "grab" the road and brakes need a lot of friction to make the wheels stop turning.

Balanced Forces

To keep an object moving at a constant speed in the presence of frictional force, a force needs to be applied that is equal in size to, but in the opposite direction of, the frictional force. This applied force balances the force of friction so that the combined force acting on the object, or the **net force**, is zero (0). The engine of a car that is moving at a constant speed is applying a force exactly equal to the frictional forces that are pushing against it. When the net force is zero, there are balanced forces and there is no change in motion, just as Newton's first law states.

The bobsled and its passengers try to reduce friction. Snow tires increase friction to bring the wheels to a stop.

As the train travels at constant speed, the engine must produce enough force to equal the friction caused by the air and the wheels on the track.

STOPPING TO THINK 3

A car travels along a straight road at a steady 40 MPH. Are the forces on the car balanced or unbalanced? Explain.

Newton's Second Law:
The Relationship Between Force, Mass, and Acceleration

Unlike the first law, Newton's second law is confirmed by our everyday experiences and is easier to understand. It states that:

1. To equally change the motion of two objects of different mass, more force must be applied to the more massive object. For example, when you add weight to a wagon, you have to push it harder to speed it up because it has more inertia.

2. The bigger the force that is applied to an object, the greater the resulting acceleration. For example, if you give a soccer ball a soft tap with your foot (a small force over a short period of time) it doesn't speed up much. If you give it a hard kick (a larger force over an equally short period of time) it speeds up more.

Newton summed up these ideas with a single equation that shows the net force (F) needed to accelerate (a) any mass (m):

$$F = ma$$

STOPPING TO THINK 4

Can a light object that was hit with a small force accelerate as rapidly as a heavier object hit with a big force? Why or why not?

Unbalanced Forces

Newton's second law describes the change in motion that is a result of unbalanced forces. If net force on an object is not zero, the forces are unbalanced and the object accelerates. Even a tiny force will cause an object to speed up if it is not balanced by another force. In a frictionless world, an object that has a continually applied force would speed up until it is traveling as fast as it possibly can.

Race horses accelerate out of the starting gate.

Newton's Third Law: Action-Reaction with Two Objects

Newton was the first one to notice that it is impossible to have a single force. Forces always happen in pairs. Newton's third law, also know as the Law of Action-Reaction explains how a pair of forces work. It states that when one object applies a force on a second object, the second object applies the same size force in the opposite direction, and for the same amount of time, on the first object. Another way to think about this is that when one object pushes or pulls on another object the other object will always push or pull back with the same force.

The force of the gases pushes downward at the same time that the gases push the rocket upwards.

An example Newton used was that if you push a rock with your hand, the rock pushes back on your hand. Another example is a launching rocket. It is propelled because, at the same time as the rocket is pushing the gases down, the force of the gases is pushing the rocket up.

It may seem that the third law contradicts the second law. If there are always equal and opposite forces, how can there ever be an unbalanced force? In the second law, Newton talks about the net force acting on a single object. The opposing forces in Newton's third law are two forces acting on a pair of different objects. When the second law is used to describe motion, the action-reaction forces are still there, but they are often ignored since they are equal and opposite.

STOPPING TO THINK 5

If you hold a backpack in your hand, the force of gravity pulls it downward. What force keeps it from falling to the ground?

ANALYSIS

1. Spaceships that travel millions of miles into outer space use very little fuel. How can they go so far on so little fuel?

2. Use Newton's laws to explain why it is easier to turn a truck when it is empty than when it is carrying a heavy load.

3. An engine can exert a force of 1,000 newtons. How fast can this engine accelerate:

   a. a 1,000-kg car?

   b. a 2,000-kg car?

4. Use Newton's third law to explain why a blown up but untied balloon will fly around the room when you let it go.

5. Motor oil, axle grease, and other lubricants are slippery. Why do you think people spend the money to put these lubricants in their cars?

INVESTIGATION

Imagine a car that is moving at a constant speed in a straight line. The frictional forces that would slow the car down are balanced by the engine force that moves the car forward. The result is a balanced, or zero (0), net force on the car. According to Newton's second law, the car is not accelerating—it's not speeding up, not slowing down, and not changing direction. An object's acceleration only changes when there is an unbalanced (nonzero) net force acting on it.

CHALLENGE

How can you tell if the forces on an object are balanced or unbalanced?

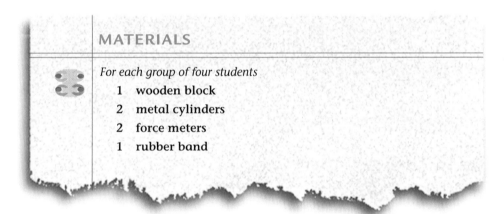

MATERIALS

For each group of four students
1 wooden block
2 metal cylinders
2 force meters
1 rubber band

PROCEDURE

Part A: Balanced Forces

1. Place the block on the table, and hook both force meters to it as shown below.

   Note: Each mark on the force meter is 0.1 N.

2. While *not* moving the block, have one group member pull gently with **1.0 N** on one force meter, while another pulls gently with **1.0 N** on the other force meter.

3. In your science notebook, draw a force diagram of the block, similar to the example below. On your diagram record the forces on the block from Step 2.

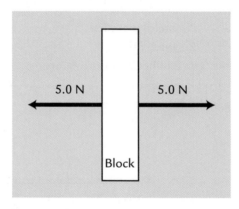

Part B: Unbalanced Forces

4. Pull gently with **1.5 N** on one force meter, while another group member pulls gently with **1.0 N** on the other force meter. The other two group members should watch the block and observe its motion.

5. Switch roles, and repeat Step 4 until each group member gets to pull the block and observe its motion.

6. Discuss with your group members the motion of the block. In particular, decide if the block was accelerating or not. Record your conclusion in your science notebook.

7. Draw another force diagram of the block in your science notebook. Record the forces from Step 4. Title your diagram "Unbalanced Forces."

Part C: The Challenge

In this part of the activity, your challenge is to decide if the forces on the block are balanced or unbalanced.

8. Unhook one of the force meters. Place two metal cylinders on the block and secure them with the rubber band as shown below.

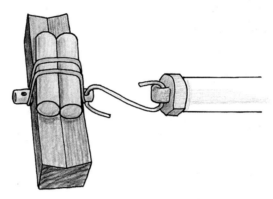

9. Practice pulling gently on the force meter so that the block slides steadily and as slowly as possible.

10. When you can do this well, read the force needed to pull the block slowly and steadily.

11. Switch roles, and repeat Steps 9 and 10 until each group member gets to pull the block and observe its motion.

12. With your group members, discuss the motion of the block. In particular, identify all the forces on the block, and then decide if the block was accelerating or not. Record your conclusion in your science notebook.

13. Draw a force diagram of the block at Step 10. Title your diagram "Balanced Forces" or "Unbalanced Forces," depending on the conclusion of your group.

ANALYSIS

1. Describe an example and draw a force diagram of a situation with:

   a. balanced forces.

   b. unbalanced forces.

2. Imagine that a parked car is hit from the left with 30,000 N of force at the exact same time it is hit from the right with 40,000 N of force.

   a. Draw a force diagram showing the two forces acting on the parked car.

   b. Draw another force diagram showing only the net force on the parked car.

3. The force diagram below shows an object with zero net force, but there is one force missing. What is the missing force? Draw the diagram in your notebook, and complete it by drawing and labeling the missing force.

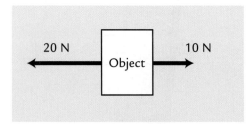

4. Look back at your work from Part A. Could the block in Part A have been moving? Explain.

5. For each situation in a–e below, explain why there is or is not a zero net force acting on the car.

   a. A car is parked on a level parking space.

   b. A traffic light turns green, and a car starts to move.

   c. A car drives steadily at 25 MPH.

   d. A car is slowing down from 30 MPH to 10 MPH.

   e. A car goes around a corner at 10 MPH.

LABORATORY

One very important force frequently used in a car is the force applied by the brakes. Sometimes drivers can avoid an accident by coming to a stop before the accident occurs. The braking distance is the distance the car travels after the driver applies the brakes, until the car comes to a full stop. Other things being equal, the vehicle with the shorter braking distance is safer.

When the brakes of a car are applied, the brake pads push against a metal section of the wheels. The increased friction acting against the wheels' motion slows down the turning of the wheels.

CHALLENGE → **How can friction lower the risk of getting into an accident?**

The space shuttle Endeavor uses a drag chute when it lands back on earth. The friction between the chute and the air reduces the shuttle braking distance by about 600 meters.

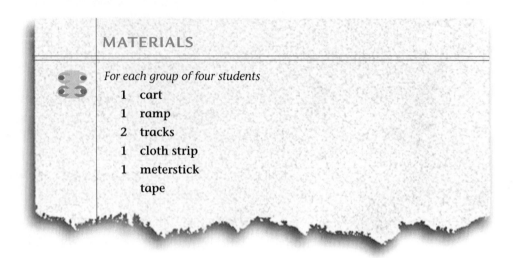

MATERIALS

For each group of four students

- 1 cart
- 1 ramp
- 2 tracks
- 1 cloth strip
- 1 meterstick
-    tape

PROCEDURE

1. In your science notebook, make a table like the one below.

Effect of Speed on Braking Distance

Speed of Cart (Notch)	Braking Distance (cm)			Average Braking Distance (cm)
	Trial 1	Trial 2	Trial 3	
Fast (A)				
Medium (B)				
Slow (C)				

2. Set up the equipment as shown below.

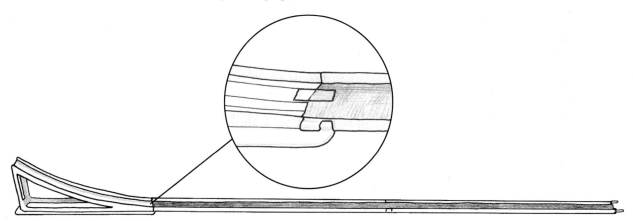

3. Place the cart so that the rear axle is at the high notch, Notch A, on the ramp. As you learned in a previous activity, this release height results in the fastest cart speed.

4. Release the cart, and let it roll to a stop.

5. Measure the distance it rolled along the flat track. Record this distance as Trial 1 in your table.

6. Repeat Steps 3–5 twice, and record the distances as Trial 2 and Trial 3 in your table.

7. Repeat Steps 3–6 with the cart starting at the middle notch, Notch B, on the ramp. This release height results in a medium cart speed. Record your data in your science notebook.

8. Repeat Steps 3–6 with the cart starting at the low notch, Notch C, on the ramp. This release height results in the slowest cart speed. Record your data in your science notebook.

9. Find the average distance the cart traveled for each speed. Record this in the right-hand column of your table.

ANALYSIS

1. In this model of a stopping car:

   a. What does the cloth represent?

   b. List some strengths and weaknesses of this model.

 2. What effect does speed have on braking distance? Explain, using evidence from this activity.

 3. Does the evidence you gathered in this investigation support the statement below? Explain why or why not, using evidence from your investigation.

   A car moving at 55 MPH needs less distance to stop than an identical car moving at 45 MPH.

4. **Reflection:** Why do you think excessive speed is a factor in about 20% of fatal car accidents?

EXTENSION

Post your results on the *Issues and Physical Science* page of the SEPUP website, and compare your data sets to those of students in other classes.

READING

Acar's braking distance, as you learned in the last activity, is the distance it travels after the brakes are applied until the car comes to a full stop. Braking distance is affected by the speed of the car, the type and quality of brakes, the surfaces of the tires, and the condition of the road.

There is some time that passes, sometimes as long as a few seconds, between the moment a driver realizes there is a problem and the moment his or her foot applies the brakes. This time interval, the driver's **reaction time**, depends primarily on the driver's level of alertness. Drugs, alcohol, sleepiness, and distractions impair alertness, slowing reaction times. The distance the car travels during the reaction time depends on how long it takes the driver to react and how fast the car is traveling.

The **stopping distance** of a car is the total of the distance the car traveled during the reaction time plus the distance traveled while braking.

CHALLENGE

How does a car's stopping distance change in different situations?

This distracted driver could be more likely to get in an accident than an alert driver. He has a longer reaction time than does a driver who is not distracted.

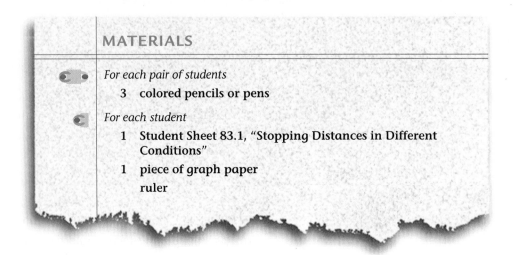

MATERIALS

For each pair of students
   3   colored pencils or pens

For each student
   1   Student Sheet 83.1, "Stopping Distances in Different Conditions"
   1   piece of graph paper
       ruler

PROCEDURE

1. Using the data on Student Sheet 83.1, "Stopping Distances in Different Conditions" and the equation below, calculate the distance a vehicle travels during the driver's reaction time.

   Reaction distance = initial speed × reaction time

   Record your calculations in the "Reaction Distance" column in the three tables.

2. Using the equation below, calculate the vehicle's total stopping distance.

   Stopping distance = reaction distance + braking distance

   Record your calculations in the "Stopping Distance" column of your student sheet.

3. Make a graph of stopping distance (y-axis) versus driving speed (x-axis). Use three different-colored pencils to plot three data sets on the same graph:

   - Plot the points for an alert driver on a slippery road. Label this line "Alert Driver, Slippery Road."

   - Plot the points for an alert driver on a dry road. Label this line "Alert Driver, Dry Road."

   - Plot the points for a distracted driver on a dry road. Label this line "Distracted Driver, Dry Road."

ANALYSIS

1. Why does stopping distance depend on road conditions?

2. What might cause:

   a. slippery road conditions?

   b. driver distractions?

3. In which of the three driving situations (alert and dry, alert and slippery, distracted and dry) does it take:

   a. the least distance to stop? Explain using evidence.

   b. the most distance to stop? Explain using evidence.

4. You are alertly driving a car at 40 MPH (18 m/s). You come around a bend and see a tree that has fallen across the road 50 meters away. Will you be able to stop before you hit the tree:

   a. on a dry road? Show your evidence.

   b. on a wet road? Show your evidence.

5. Would your answers to Analysis Question 4 change:

   a. If something were distracting you as you came around the bend? Explain.

   b. If you were driving 20 MPH instead of 40 MPH? Explain.

6. Your friend says that when a car goes twice as fast, the braking distance doubles. Do you agree or disagree? Use evidence from this investigation to support your ideas.

7. Create a concept map using the following terms:

stopping distance	tires	alertness
reaction distance	brakes	distance
road surface	speed	distraction
braking distance	time	friction

EXTENSION

The table below shows the stopping distances for a distracted driver on a slippery road. Using the graph you made in this activity, plot this data on your graph. Label the line, "Distracted Driver, Slippery Road."

Stopping Distance: Distracted Driver on Slippery Road	
Initial Speed (m/s)	**Stopping Distance (meters)**
5	17
9	40
18	108
27	203
36	326

READING

When a car crashes into something, the driver's and passengers' inertia keeps them moving forward until something stops their motion. Stopping or slowing motion is called **deceleration.** How a person in a car decelerates often determines the seriousness of that person's injuries. Most injuries and deaths occur when internal body parts, such as bones or brains, are decelerated very quickly by a large force.

CHALLENGE

How can a person's deceleration be controlled during a collision?

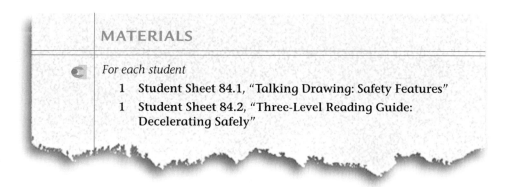

MATERIALS

For each student

1 Student Sheet 84.1, "Talking Drawing: Safety Features"
1 Student Sheet 84.2, "Three-Level Reading Guide: Decelerating Safely"

READING

Use Student Sheet 84.1, "Talking Drawing: Safety Features" and Student Sheet 84.2, "Three-Level Reading Guide: Decelerating Safely" to prepare yourself for the following reading.

Safety Features

To design safer cars, it is important to understand friction, forces, and deceleration. Many safety features help reduce the speed before impact, and other features help protect passengers during a collision. Automobile safety engineers use their knowledge of forces and motion to develop, and continue to improve, many safety features that help avoid accidents or reduce injuries in accidents.

Before the Accident

Driving on a worn-out tire is dangerous because there isn't enough friction between it and the road.

Two of the most important safety features of a car are its brakes and tires. Good tires and brakes help to avoid accidents by using friction to decelerate a car quickly, yet in a controlled way.

The friction between the tires and the road affects braking distance. The amount of this friction depends mostly on the contact area between the tire and the road, the material and tread design of the tire, the type and condition of the road surface, and the temperature of the tire. All new tires are rated for various aspects of safety.

The disc brakes commonly used on cars, like bicycle brakes, work because brake pads squeeze against the two sides of a rotating wheel. The friction between the brake pads and the wheel slows the rotation of the wheels. The larger the surface area of the brake pads, the more friction and, therefore, the greater the braking power. More braking power, however, is not always better.

When a car's brakes clamp down so tightly that they "lock" the wheels, the tires stop rolling and begin to slide on the road. When this happens, the car skids, and the driver can lose control. In this situation there is actually less friction between the tires and the road than when the tires roll. To bring the car to a stop as quickly as possible, friction between the tires and road needs to be maximized. Antilock brake systems (sometimes referred to as ABS) automatically engage and release the brakes many times per second. During the moments when the brakes are released, the tires stop skidding and briefly roll. The overall amount of friction during the pulsing of the

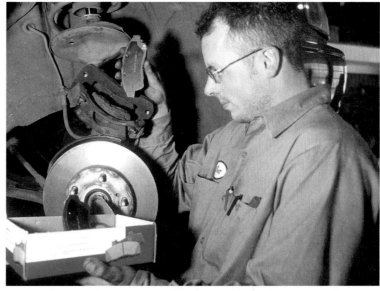

A bicycle brake, above, uses friction between the brake pads and the wheel rim to stop or slow down. In the photo on the right, a mechanic inspects a brake. If the parts become too worn, they won't generate enough friction to stop the car quickly.

ABS brake is higher than if the tires were simply skidding. By maximizing the friction between the tire and the road, antilock brakes help a vehicle stop more quickly and with more control.

During the Accident

When a vehicle is moving, everything inside it, including the passengers, is moving at the same speed as the vehicle, as shown below left. When a vehicle collides with a solid object, the car stops quickly, but the inertia of the passengers keeps them moving forward until a force changes their motion and slows them down, as shown below right. If that force is from the steering wheel, dashboard, or windshield, the injuries are often very serious.

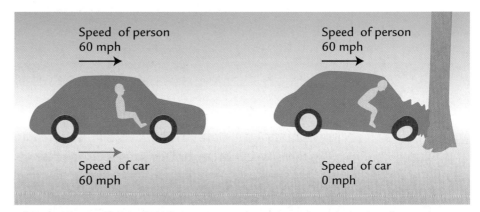

The stopping time of a seat-belted passenger may be up to ten times slower than the stopping time for the car.

Seat belts are designed to reduce the force that a passenger experiences. To reduce the force, seat belts increase the amount of time that it takes to decelerate the passenger. If it takes longer to come to a stop, the deceleration has been reduced. According to Newton's second law, a reduced acceleration (or in this case, deceleration) results in a reduced force:

$$F = m a \qquad\qquad F = m a$$

Smaller deceleration (a) results in a smaller force (F)   Larger deceleration (a) results in a larger force (F)

For example, a car that hits a tree may take about 0.01 seconds from the moment of impact until it comes to a full stop. Without a seatbelt it may take the same amount of time for the driver to also stop. If the driver is wearing a seatbelt, the seatbelt will slow her or him down to a complete stop closer to 0.1 seconds. These time intervals may both seem very fast, but the passenger has taken 10 times longer to come to a stop than the car. This can reduce the maximum force between the seatbelt and the passenger to 1/10 that of the force between the car and the tree. If the driver is not wearing a seatbelt, he or she is likely to be decelerated with a force close to that applied to the car by the tree.

Stopping time for car is 0.01 seconds

Stopping time for seat belted person is 0.1 seconds

Like seatbelts, air bags also reduce the deceleration a person experiences during a collision. Air bags also help by spreading out the deceleration force over a large area. This reduces the pressure, or force per unit area, on the body. When a car hits a tree, if there is no air bag and the driver's forehead hits the steering wheel, the entire force needed to decelerate the driver is applied to the forehead. This pressure could be great enough to break the skull. With an air bag, the same force is needed to decelerate the

driver, but it is spread out evenly over the larger area of the driver's body—head, arms, shoulders, and chest—that hit the air bag. The pressure on any one part is much lower and much less likely to cause injuries. Seatbelts also reduce the pressure on the body by distributing force over the belt, but they have a smaller effect than air bags.

Other Safety Features

A well designed car has a strong occupant compartment, known as the safety cage. The safety cage is important because once it starts to collapse during a collision, the likelihood of injury increases rapidly. Crumple zones are sections in cars that are designed to crumple up when the car collides with something. In a collision, forces are directed to that section of the vehicle instead of being transmitted to the safety cage. Crumple zones increase the damage to the car but reduce the harm done to the occupants. Crumple zones, like air bags and seatbelts, make deceleration more gradual and spread out the area of impact. This can significantly reduce the force felt by the passengers.

Modern steering columns are designed to collapse, as this telescope can.

Cars have not always had as many safety features as today's vehicles. For example, it wasn't until the 1970s that steering wheels were made to be collapsible. Before then, steering wheels were attached to rigid steering columns. If a driver hit the steering wheel with enough force, the rigid steering column could push through the steering wheel and spear the driver. Today's cars have steering columns designed to collapse on impact like a ship captain's telescope. This reduces the chances of being speared. Similarly, headrests, padded dashboards, padded steering wheels, side impact beams, even plastic-covered car keys, and other devices must, by law, be built into new cars.

Safety features in vehicles have come a long way since the automobile was first invented. Although every new generation of cars has better safety features than the previous cars, even the most innovative designs are based on the understanding that passengers are best protected if they decelerate as slowly as possible and if the force is spread over the largest surface possible.

ANALYSIS

1. Choose one of the safety features described in the reading. Use the terms inertia, force, and deceleration to describe how the safety feature helps keep people safe in a collision.

2. As a collision is about to happen, if you had enough time to chose between hitting a large haystack or a telephone pole, which one would you choose to hit? Explain why in terms of force and deceleration.

3. In the accident mentioned in Activity 73, "Choosing a Safe Vehicle," Noah's family car had old tires that were worn down. Explain how this could have contributed to the car accident.

4. Reflection: Since the 1920s, the rate of fatalities per billion miles traveled has dropped steadily. However, the rate has been about the same for the past 20 years. Why do you think this is?

Automobile and safety engineers use crash tests to find out how well each kind of car keeps people safe in an accident. In a standard frontal or front-end crash test, the car travels down a track at 35 MPH and smashes into a barrier. In a standard side-impact test, a barrier moving down a track at 31 MPH crashes into the side door of a stationary car. The results of the crash tests show whether the car meets government safety standards and help consumers evaluate and compare the safety of different kinds of cars.

Life-sized human dolls, called crash-test dummies, are used as models for actual passengers. To help predict how badly drivers and passengers could be injured, sensors that measure changes in motion and pressure are placed on various parts of the dummies.

CHALLENGE

How is a crash-test dummy designed?

This high speed photograph of a crash test shows the movement of the crash-test dummies placed in the front and back seats.

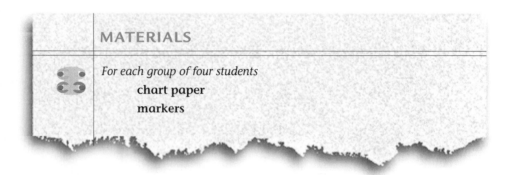

MATERIALS

For each group of four students
   chart paper
   markers

PROCEDURE

1. Within your group, discuss the following design elements for the crash-test dummy that will be placed in a car's driver's seat. Listen to the ideas of others. If you disagree with others in your group, explain why you disagree. The design considerations are:

   • How should the dummy be like and not like a person?

   • What material(s) should the dummy be made of?

   • How tall and how heavy should the dummy be?

   • What should the sensors measure?

   • Where should the sensors be placed on the dummy?

2. Draw your crash-test dummy design. Include labels and explanations of its different parts.

3. Use an "X" to show the locations of sensors on your drawing. You should show at least five sensors.

4. With your partner, share your design ideas with another pair of students. Get their feedback on what could improve your crash-test dummy. Then switch roles and provide ideas on how to improve the other pair's design.

5. With the feedback from the previous step, redesign the crash-test dummy to improve it.

6. Prepare a presentation to the class explaining your group's design. Make sure to show all the design elements you discussed in your group, and the scientific reasons for your choices.

ANALYSIS

1. The crash-test dummy that is most often used in frontal crash tests is the Hybrid III dummy. It is 5 feet 9 inches tall, weighs 170 pounds (the size of an average man), and costs about $100,000. What are the advantages and disadvantages of using the Hybrid III in all vehicle crash tests?

EXTENSION

Go to the *Issues and Physical Science* page of the SEPUP website to learn more about vehicle crash testing. Then investigate careers in automotive engineering.

Mass is an important characteristic of an object. Another important characteristic is the object's center of mass. The **center of mass** is the point where the distribution of an object's mass is centered. While mass describes an amount, the center of mass describes a location. For example, a meterstick's center of mass is the point where the mass of the stick is evenly distributed to the left and right ends, to the front and the back, and to one edge and the other. This is where it balances, as shown below.

The center of mass for a vehicle is somewhere inside the vehicle. Vehicles that are tall or ride high off the ground usually have higher centers of mass than vehicles that are less tall and ride closer to the ground. In certain kinds of accidents the vehicle's center of mass can affect what happens to the vehicle and the people inside it.

CHALLENGE ⟶ **How does the center of mass affect what happens in a collision?**

The center mass of this meterstick is in the middle.

The center mass of the ruler and eraser is toward one end of the meterstick.

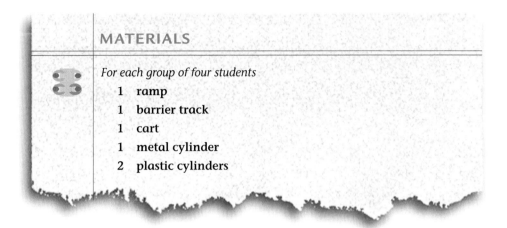

PROCEDURE

1. Attach the barrier track to the ramp.

2. In your science notebook, make a table like the one below.

Center of Mass and Collisions

Mass	Observations	Stability Ranking
Empty Cart		
Loaded cart, Low center of mass		
Loaded cart, High center of mass		

3. While holding the ramp in place, hold the cart so its rear axle is at Notch A of the ramp. Observe what happens when you release the cart and it hits the barrier.

4. Repeat Step 3 several times, and observe what the cart tends to do when it hits the barrier. Record your observations in your table.

5. Place all the cylinders in the cart with the metal one on the bottom. This loaded cart has a low center of mass.

6. With your group, predict what will happen when this loaded cart hits the barrier. Record your prediction in your science notebook.

7. Repeat Steps 3 and 4 using the loaded cart.

8. Now, place all the cylinders in the cart so that the metal one is at the top. This reloaded cart has a high center of mass.

9. With your group, predict what will happen when this reloaded cart hits the barrier. Record your prediction in your science notebook.

10. Repeat Steps 3 and 4 for the reloaded cart.

11. Discuss the results with your group, and compare what happened to the carts when they hit the barrier. In your table, rank with a 1, 2, or 3 the stability of each type of cart: 1 for the most stable cart, and 3 for the least stable cart.

ANALYSIS

1. How did you rank the stability of the carts with three different centers of mass? Describe the observations that determined your ranking.

2. How did a higher center of mass affect the cart's motion after it hit the barrier?

3. Imagine three identical barrels, one empty, one half-full of water, and one full of water. Make a sketch of the barrels in your science notebook, like the ones below.

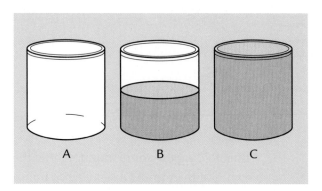

a. Place an "X" on each barrel to show the approximate location of its center of mass.

b. Label the barrel that has the most mass "most mass."

c. Label the barrel with the lowest center of mass "lowest center of mass." Explain why the center of mass is located there.

d. Label the barrel that is easiest to tip over "least stable." Then explain why that barrel is the least stable.

4. Your friend's parents want to haul some lumber in their station wagon. His parents are not sure whether to put the lumber in the wagon or tie it on the roof rack. What advice do you give them? Explain in terms of center of mass.

5. Why do think pick-ups and SUVs tend to roll over more often than passenger cars of similar mass? Explain in terms of center of mass.

EXTENSION

Design an experiment to determine how the cart's speed affects the motion of the cart after it hits the barrier.

TALKING IT OVER

There are many types of vehicles and even more types of accidents. Unfortunately, people are hurt or killed in car accidents every day. Many accidents are caused by driver error, road conditions, vehicle design, or any combination of those. Even when vehicle design is not the cause of an accident, it can contribute to the severity of the damage.

The design of a car affects how well the car protects its occupants. It also determines how much damage and injury the car can inflict on other vehicles and their occupants. Cars with more mass, for example, will hit something with more force than a similar, but lighter, car.

CHALLENGE

Are some types of cars more dangerous than other types?

MATERIALS

For each student
1   **Student Sheet 87.1, "Ranking Fatality Risk"**

Accidents can be caused by driver error, distractions, weather, vehicle design, or a combination of factors.

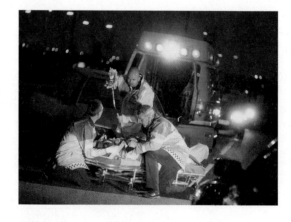

PROCEDURE

1. Using the data tables below, discuss with your partner which vehicles have the highest and lowest risk for each kind of accident.

2. Use Student Sheet 87.1, "Ranking Fatality Risk," to help analyze the data. Record the type of vehicles that have the highest and lowest risk for each kind of accident.

3. With your group, discuss the limitations of the data in the tables. Make a list of information about traffic fatalities that the tables do not include.

Number of Fatalities per Billion Vehicle Miles*			
Vehicle Type	All Accidents, Any Fatality in Any Vehicle	Rollover Accidents Occupant Fatalities	Fixed Object, Occupant Fatalities
Very small 4-door cars	20.6	1.1	4.0
Small 4-door cars	15.3	.8	2.9
Mid-sized 4-door cars	12.4	.8	2.6
Large 4-door cars	9.3	.5	2.1
Large pickup trucks	13.0	1.0	2.2
Mid-sized 4-door SUVs	16.7	4.4	2.6
Large 4-door SUVs	13.0	2.1	2.1
Minivans	10.6	1.1	1.4

Two-Vehicle Accidents: Number of Fatalities per Billion Vehicle Miles*		
Vehicle Type	Occupant, Fatalities	Fatalities in Other Vehicle
Very small 4-door cars	7.1	2.7
Small 4-door cars	4.9	2.2
Mid-sized 4-door cars	2.8	2.5
Large 4-door cars	1.7	2.2
Large pickup trucks	1.3	4.9
Mid-sized 4-door SUVs	2.2	4.5
Large 4-door SUVs	1.3	4.3
Minivans	1.8	3.0

SOURCE: U.S. Dept of Transportation: National Highway Traffic Safety Administration (NHTSA)

Case vehicles are model year 1996–1999 with air bags, and the accidents occurred 1996–2000.

ANALYSIS

1. How can the following aspects of a car's design help avoid accidents:

   a. mass and inertia?

   b. center of mass?

   c. braking distance?

2. Use the data from the tables to explain which vehicle type:

   a. is most likely to be in an accident that includes fatalities.

   b. is least likely to be in an accident that includes fatalities.

3. Use the data from the tables to explain which vehicle type in a two-car accident is most likely to cause a death:

   a. of people in the other vehicle.

   b. of its own occupants.

4. Use evidence from this and other activities in this unit to explain why mid-sized cars and SUVs have:

   a. different rollover fatality rates.

   b. the same fixed-object fatality rates.

5. Noah's family of four wants to buy a safe car. Which type of car would you recommend? Use evidence from the data tables in this activity and ideas from this unit to explain your decision.

6. Reflection: Americans 15–24 years old have almost twice the risk of dying in a motor vehicle accident as Americans aged 25–34. Why do you think the risks are so different for these two age groups?

ROLE PLAY

The severity of a car accident depends on many factors. These factors tend to fall into two categories: driving habits and vehicle characteristics. Because people's driving habits are harder to control than vehicle characteristics, some people think the best way to reduce the number of injuries and deaths caused by car accidents is to pass laws that standardize the features of noncommercial cars, such as their mass, bumper height, and front-end and roof stiffness.

CHALLENGE ➡ **Should noncommercial vehicles be more alike?**

MATERIALS

For each student
1   **Student Sheet 88.1, "Discussion Web: Safety For All"**

PROCEDURE

1. Decide which group member will play each of the roles shown on this and the next page.

2. Each person should read his or her role aloud while the rest of the group listens.

3. After each role is read, identify the evidence each character has presented.

4. Discuss whether each character's piece of evidence supports or does not support making cars more alike. Use Student Sheet 88.1, "Discussion Web: Safety For All," to sort the evidence.

    *   Under the "Yes" column, explain how a particular piece of evidence *supports* making cars more alike.

    *   Under the "No" column, explain how a particular piece of evidence *does not support* making cars more alike.

Hope Ezersky, founder of Families For Larger Cars

Both my legs were broken when a large SUV slid into my very small four-door sedan on a wet road. Now I drive a large family sedan so that I will have less chance of getting hurt if a car hits me again. I think all cars should be about the same mass so that the risk is even for everyone in an accident. Right now, larger passenger vehicles can weigh 1,000–2,000 pounds more than small ones. That means all vehicles do not hit with the same force. Since the average American family is three or four people, cars should be large enough to easily hold that many. So help make accidents fair by banning all small cars.

Damion Reese, President of Equitable Vehicles Now

I think some features of larger vehicles make driving more dangerous. With their higher centers of mass, SUVs and pickup trucks roll over more easily than ordinary passenger cars. Of all accident types, rollovers are most likely to lead to fatalities. In addition to putting their own occupants at risk, large SUVs, pickups, and vans put the occupants of other passenger cars at high risk. Large vehicles cause more damage in accidents because of their high mass, higher frames, and stiff front ends. All vehicles should have similar features to help avoid fatalities. Increased costs from making vehicles similar will be worthwhile if it makes the roads safer for everyone.

Hugo LaPierre, Physics Student and Teacher

Don't ban certain types of cars, ban certain kinds of drivers. Most accidents happen because people are bad drivers. I don't think people understand how much the braking distance changes when the road conditions change. As a result, people often drive too fast and too closely to other cars in the rain and snow. I always make sure to leave extra braking room when I drive. People also drive when they're sleepy or distracted. The worst ones drive under the influence of drugs and alcohol. I think we need to educate drivers more and pass laws requiring tougher and more frequent driving tests. The cost for the extra education can be spread out among all drivers.

Wilma Chang, Owner of Haul It, Inc.

I think the current laws work for everyone. I haul lumber and other supplies in my free time, so I need a large pickup truck. Sometimes I use the truck to help a neighbor, pick something up, or move things for a local charity. If automakers redesign pickups to add more safety features, trucks will cost more for people like me who can't afford to pay more. I've never caused an accident, and the one time I was hit, I wasn't hurt. This country is based on freedom, and that should include the freedom to choose what type of car you drive.

ANALYSIS

1. Make a list of car features that contribute to the safety of the vehicle but are not the same in all vehicle classes. Explain how each feature contributes to the safety of the vehicle.

2. Write a letter to the head of the U.S. Senate Committee for Highway Safety, explaining your position on whether cars should be required by law to be alike. Use evidence to support your position and describe at least one trade-off of your decision.

Waves

F

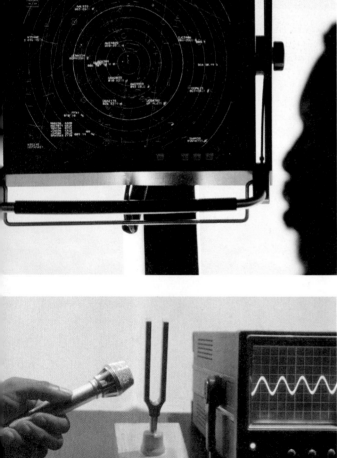

Waves

Gemma looked outside. After days of rainy weather it was finally a bright and sunny day. "Ma, I am heading outside to meet Sam," she called to her mother. She grabbed her headphones and headed for the door.

"Remember your sunglasses!" said her mother. Gemma swept them off the kitchen counter as she left and put them on. Listening to her music, she walked down the street and joined her friend Samantha at the corner.

"Hey," said Sam, pointing at Gemma's sunglasses. "My glasses are just like those. Only blue."

Gemma took out her headphones to be able to hear to her friend. "Well, why aren't you wearing them?"

"Oh, I don't like wearing them. They make my nose itch," Sam said.

"My mom says the sun can damage your eyes. Have you ever heard of that? We have a lot of bright days around here, so maybe you should wear them," Gemma said with concern.

"Yeah, you're probably right. But aren't you worried about hurting your ears with those headphones turned up so loud?" said Sam with equal concern for her friend.

• • •

How is sound energy transmitted? Can light go through an object? What is ultraviolet?

How are sound and light waves similar?

In this unit, you will learn about several kinds of waves and investigate the transmission of sound and light. You will also investigate the situations in which some waves may be harmful to your health.

INVESTIGATION

José and Jenna were talking at lunch. The cafeteria was noisy, though, and José was having a hard time understanding Jenna. Jenna thought it was weird that he wasn't able to hear her very well. Later they talked in a quieter place.

"José, I'm a little worried about your hearing," Jenna said.

"What do you mean?" José asked.

"Well, I noticed that sometimes you don't hear me call to you. I have to repeat myself really loudly."

"Well, actually, sometimes I don't hear my teacher right. Like yesterday I wasn't aware of what she said in class and I ended up doing the wrong thing."

"You should get your hearing tested."

"I've had it tested before, and it was fine. I don't see why it would change."

There are a number of causes of hearing loss. It can be present at birth or develop later in life. Some people are genetically more likely to lose their hearing, although it is not yet known which people are at higher risk. Occupational noises, recreational noises, some medications, and illnesses can all cause hearing loss.

When we hear something it is because sound waves have transferred energy to our ears. A **wave** is a disturbance that repeats regularly in space and time and that transmits energy from one place to another with no transfer of matter. Some sound waves are more intense than others. **Sound intensity** is a measurement of how much sound energy passes by a point in a certain amount of time as it spreads out from the source. Scientists measure sound intensity in watts per square meter (W/m^2). A common way of describing sound is with the decibel scale. The **decibel** (dB) is a unit of measure that indicates the relative intensity of a sound. In this activity you will investigate the decibel scale and how the human ear responds to different levels of intensity.

CHALLENGE ⟹ What is the range of sound intensity that humans can hear?

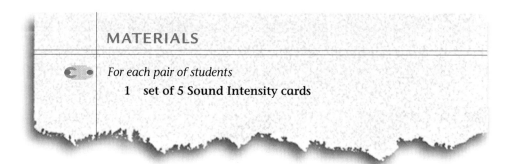

MATERIALS

For each pair of students
1   set of 5 Sound Intensity cards

PROCEDURE

1. With your partner, examine the Sound Intensity cards. Each card represents a particular sound. The number of shaded squares in relation to the total squares on the card shows the relative intensity of the sound.

2. Make a data table similar to the one below.

Relative Intensity of Certain Sounds

Card	Type of Sound	Number of Squares Shaded	Total Number of Squares on the Card	Proportion of Shaded Squares on the Card (relative intensity)	Decibel Level (dB)
A					
B					
C					
D					
E					

3. Based on the data for each card, complete the table.

4. With your partner, examine the data in the table, and look for a relationship between the changes in relative intensity and the change in decibel level. Record your findings in your science notebook.

5. The table below shows the sound levels of some common sounds. In your science notebook, copy the first two columns of the table. Complete the second column of the table. Do this by using the relationship you determined in Step 4 to calculate how many times more intense each sound is compared to a whisper.

Sound Levels of Common Noises		
Decibels	Relative Intensity	Noise Source
Safe range		
0	1	Threshold of hearing
10		Breathing
20		Whisper; rustling leaves
30		Quiet bedroom; park
40		Quiet library
50		Average home or office
60		Normal conversation, 1 m away; clothes dryer
70		Vacuum cleaner, 1 m away; average road noise, 25 m away; inside car; headphone use in quiet environment
Risky range		
80		Heavy city traffic, at curb; power lawn mower; hair dryer; freight train @ 40 km/h; noisy restaurant; headphone use most places outdoors
90		Diesel truck, 1 m away; average factory floor
100		Snowmobile, 15th row of rock concert, circular saw; typical musical instrument
110		Chain saw, 1 m away; leaf blower close by
Injury range		
120		Ambulance siren; jackhammer; car horn; front row of rock concert or symphony; max headphone level
130		Threshold of pain
140		Jet engine, 50 m away; firecracker; gunshot
Instant perforation of eardrum		
160		some explosions

6. Use the table and data from the Sound Intensity cards to calculate how many times more intense a noise at the threshold of pain is than a whisper. Discuss with your partner the range of intensities that the human ear can hear.

ANALYSIS

1. What is the range of sound intensities that the human ear can hear, from the quietest sound to one that causes pain?

2. What is the advantage of using the decibel scale to indicate intensity of sound?

3. If a sound increases by 10 dB, how many times more intense is the sound?

4. Most people perceive an increase of 10 dB as a doubling in volume of a sound. How many times louder would a 70 dB sound seem to be when compared to a 40 dB sound? Explain your answer.

LABORATORY

José made an appointment with his doctor, who referred him to a hearing center. At the center José was seen by an audiologist, who conducted a hearing test. She asked José to wear headphones and then played different tones with varying loudness levels to one ear at a time. Each tone was a different frequency to allow the audiologist to measure at which decibel level José could hear a particular frequency. She repeated the tests several times for each ear.

Hearing loss does not necessarily mean a person hears all types of sound less clearly. The results of José's hearing tests indicated that his hearing was fine for some frequencies, but not all. The **frequency** of the sound is the number of vibrations per second the ear receives, otherwise known as the sound's pitch. High-frequency sounds have a high pitch, like a flute, while low-frequency sounds have a low pitch, like a bass drum.

An audiogram is a graph that shows the sensitivity of a person's hearing for different frequencies. Frequencies are measured in **hertz** (Hz), or wave cycles per second. José's audiogram showed that José's hearing was most affected in the 3,000 Hz-and-higher range. This means he could have difficulty distinguishing female speech in a noisy environment.

An audiogram for someone with normal hearing.

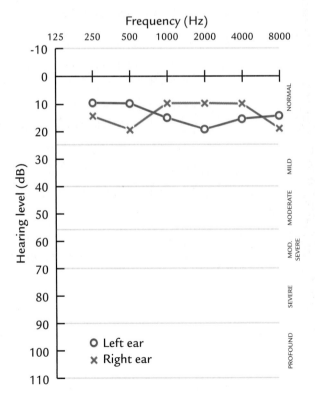

CHALLENGE ⟹ How are frequency and wavelength related?

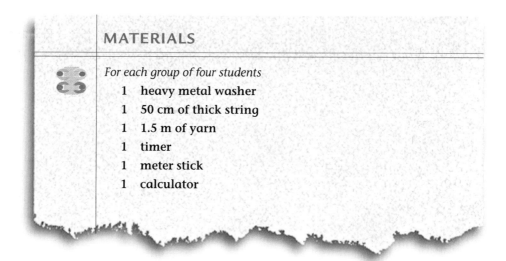

MATERIALS

For each group of four students
1 heavy metal washer
1 50 cm of thick string
1 1.5 m of yarn
1 timer
1 meter stick
1 calculator

PROCEDURE

1. Tie the thick string firmly to the washer, making sure that 50 cm of the string extends from the washer.

2. Tie the yarn firmly to the opposite side of the washer, making sure that 150 cm extends below the washer.

3. Assign one of the following roles to each member of your group.

Role	Task
Swinger	This person holds the thick string high enough that the last few centimeters at the bottom of the yarn lie on the ground. This person will keep the pendulum washer swinging at a steady rate.
Timer	This person times how long it takes for the washer to complete 10 swings.
Measurer	This person estimates the length of the wave produced in the yarn.
Recorder	This person creates the data table for Step 5. This person also records the data in the table.

4. Find a safe place for the swinger to stand so that the top of the thick string can be held in the air and the bottom few centimeters of the yarn lie on the ground, as shown in the picture at left.

5. *Recorder:* Create a data table like the one below.

Thick String Length (cm)	Time for 10 Swings (s)	Time for One Swing (s)	Frequency (Hz)	Wavelength

6. *Swinger:* Hold the thick string at a point 5 cm above the washer, and move your wrist just enough to keep the washer swinging at a steady rate. Generate a steady **amplitude**, which is the wave's displacement from its state of rest. After a few seconds it should be possible to observe a wave in the yarn.

7. *Measurer:* Estimate the distance between any two successive places where the shape of the wave repeats itself. This is the **wavelength**, or the length of one wave cycle. The distances AB and CD in the figures below show examples of how wavelength can be measured.

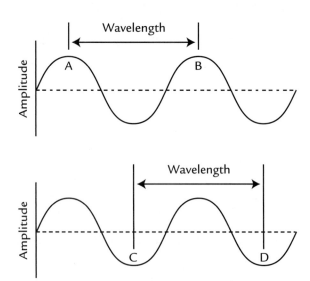

8. *Timer:* When the wave is seen clearly, time 10 full swings of the washer. A full swing of the washer includes both its swing away and its return.

9. *Recorder:* Record your results for wavelength and time for 10 swings in the data table.

10. As a group, calculate the time for one swing. Use this value to calculate the wave's frequency by taking the inverse of the time for one swing. Record the results in the data table.

11. Increase the length of the thick string to 25 cm, and repeat the experiment. Add those results to the data table.

12. Look for a relationship between the frequency of the washer and the wavelength of the wave produced in the yarn. Record your ideas in your science notebook.

13. Discuss your conclusions with the class.

ANALYSIS

1. Waves involve some type of disturbance that causes the transfer of energy from one point to another.

   a. What was the disturbance that caused the wave in the yarn?

   b. What evidence do you have that energy was transferred from one end of the yarn to the other?

2. The frequency of the swing of the washer can be calculated if the time for one swing is known. Suggest reasons why you were instructed to measure 10 swings instead of one swing.

3. Look at the diagram of a wave below.

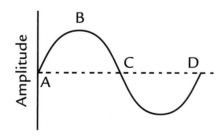

   a. Describe the motion of the yarn at positions B and C.

   b. Between which two points is the energy transferred?

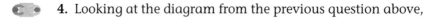

4. Looking at the diagram from the previous question above,

   a. draw what the wave would look like if the frequency were doubled.

   b. draw what the wave would look like if the wavelength were doubled.

5. Match the following descriptions of people to their audiogram:

   a: José has decreased hearing in the right ear at higher frequencies.

   b: Leon has noticed lately that he has trouble deciphering women's speech.

   c: Shannon has moderate hearing loss involving sounds of 3,000–6,000 Hz.

   d: Sophia has less than 50% hearing in both ears.

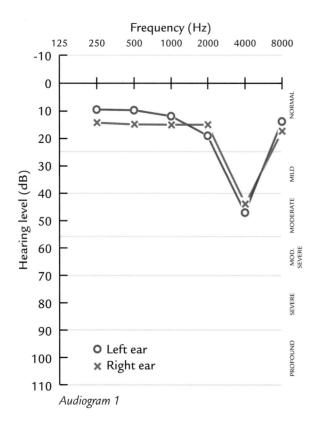

Audiogram 1

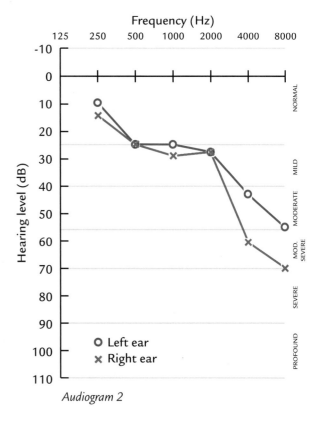

Audiogram 2

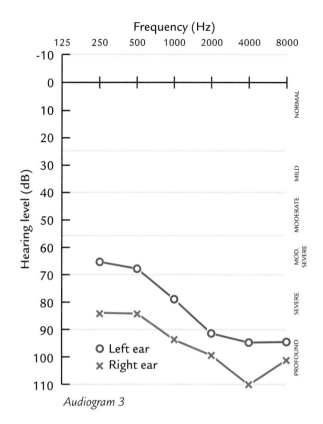

Audiogram 3

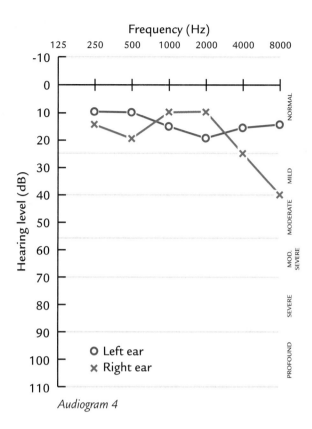

Audiogram 4

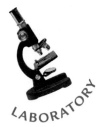

LABORATORY

Sound is one of many kinds of waves. Other common waves include those on the surface of water, light waves, radio waves, and seismic waves. All waves share some of the same characteristics, but they also differ in certain ways. For example, all waves (including sound waves and water waves) carry energy. However, one difference is that a sound wave is a longitudinal wave, while a water wave is a transverse wave. A **longitudinal wave** is one that transfers energy through compressions and rarefactions in the material through which the wave travels. A compression is the region of the wave in which the material through which the wave is transmitted is pressed together. A rarefaction is the region in which the material is spread apart. A **transverse wave** does not have compressions and rarefactions. For a transverse wave to be transmitted through a material, the motion of the material is perpendicular to the direction that the energy travels. In this activity you will investigate the similarities and differences between a transverse and a longitudinal wave.

CHALLENGE **How are sound waves similar to, and different from, other types of waves?**

MATERIALS

For each group of four students
1 **long metal spring**

A longitudinal sound wave from a tuning fork is displayed as a transverse wave on the screen.

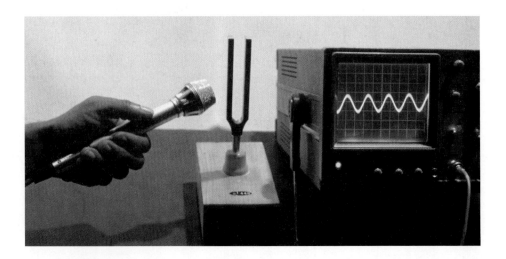

PROCEDURE

Part A: Longitudinal Waves

1. Assign each member of your group to one of the following roles:

Role	Task
Holder 1	This person holds one end of the spring on the ground so that the circular end of the spring is flat against the floor.
Holder 2	This person holds the other end of the spring vertically above the bottom end.
Wave maker	This person creates wave pulses from the top of the spring.
Recorder	This person observes and records what happens to the spring.

2. *Holders:* Set the spring up so that one end is on the floor and it stretches vertically. The other end should be about 2 m above the ground.

3. *Wave maker:* Gather about one half of the coils of the spring and compress them into the top 10 cm of the spring. When everyone is ready, release a few of the compressed coils to make a wave pulse.

4. All group members should observe the pulse as it travels down the spring. *Recorder:* Record the group's observations.

5. *Wave maker:* Create additional pulses by releasing more coils. *Recorder:* Observe and record what happens as the pulse travels down the spring each time.

6. Change roles, and repeat Steps 3–5, beginning with slightly more than half of the spring compressed.

Part B: Transverse Waves

7. Change roles again. *Holders:* Put the spring on the floor or a long table, holding the ends about 2 m apart.

8. *Wave maker:* Pull a handful of coils to one side at the end of the spring, close to one of the Holders. When everyone is ready, release the coils to make a wave pulse.

9. All group members should observe the pulse as it travels down the spring. *Recorder:* Record the group's observations.

10. *Wave maker:* Create additional pulses by pulling and releasing more coils. *Recorder:* Each time observe and record what happens as the pulse travels down the spring.

11. Change roles, and repeat Steps 8–10 with the spring held to about a 4-m length.

Part C: Additional Investigations

12. Try experimenting with a series of transverse wave pulses, instead of a single pulse. To do this, continuously move one end of the spring to the left and right. Record your observations in your science notebook.

13. Try creating longitudinal wave pulses while the spring is laid along the floor or table. Record your observations in your science notebook.

ANALYSIS

 1. Create a larger version of the Venn diagram shown below. Record the characteristics of longitudinal and transverse waves in the circle with that label. In the spaces that overlap, record common features.

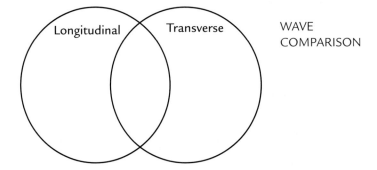

Longitudinal   Transverse   WAVE COMPARISON

 2. Describe what happened when

    a. the longitudinal wave pulses hit the floor in Part A.

    b. the transverse wave pulses reached Holder 2 in Part B.

 3. Describe what happened in Part B when the spring was stretched to double its length.

 4. What happened to the amplitude of the wave pulse when it traveled along the spring in Part B? Suggest an explanation for your observations.

5. Make two tables like the ones on the next two pages, and fill in the missing diagrams to show changes in amplitude or frequency.

Wave Characteristic: AMPLITUDE

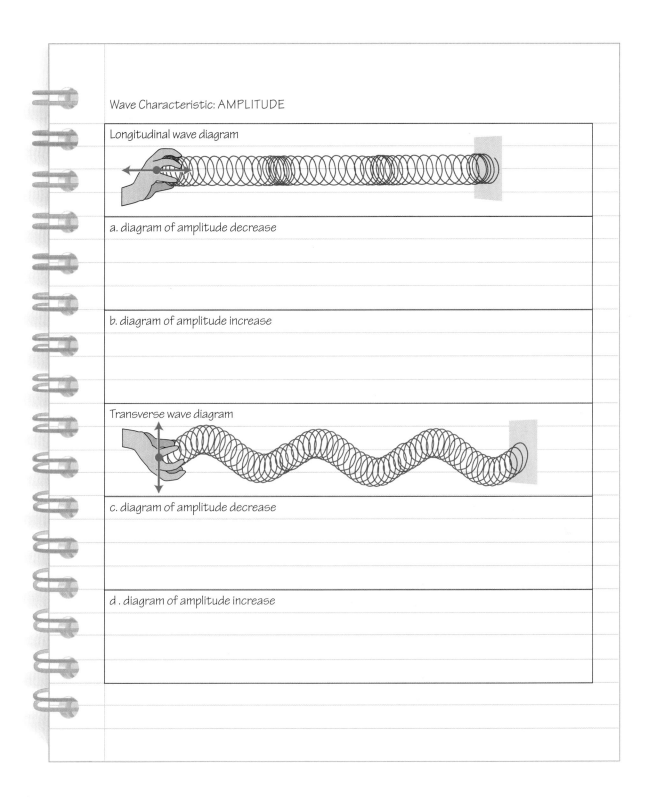

Longitudinal wave diagram

a. diagram of amplitude decrease

b. diagram of amplitude increase

Transverse wave diagram

c. diagram of amplitude decrease

d . diagram of amplitude increase

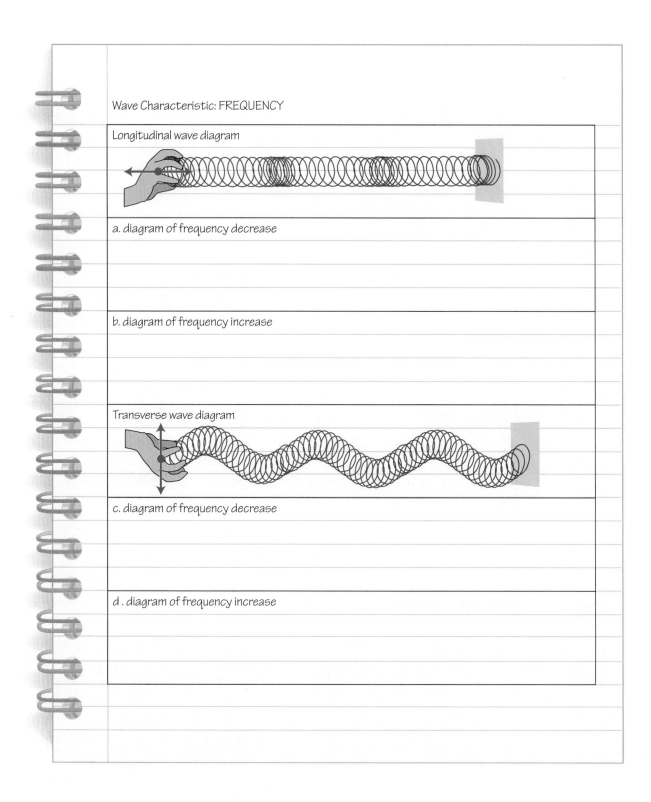

Wave Characteristic: FREQUENCY

Longitudinal wave diagram

a. diagram of frequency decrease

b. diagram of frequency increase

Transverse wave diagram

c. diagram of frequency decrease

d . diagram of frequency increase

INVESTIGATION

Noise-induced hearing loss (NIHL) occurs when sounds damage hearing, either temporarily or permanently. Harmful noises are sounds that are too loud or loud sounds that last a long time. Long-term exposure to loud noises causes permanent hearing loss by damaging the inner ear. The small sensitive cells in the inner ear, called hair cells, ordinarily convert sound energy into electrical signals that travel to the brain. Once damaged, hair cells send an incomplete message to the brain, which results in sensorineural hearing loss, or "nerve deafness."

Exposure to excessive noise is the most frequently avoidable cause of permanent hearing loss. This exposure puts people at risk, which is the chance that an action or event could result in something unfavorable happening, such as injury. People at risk for NIHL are those who are exposed to loud sounds regularly, such as firemen, musicians, truck drivers, and headphone users. People exposed to a sudden burst of noise may suffer hearing loss, but NIHL more commonly occurs gradually from long-term noise exposure. People at risk for damage can prevent permanent damage with a few simple strategies. Unfortunately, most people are not aware of the degree of risk.

Middle ear
Inner ear
Outer ear
Auditory nerve
Cochlea
Ear canal
Ear drum
Eustacian tube

CHALLENGE ➡ **What can be done to prevent noise-induced hearing loss?**

Headphones are often turned up significantly when users are in noisy places.

MATERIALS

For each student
graph paper

PROCEDURE

Part A: How Much Is Too Much?

1. Review the intensity table, "Sound Levels of Common Noises," provided in Activity 89, "It's a Noisy World." Compare it to the table below, "Federal Noise Standards," which shows the maximum job-related noise exposure for unprotected ears allowed by federal regulation.

Federal Noise Standards		
Sound Level, Decibels	Typical Activities	Maximum Allowed Job-Noise Exposure, Daily Duration
90	Typical factory work	8 hr
95	Driving a subway, tractor	4 hr
100	High-volume headphone use; playing musical instrument; power boating; riding snow mobile, motorcycle	2 hr
105	Sporting events, mowing the lawn	1 hr
110	Dancing at a club, playing drums; using power tools, chain saw	30 min
115	Front-row rock concert; cheering stadium crowd	15 min or less

2. Plot a line graph of daily duration (y-axis) vs. sound level (x-axis). Use the graph to determine the maximum allowed time for a sound level of 97 dB.

Part B: What Can Be Done?

3. With your partner, discuss ideas you have for reducing your chance of getting noise-induced hearing loss. Make a list of strategies in your science notebook.

4. With your group, compile a list of strategies that would help reduce the risk of hearing loss. Then go through the list, and identify types of activities that each strategy might succeed with.

5. For each person described in the profiles below use the table to decide

    a. if they have a high-, medium-, or low-level risk for noise-induced hearing loss.

    b. why you gave them the rank.

    c. what could be done to protect their hearing.

José

José is an active middle school student who recently has had trouble hearing. When he went to the doctor, she didn't find any structural problems or inflammation in his ears. She sent him for a hearing test, which showed he has some difficulty being able to hear higher frequencies in one ear. It is not clear at this time whether his hearing will return, or what is the exact cause. José will continue to undergo tests to determine the cause. In his free time, José likes to read, plays the drums in a band, and often listens to music loudly on his MP3 player with the earpiece in his right ear only.

Leon

Leon is 68 years old and just retired from his work as a computer engineer. He has always loved anything electronic, including games and robots. As a child he was fascinated by robots, a passion that led him to study robotics in graduate school. Eventually he began programming them full-time. His other love is music, and he goes to concerts regularly. He loves rock concerts as much as symphony concerts. He has been a band technician for many years, and when he noticed ringing in his ears that wasn't going away, he started getting concerned. Over the years, he has lost some hearing but has only recently noticed it. In particular, he has trouble understanding women when they are talking to him. His doctor has told him that he should buy hearing aids.

Shannon

Shannon is a middle-aged woman who has worked at a paper mill for many years. Lately her work has involved running the big trucks that pull the felled trees into the mill entrance. Her favorite part of the paper mill is watching the massive automated machines run paper rolls at high speed. She knows she should wear ear protection because she has some hearing loss at 3,000–6,000 Hz, but admits she occasionally forgets to bring them to work.

Sophie

Sophie is a high school student with congenital deafness in both ears, which means she was born with little hearing. The cause of her deafness is most likely genetic as her father is also deaf. She has some hearing in one ear, and she would like to protect it. She has studied lipreading and had speech training, which is helpful in her every-day life but not particularly natural for her. She is most comfortable communicating through American Sign Language (ASL), which she learned from her parents and at school. She wonders if she might be making her hearing worse when she hangs out with her brother, who loves to take her to college soccer games.

ANALYSIS

1. List the people in the profiles from highest to lowest risk of further hearing loss, and explain how you choose their rank.

2. What kinds of things should be done to make people aware of the common risks to their hearing?

3. How does your own risk compare to the case studies in this activity? Explain how you will or will not change your behavior based on what you learned here.

4. What would you recommend for the following people to help them protect their hearing?

    a. Snowmobile driver

    b. Concertgoer

    c. Hair stylist

    d. MP3 user

READING

Sound is only one of several kinds of waves. Some waves carry small amounts of energy, such as the waves you observed in the long coil on the floor, a whisper, or gentle water waves. Other waves transfer tremendous amounts of energy, such as the energy transferred in earthquakes, tsunamis, or gamma waves. There are waves that humans cannot detect directly, even though some of them carry a lot of energy. In this activity you will learn more about the nature of various kinds of waves. You will also learn about how certain devices have extended humans' sensory capabilities.

CHALLENGE ➡ **What are the properties of certain kinds of waves?**

Some animals, such as the bat and dolphin shown here, navigate their environments with sonar.

READING

Wave Media

No matter what kind of wave or what amount of energy it transmits, it is important to note that when waves transmit energy, the individual molecules or particles in the medium are not transmitted. In other words, the medium does not move along with the wave. A **medium** (plural is media) is the material in which wave energy travels. Mechanical waves, such as sound or seismic waves, move through the ground, water, air, and other materials. For example, when making waves in the long metal spring in Activity 91, "Longitudinal and Transverse Waves," the metal of the spring was the medium. The disturbance moved away from the source. The coils of the spring temporarily moved up and down or closer together and farther apart, but the spring did not undergo a permanent change of position relative to the source. In this case, the medium itself—the metal of the spring—was not transferred from the wave maker to the other end.

STOPPING TO THINK 1

What is the medium for an ocean wave? Provide evidence that the medium is not transferred when a water wave moves on a lake.

Two Major Kinds of Waves

In Activity 91, "Longitudinal and Transverse Waves," you investigated two fundamentally different kinds of waves, longitudinal and transverse. A longitudinal wave is one that transfers energy through compressions and rarefactions in the medium through which the wave travels. Sound is an example of a longitudinal wave. When you hear a sound wave through the air, you are detecting a disturbance in the pressure of the air. When the pressure is increased the air molecules are pushed closer together, into a compression. When the pressure is reduced and the air molecules move farther apart, it is referred to as a rarefaction. A longitudinal wave is one that causes the medium to move parallel to the direction of transmission, or propagation of the wave.

A transverse wave that travels through a medium is a result of the medium moving perpendicular to the direction of propagation. The long coil used in a previous activity was an example of a transverse wave. Light is another example of a transverse wave.

LONGITUDINAL WAVE

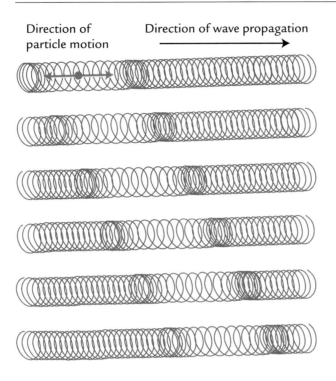

TRANSVERSE WAVE

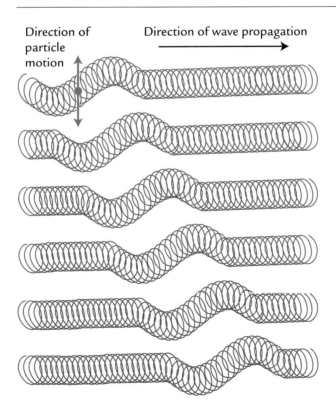

How is a transverse wave different from a longitudinal wave?

Transmission of Waves Through Various Media

Mechanical waves, such as earthquakes, sound waves, or waves in a coil will travel differently depending on the medium. The same wave will travel at different speeds through two different substances. In general, waves travel faster through materials that have "springier" molecules. This means sound moves faster through solids than liquids and faster through liquids than gases. For example, sound travels about five times faster through metal than through air.

Because sound waves always involve the physical disturbance of atoms or molecules they are referred to as mechanical waves. A mechanical wave must have a medium in order to travel. Mechanical waves cannot travel through a vacuum because there are no atoms or molecules in a vacuum. Although outer space is not a perfect vacuum, the molecules are so far apart that they do not allow the production of compressions and rarefactions. Therefore, sound cannot travel in space.

Some waves, however, do not require a medium and can be transmitted through a vacuum. For example, light travels through the vacuum of outer space, whereas sound does not. Because light waves do not require the presence of atoms or molecules, they are not considered to be mechanical waves. Light is a transverse wave that carries electromagnetic energy. This energy in light waves travels about 900,000 times faster than the energy carried by sound waves.

Wave Speed

Every wave has four basic characteristics: frequency, wavelength, amplitude, and speed. **Wave speed**, measured in meters per second (m/s), is the distance traveled by a certain feature on the wave, such as a crest, in a given amount of time. The speed at which the wave travels depends on what type of material it travels through. Sound is transmitted through the air at about 340 m/s. The exact speed depends on such factors as the temperature and humidity of the air. The tables on the next page show the speeds of sound and light through various media. Although light slows down a little in air, it still travels about 900,000 times faster than sound. This is why you will see a lightning flash long before you hear the sound of thunder from a storm several miles away.

STOPPING TO THINK 3

What does it mean if you hear thunder and see lightening at almost the same time?

Speed of Sound	
Medium	**Speed (m/s)**
Vacuum	0
Carbon dioxide (0°C)	258
Air (20°C)	344
Helium (20°C)	927
Water, fresh (20°C)	1,481
Wood	3,500
Aluminum	6,400

Speed of Light	
Medium	**Speed (m/s)**
Diamond	124,000,000
Glass	197,200,000
Plexiglass	198,500,000
Water	224,900,000
Ice	228,800,000
Air	299,700,000
Vacuum	299,800,000

Extending the Senses

Although our world is full of sights and sounds of waves, there are many waves our sensory organs cannot detect directly. However, people have invented devices to detect waves having frequencies that fall out-side our range of hearing and vision. These devices include cell phones, radios, X-ray film, radar, and sonar. Each of these devices receives energy from a wave that we cannot detect and converts it into some-thing that we can see or hear.

Airport radar towers, left, show plane positions on a screen, above.

Radar works by sending radio waves from a radar source to the surface of a target, such as an airplane or a cloud. The waves are reflected back to the radar source, and the location or speed of the target is calculated from the measurements. Radar systems are based on radio waves or microwaves. Sonar works in a similar way but relies on sound waves at frequencies that are not detectable by human ears. Sonar allows personnel on ships and submarines to detect the depth of water and the presence of fish and other boats on or under the surface. Seismic waves are low-frequency mechanical waves that move through the Earth. They are caused by such events as explosions and earthquakes. By measuring seismic waves with a seismograph, even those waves that are not felt by humans on the surface of the Earth, scientists locate earthquake epicenters and create maps showing regions at risk of earthquakes. All of these examples illustrate ways in which people have invented devices to employ the energy of waves to hear things we wouldn't normally hear and discover things we wouldn't normally see.

STOPPING TO THINK 4

What is another example of a device that uses waves to extend our senses?

ANALYSIS

 1. Create a larger version of the Venn diagram shown at right. Record the characteristics of sound and light waves in the circle with that label. In the spaces that overlap, record common features.

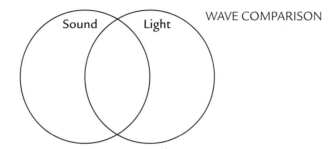

2. Explain why a satellite orbiting Earth could use radar to detect other objects but not sonar.

3. If you started the motor of a boat in the middle of a lake, who would detect the sound of the motor first: a friend sitting on the shore of the lake, or a friend snorkeling just below the surface of the water along the same shore? Explain your answer.

4. Dolphins and whales communicate with other dolphins and whales, respectively, by making low-frequency sounds. They navigate by making high-frequency sounds that echo back to them. Military sonar systems on ships produce sounds as loud as 200 dB, and these sounds travel great distances across oceans. Describe how such systems might affect whales and dolphins.

LABORATORY

During first period, Jenna noticed that her friend José looked worried. After class she asked, "José, is everything okay with you?"

José replied, "Well, actually, I'm a little worried because my favorite great-aunt, Tía Ana, is having eye surgery."

"Surgery!" replied Jenna. "What happened?"

José explained, "Everything started to look blurry for her, and when she went to her doctor, she found out she had cataracts. Today the eye surgeon is going to take out the cloudy lens in her right eye and put in an artificial one."

We use our eyes for almost everything we do, and so it is important to take care of them. One thing that hurts our eyes is too much exposure to the sun. Even people with limited vision may damage their eyes further by exposing them to too much sunlight.

In this activity, you will explore some of the characteristics of white light, or the light we can see, to investigate what might have damaged Tía Ana's eyesight. White light can be separated into the **visible light spectrum**, which is the scientific name for the colors of the rainbow.

CHALLENGE

How are the colors of the visible light spectrum similar to and different from each other?

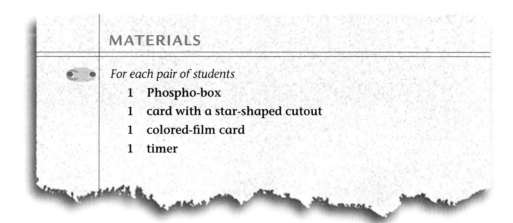

MATERIALS

For each pair of students
1   Phospho-box
1   card with a star-shaped cutout
1   colored-film card
1   timer

PROCEDURE

Part A: The Visible Light Spectrum

1. Observe how your teacher splits white light into the colors of the visible spectrum.

2. List the colors that you see in the order that they appear.

3. Describe whether the colors blend from one to the next or have distinct boundaries between them.

4. Which color of light seems to be

   a. the brightest?

   b. the least bright?

Part B: Colored Light

5. Open the top of the Phospho-box, and examine the bottom of it. The strip on the bottom of the Phospho-box is sensitive to a particular high frequency wave. Sketch and describe what you observe.

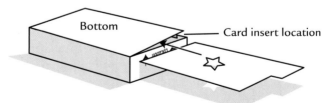

6. Turn the Phospho-box over so that the top with the viewing slit is on the table. Slip the card with the star-shape cutout into the card insert locatsision at the bottom of the box, as shown above. Leave the box in this position for 30 seconds.

A rainbow shows the colors of the visible light spectrum.

7. Turn the Phospho-box right side up, open the top, and let light hit the entire bottom of the box for 20 sec.

8. Close the top of the Phospho-box, and remove the card with the star-shaped cutout. Quickly look through the viewing slit, and record your observations.

9. Turn over the Phospho-box as you did in Step 6. Lay the colored-film card on top of the Phospho-box.

10. Describe or sketch what you see. Rank the colors from brightest to least bright.

11. Describe or sketch what you predict you will observe if you repeat Steps 6–8 using the colored-film card instead of the card with the star-shaped cutout.

12. Repeat Steps 6–8, but use the colored-film card instead of the card with the star-shaped cutout.

13. Rank each color and the cutout shape according to how brightly it caused the strip on the bottom of the Phospho-box to glow.

14. Describe or sketch what you predict you will observe if you repeat Steps 6–8 with the colored-film card, but this time let the sunlight hit the bottom of the box for 40 sec.

15. Repeat Steps 6–8 within the colored-film card, but this time let the light hit the bottom of the box for 40 sec.

16. Record your results in your science notebook.

ANALYSIS

1. What is the purpose of the card with the star-shaped cutout?

2. How do you think the colored-film card changes the white light into colored light?

3. Why do you think only some colors make the strip on the bottom of the Phospho-box glow? Explain.

4. Is there enough **evidence**, or information that supports or refutes a claim, that supports the idea that the higher-energy colors of white light are damaging Tía Ana's eyes?

5. Look at the graph of the visible light at the surface of the earth, below. Why do you think sunlight is yellow instead of blue?

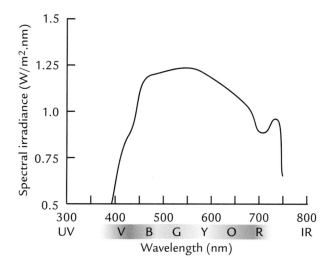

6. Sunglass lenses are an example of a material that blocks some white light and some other high-frequency light that is harmful to the eyes. Examine the transmission graphs about three pairs of sunglasses below.

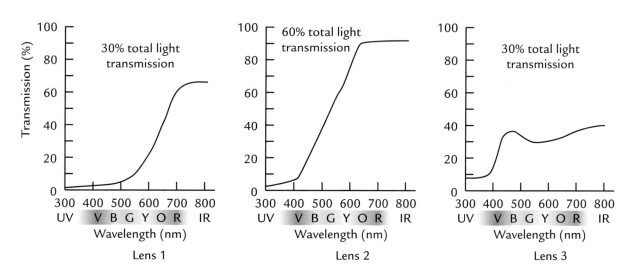

a. Which lens has the best high-energy protection for the eyes? Explain how you decided.

b. The price for each pair of sunglasses is shown below. Which pair would you buy? Why? Describe any trade-offs you made in your choice.

Lens 1: $80
Lens 2: $10
Lens 3: $20

In the last activity, you saw colors of the visible light spectrum being **transmitted**, which is when light energy quickly enters the material and is reemitted on the other side. Any light that is not transmitted through an object is either reflected or absorbed by the object it hits. Light waves are **reflected** when light bounces off the object, either in one direction or scattered in many directions. Reflected light is what enters our eyes so that we can see an opaque object. Light waves are **absorbed** when light enters the object and it does not come out of the object again as light, thereby adding energy to the object. Often light that is absorbed by an object is converted into heat that warms up the object.

Sunlight is selectively transmitted through the stained glass window.

In the last activity, you learned that not all frequencies of sunlight are transmitted through a translucent object, such as a colored film. In this activity, you will investigate the transmission, reflection, and absorption of waves from the sun that are not visible to the human eye.

CHALLENGE **What part of sunlight is transmitted through selected films?**

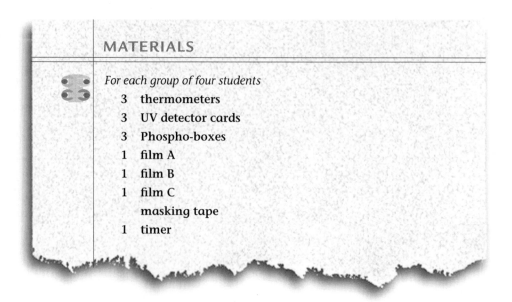

MATERIALS

For each group of four students

3	**thermometers**
3	**UV detector cards**
3	**Phospho-boxes**
1	**film A**
1	**film B**
1	**film C**
	masking tape
1	**timer**

PROCEDURE

Part A: Comparing Temperatures

1. In your science notebook create a data table similar to the one below.

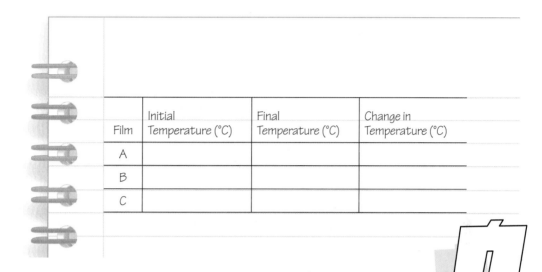

Film	Initial Temperature (°C)	Final Temperature (°C)	Change in Temperature (°C)
A			
B			
C			

2. Place one thermometer face up in the bottom of each of the boxes, and tape it in place so that it will not move. Place a film on each open box, and secure it with tape, as shown in the diagram at right. Make sure to tape the film on all four sides to keep air from blowing into the box during testing.

3. Close the Phospho-box lids until you are ready to perform the experiment in the sun.

4. When in the sunlight have one member of your group hold the closed Phospho-boxes together so they are oriented toward the sun in the same way. Do this so no shadow falls on the thermometer.

5. Record in the data table the initial temperature inside each box.

6. Have another group member open each box and expose it to the sun.

7. Hold or prop the boxes in this position for 5 minutes. Then record in the data table the final temperature inside each box.

8. Calculate the change in temperature for each thermometer. Record these data in your data table.

9. Rank each film from 1 (smallest change) to 3 (highest change). Record your results in your science notebook.

Part B: Comparing Ultraviolet

10. Gently remove the films, and replace the thermometers with the UV detector cards. Replace the films as instructed in Step 2.

11. Make a new data table with titles changed accordingly.

12. Repeat Steps 4–8.

13. With your group, discuss if the results from either Part A, Part B, or both give evidence for invisible waves transmitted into the Phospho-box.

ANALYSIS

1. Which film transmits the most energy? What is your evidence?

2. What evidence from this investigation supports the idea that sunlight contains invisible waves that behave similarly, but not identically, to visible light waves?

3. Films, like the ones used in this activity, are commonly put on glass windows as energy-saving devices and to prevent sun damage. If the costs of the films A, B, and C from this activity are those listed below, which material would you choose to put on

   a. your car windows?

   b. windows in a home located in a desert?

   c. windows in a home located in a snowy mountainous region?

   Explain your choices, citing evidence from this activity. Explain any trade-offs you made.

   Film A: $20/$m^2$

   Film B: $100/$m^2$

   Film C: $50/$m^2$

READING

Sunlight is a combination of light-waves of various frequencies. Some of the frequencies can be seen and some cannot be seen by the human eye. The reading in this activity explores the nature of these waves, which are electromagnetic. An **electromagnetic wave** transmits energy that is emitted from vibrating electrical charges, such as electrons. The vibrations send energy across distance as moving electrical and magnetic fields, which act as waves.

CHALLENGE

What are the characteristics of electromagnetic waves?

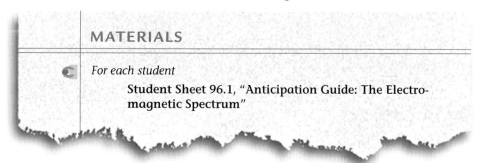

MATERIALS

For each student

    Student Sheet 96.1, "Anticipation Guide: The Electro-magnetic Spectrum"

PROCEDURE

1. Fill in the Before column of Student Sheet 96.1, "Anticipation Guide: The Electromagnetic Spectrum."

2. Complete the Reading.

3. Fill in the After column of Student Sheet 96.1, "Anticipation Guide: The Electromagnetic Spectrum."

READING

Herschel's Famous Experiment

In 1800, British astronomer Sir Frederick William Herschel made an important discovery. While observing the sun through colored lenses, he noticed that some colors of light felt warmer than others. This observation interested him so much that he designed an experiment to try to measure the temperatures of the different colors of light.

In his experiment, Herschel used a prism to separate sunlight into the colors of the rainbow. He then placed a thermometer so that it was only struck by one color of light at a time. He discovered that violet light had the lowest

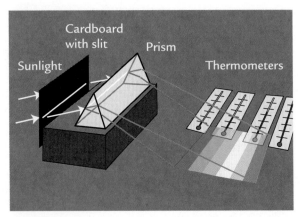

HERSCHEL'S
EXPERIMENT

temperature as shown in the diagram at left. Herschel was surprised at this, because he knew that violet light was a higher frequency than red light and carried more energy. He then decided to investigate of the unlit area just past the red end of the spectrum. He found the temperature on the thermometers rose even higher than it had in the red light.

The only explanation for this data that made sense to Herschel was that sunlight must contain invisible "calorific rays" of low frequency that heat the thermometer. Herschel performed other experiments and found that these waves behaved just like visible light. They were reflected, absorbed, or transmitted. Because these "calorific rays" have a frequency just below visible red light, later scientists, in 1881, established a name for them: infrared. This name was chosen because the prefix "infra-" means "below." Herschel was the first to detect an electromagnetic wave that was not visible to humans.

The reason infrared heats things up more than visible light does is related to its frequency. When infrared hits the molecules that make up many substances, it is often just the right frequency to be absorbed by the molecules. This increases the molecules' energy. The increase in energy makes the molecules move faster, which heats up the substance. In a separate process, warm objects also give off infrared radiation as well as other wavelengths of electromagnetic energy.

Ultraviolet Energy

A year after Herschel's experiment, Johann Wilhelm Ritter in Germany decided to find out if there were waves beyond the violet end of the visible spectrum as well. He conducted an experiment similar to Herschel's, but directed the light onto a chemically coated paper that turned black when exposed to light. He chose this chemical, silver chloride, because it darkened more at the violet end of the spectrum. When he separated the light, the silver chloride was darkest just beyond the visible violet end of the spectrum. He called them "chemical rays," which later became known as ultraviolet because "ultra-" means "beyond."

Ultraviolet waves transmit more energy than infrared and visible light. In fact, ultraviolet has the most energy of all of the waves that commonly reach Earth's surface. The energy transmitted to us by ultraviolet waves can be helpful. For example, human bodies transform some of the sun's ultraviolet energy into vitamin D, which is necessary for bone growth. Those people whose diets lack vitamin D and who do not have much sun exposure may develop a vitamin deficiency. This results in defective bone growth in children

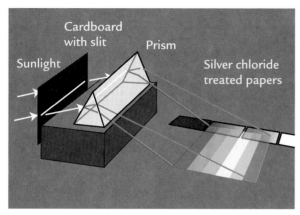

RITTER'S EXPERIMENT

or soft bones in adults. Lack of sun exposure, including ultraviolet wavelengths, also results in seasonal affective disorder for some individuals who are prone to depression. Scientists have invented machines with which to use ultraviolet light to sterilize equipment because it destroys bacteria, viruses, and molds.

At the same time, the high energy of ultraviolet waves poses a danger to people and other living things. They cause damage to living cells, which can result in cancer and cataracts, like those in Tía Ana's eyes. Ultraviolet waves also cause materials, such as those used in clothes, furniture, curtains, and car interiors, to fade and become brittle.

Light From the Sun

Herschel's and Ritter's experiments showed that there is more energy in sunlight than meets the eye. As shown in the diagram below, most of the energy that reaches Earth is in the form of infrared, visible, and ultraviolet light waves. The diagram also shows that much of the energy given off by the sun never reaches Earth's surface. This happens because the gases of Earth's atmosphere reflect and absorb some of the energy. The atmosphere acts as a shield that protects all living things from most of the very dangerous high-frequency, high-energy ultraviolet waves, x-rays, and gamma rays. Although ultraviolet light has less energy than other high-frequency waves (like gamma rays and x-rays), it poses more of a hazard to living things because of the large amount of it that the sun emits. If Earth's atmosphere did not have a thick ozone layer, much more electromagnetic energy would reach Earth's surface, causing more harm to living things.

ENERGY FROM SUNLIGHT THAT REACHES EARTH

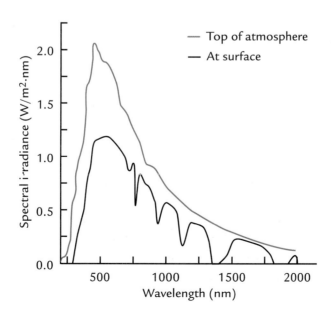

The Electromagnetic Spectrum

In addition to infrared, visible, and ultraviolet waves, the sun emits a large amount of other kinds of invisible electromagnetic energies. They include radio waves, microwaves, x-rays, and gamma rays. Together, the continuous range of all possible electromagnetic frequencies makes up the electromagnetic spectrum shown below.

Although portions of the frequencies of electromagnetic spectrum are given specific names, such as radio, visible, and x-rays, the categories overlap. This is because the wavelength ranges with which scientists classify each type of energy are somewhat arbitrary. It is often hard to distinguish where one group of waves ends and the next one begins. Fundamentally, all electromagnetic energy is of the same nature. For example, all electromagnetic waves can travel through a medium or through a vacuum. They can all be reflected, absorbed, and transmitted through various materials. The degree to which each type will reflect, absorb, or transmit depends on the wavelength of the wave and the surface it hits.

Although electromagnetic waves have common properties, there is an astounding difference in wavelength from one end of the spectrum to the other. The range of wavelength from gamma rays to typical radio waves is over 1,000 meters. Each range has some unique characteristics. Shorter wavelengths—those from ultraviolet to gamma rays—have the ability to penetrate living cells and damage them. Longer wavelengths of energy, like those in the radio range, can be generated or received by antennae. Our eyes can only detect a very small range of wavelengths from 380–620 nanometers (1 nanometer is one billionth of a meter).

THE ELECTROMAGNETIC SPECTRUM

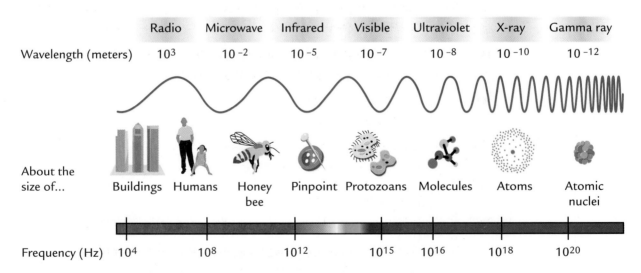

An astronomer investigates a radio telescope in Germany.

Extending Our Senses with Electromagnetic Energy

There are hundreds of applications of electromagnetic energy. For example, x-rays are used to scan bones and teeth. Remote controls send an infrared signal to a device. WiFi relies on radio or microwaves to send and receive data. Microwave ovens create microwaves to transmit energy to the water in food, thereby heating it up.

Some technologies allow us to extend our senses by using electromagnetic waves. One example is infrared imaging in night-vision goggles. Night-vision technology lets us see objects by changing the invisible infrared light given off by objects into an image we can see with visible light. Since warm bodies give off infrared energy, a person wearing night-vision goggles can scan an area to see people and other warm-blooded animals in the darkness. Additionally, there are detectors that can sense all kinds of electromagnetic energy. For example, astronomers use radio telescopes that detect radio waves by which astronomers "see" distant objects in the universe.

ANALYSIS

1. With what evidence did Herschel support his discovery of infrared waves?

2. With what evidence did Ritter support his discovery of ultraviolet waves?

 3. Compare infrared and ultraviolet. In what ways are they similar? In what ways are they different?

4. From the following list, choose the one that describes the portion of the range of electromagnetic waves that is visible.

   a. More than ½

   b. about ½

   c. ¼–½

   d. 1/10–¼

   e. much less than 1/10

   Explain your reasoning, citing evidence from this activity.

 5. Is it likely that light frequencies higher than ultraviolet were the main cause of Tía Ana's cataracts? Explain why or why not.

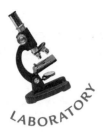

In Activity 95, "Selective Transmission," you learned that electromagnetic energy is selectively transmitted. This means that not all frequencies of light are transmitted through an object when light hits its surface. Energy transmission depends on the combination of the wave's frequency the properties of the material it hits. In this activity, you will gather evidence on whether electromagnetic energy can be selectively absorbed and reflected.

CHALLENGE ➡ **How do different materials absorb or reflect light?**

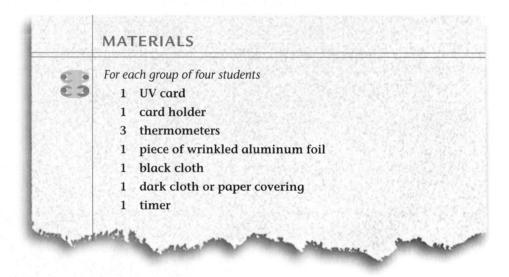

MATERIALS

For each group of four students
1   **UV card**
1   **card holder**
3   **thermometers**
1   **piece of wrinkled aluminum foil**
1   **black cloth**
1   **dark cloth or paper covering**
1   **timer**

An Inupiaq guide protects his eyes, left, by wearing glasses that reflect light. The black asphalt, right, absorbs more sunlight than the surrounding land.

PROCEDURE

Part A: Reflection

1. Before going outside, assemble the ultraviolet (UV) card in the card holder with the card facing down. Cover the assembly with the cloth covering before going outside.

2. Go outside, and spread out the black cloth and the piece of wrinkled aluminum foil next to each other in the sunlight.

3. With the dark covering over the UV card assembly, place it on the wrinkled aluminum foil and the black cloth so that one side of the UV card is only exposed to the foil while the other side is only exposed to the black cloth as shown below. Be sure to direct the assembly toward the sun so the assembly does not cast any shadow on the cloth or foil.

4. Expose the setup to sunlight for exactly 20 sec. Remove the UV card from the sun, and look at the UV-sensitive strip. Compare both sides, and record your observations in your science notebook.

5. Place the UV card in a dark place, such as a pocket, where it will reset, or turn the sensitive strip face down.

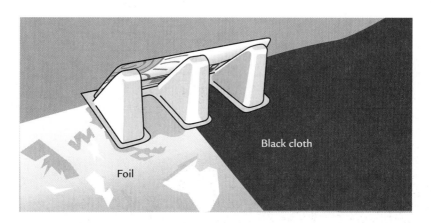

Black cloth

Foil

Part B: Absorption

6. In your science notebooks make a table like the one below.

Temperature Changes

Material	Initial Temperature (°C)	Final Temperature (°C)	Change in Temperature (°C)
Black cloth			
Aluminum foil			
Control			

7. Place the three thermometers next to each other in the shade outside. Wait 1 min, and record the initial temperatures of each thermometer in your data table.

8. Place one thermometer on top of the aluminum foil and the other on top of the black cloth. Fold over the bottom of each material so that it covers the bulb of the thermometer as shown below. Leave the third one uncovered to serve as a control.

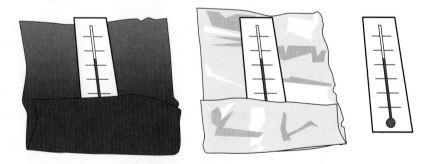

9. Expose all three thermometers to sunlight for 5 minutes. After 5 minute record the final temperatures of each thermometer.

10. Calculate the change in temperature of each thermometer, and record it.

ANALYSIS

1. Which surface—the black cloth or the aluminum foil—relected more ultraviolet on the UV card? Cite evidence from this activity to support your answer.

2. Copy the diagram below.

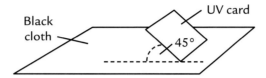

Draw a line that traces the path of the light from the sky to the aluminum foil and then onto the UV card.

3. In this activity, the black cloth models the dark ground. What could the aluminum foil and the UV card model?

4. Use evidence from this activity to support one of the following two statements:

   a. There is a decreased risk for ultraviolet exposure when playing at the beach or in the snow compared to playing at the park.

   b. There is an increased risk for ultraviolet exposure when playing at the beach or in the snow compared to playing at the park.

5. Which surface—the black cloth or the aluminum foil—caused a greater temperature increase when covering the thermometer? Explain why you think this happened.

6. Explain why the temperature will increase more in a house with a black roof than in one with a reflective roof.

7. Provide an example of a material that transmits, reflects, and absorbs light simultaneously.

LABORATORY

In this investigation, you will apply what you know about transmission, absorption, and reflection to the use of sunscreens. People often rub sunscreens on their skin to reduce the ultraviolet energy that reaches the skin. The evidence you gather will help you decide if sunscreen absorbs or reflects the electromagnetic energy that is not transmitted.

CHALLENGE → **Does sunscreen transmit, absorb, or reflect ultraviolet waves?**

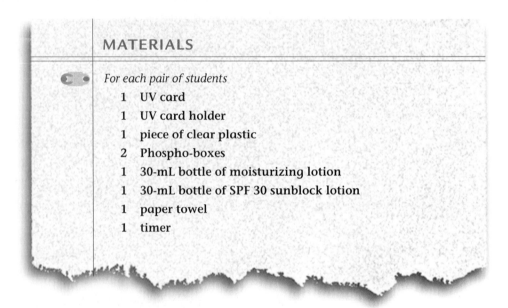

MATERIALS

For each pair of students
1 UV card
1 UV card holder
1 piece of clear plastic
2 Phospho-boxes
1 30-mL bottle of moisturizing lotion
1 30-mL bottle of SPF 30 sunblock lotion
1 paper towel
1 timer

PROCEDURE

Part A: Ultraviolet Transmission

1. Position the clear plastic so that it covers one half of the UV-sensing strip on the UV card.

2. Expose the UV card to the sun for 20 sec. Observe the UV card level of the two sides of the sensing strip, and record your results.

3. Place the UV card in a dark place, such as a pocket, where it will reset, or turn the sensing strip face down.

4. Spread a thin layer of moisturizing lotion on one half of the clear film and a thin layer of sunblock lotion on the other half, as shown in the diagram below. Make both layers as close to the same thickness as possible.

   Note: Do not put the lotion directly on the UV card as it will damage the sensing strip.

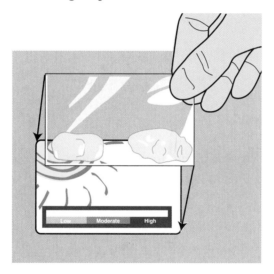

5. Position the plastic over the UV card so that about half of the sensing strip is covered with each kind of lotion.

6. Expose the UV card to the sun for 20 sec. Observe the UV levels of the two sides of the sensing strip, and record your results.

7. When you are finished, clean the lotion off the plastic with the paper towel.

Part B: Ultraviolet Absorption

8. With the equipment assigned to you design an experiment that will determine whether the sunblock lotion absorbs or reflects UV light. When designing your experiment, think about the following questions:

   What is the purpose of your experiment?

   What variable are you testing?

   What is your hypothesis?

   What variables will you keep the same?

   What is your control?

   How many trials will you conduct?

   What data will you record?

9. Record your hypothesis and your planned experimental procedure in your science notebook.

10. Make a data table that has space for all the data you need to record during the experiment.

11. Obtain your teacher's approval of your experiment.

12. Conduct your experiment, and record your results.

ANALYSIS

1. What evidence from this activity indicates that moisturizing lotion has different ingredients than sunblock lotion?

2. What effect do you think the ingredients in sunblock lotion have on the ultraviolet waves? Be sure to state any evidence you observed from the activity.

3. Do the results of this experiment allow you to predict the actual results of using sunblock lotion on your skin? Why or why not?

TALKING IT OVER

When Tía Ana recovered from her surgery, her sight was much better. José told her about the increased risk of ultraviolet exposure from sunlight. She was impressed that he knew so much about light. José gave her a pair of sunglasses in her favorite color for her birthday. Then he got a pair himself. Although he still loved spending time outside, José was a little more thoughtful about when and where he was exposed to ultraviolet waves.

Although doctors agree that people need vitamin D, there is some controversy over whether it is best to obtain it through food, from natural sun exposure, or both. Some doctors support the ideas that people should get their vitamin D through eating vitamin-D rich foods such as seafood and eggs. Other experts recommend limited exposure to sunlight, around 10 minutes a day without sunscreen, as a way to produce enough vitamin D. While excessive exposure increases risk of health problems, there are trade-offs involved in trying to avoid ultraviolet altogether. A **trade-off** is an exchange of one outcome for another—giving up something that is a benefit or advantage in exchange for something that may be more desirable. In this activity, you will analyze risk factors associated with ultraviolet exposure. Then you will make trade-offs while deciding how to protect yourself from ultraviolet waves.

CHALLENGE ➡ **What personal ultraviolet protection plan fits your risk factors and lifestyle?**

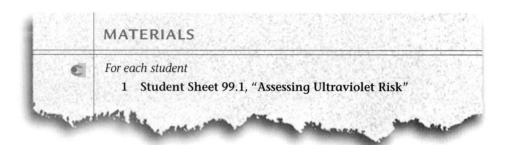

MATERIALS

For each student
   1   **Student Sheet 99.1, "Assessing Ultraviolet Risk"**

PROCEDURE

Part A: Analyzing Other People's UV Exposure

1. Read the UV exposure risk assessment table shown below.

UV Exposure Risk Assessment: Cataracts and Skin Cancer			
Factors	**Lower risk**	**Medium risk**	**Higher risk**
Age at exposure	20 and over, equal risk		Under 20
Intensity due to location: latitude	Far from equator	Mid-distance to equator	Close to, or on, the equator
Intensity due to location: altitude	Sea level–6,000 ft	3,000–6,000 ft	Over 6,000 ft
Time of day exposure	Before sunup or after sundown	Morning or late afternoon	10 a.m.–2 p.m.
Duration of exposure	Less than 1 hr/week	1–10 hr/week	More than 10 hr/week
Reflectivity	Dirt, grass	Water, sand	Snow
Family history	No relatives with history	Relatives have disease	Close relatives have disease
Skin type: skin cancer	Dark skin	Medium skin	Fair skin
Skin type: cataracts	Equal risk		
Mitigating behavior: hats, sunglasses, sunscreen	Always wear	Sometimes wear	Never wear

2. Read the case studies starting on the next page carefully. For each risk factor, assign a value of low, medium, or high risk for each case. If the case study doesn't give you enough information to assign a value, leave the space blank. Record these values on Student Sheet 99.1, "Assessing Ultraviolet Risk."

3. When you finish all of the cases, go back and make sure you rated consistently.

4. Examine each row of factors, and approximate the cataract and skin cancer risk for each case.

Case Studies

José

José is a 14-year-old, dark-skinned 8th grader who lives near the coast of Southern California. Since he got his dog Freddie five years ago, he has spent most mornings and evenings with Freddie at the park. José is amazed that his dog never seems to get tired, even when they have been playing for hours. Every Saturday, José and his friend pack lunches and take them to the beach so that they can stay all day. José is concerned about getting too much sun because his great-aunt just had cataract surgery, but he only recently started wearing sunglasses.

Shannon

Shannon is 50 years old and has lived in the mountains of Maine all of her life. She has fair skin and freckles. Because of this, she is careful to wear long sleeves and a hat during the summer when she spends part of the day outside. She also wears sunglasses all summer. As a teenager, Shannon and her twin brother worked at their dad's grocery store after school and spent all of their free time playing basketball or baseball, which she still does on weekends. Last year, her twin had a small, dark spot of skin cancer removed from his similarly fair skin.

Leon

Leon, age 65, is very proud of the garden in his backyard. Now that he's retired, he spends several hours each morning tending it. While growing up on the Gulf Coast in Mississippi, he spent afternoons fishing on his dad's small boat. Now on weekends, Leon enjoys taking his own boat to a peaceful cove in the evenings to relax and fish. A dark-skinned African American, he never thought about protecting himself from the sun. However, recently he has noticed that his vision is a little cloudy. His sister who lives nearby says she's having difficulty seeing, too, and just made an appointment to see her doctor.

Sophie

Sophie and her family live in Colorado. She has blond hair, blue eyes, and very light skin. Although Sophie was born with very little hearing, she loves participating in sports, particularly those outdoors. She spends a lot of time swimming in the summer and skiing in the winter. She enjoys skiing the most, and she spends most winter weekends at her uncle's ski area nearby. He has eye damage from years of skiing, and the weathered skin on his tanned face makes him look older than he is. Sophie always remembers to wear her UV-blocking goggles when she's skiing or sunglasses when just outside in the snow. She also tries to remember sunscreen but tends to forget.

Part B: Your Own UV-Exposure Risk

5. Create a case study about yourself in your science notebook. Write a paragraph that describes where you live, your activities, and your personal risk factors for cataracts and skin cancer.

6. Add your name at the bottom of the first column on Student Sheet 99.1, "Assessing Ultraviolet Risk."

7. Assign ratings to yourself, and approximate your cataract and skin cancer risk.

ANALYSIS

1. In the case studies that you analyzed, who has the greatest risk for
    a. cataracts?
    b. skin cancer?

2. What risk factors are common for both cataracts and skin cancer?

3. Why do you think childhood ultraviolet exposure is considered a bigger risk factor than ultraviolet exposure later in life?

4. In the activity you used a scale of low–medium–high to rate people's risk. Do you believe there can be zero risk of a particular outcome? Why or why not?

5. Prepare a personal ultraviolet protection plan by making a list of all of the things you can do to reduce your ultraviolet exposure while still participating in the outdoor activities that you enjoy the most. Then identify any trade-offs that are part of your new strategy.

Index

A **bold** page number identifies the page on which the term is defined.

Credits

Abbreviations: t (top), m (middle), b (bottom), l (left), r (right), c (center)

All illustrations by Seventeenth Street Studios/Valerie Winemiller.

Cover (front): wind power generators: Digital Vision/Getty Images

"Problem Solving" icon photo: ©Thom Lang/Corbis

"Talking It Over" icon photo: ©Michael Keller/Corbis

UNIT A

Unit title (A-1): Charles D. Winters/Photo Researchers, Inc.; Unit Opener (A-2, A-3): tl: David Woodfall/Getty Images; tr: Creatas/Fotosearch; cl: Martin Shields/Photo Researchers, Inc.; bl: ©Richard T. Nowitz/Corbis; br: Joseph Sohm, ChromoSohm Inc./Corbis; A-6 l: Jack Star/Photolink/Getty Images; r: Phanie/Photo Researchers, Inc.; A-15 ©Joel W. Rogers/Corbis; A-16 ©Richard T. Nowitz/Corbis; A-17 Joseph Sohm, ChromoSohm Inc./Corbis; A-19 Creatas/Fotosearch; A-21 David Woodfall/Getty Images; A2-6 t: MedioImages/Getty Images; b: Photo-Cuisine/Corbis; A-27 ©Roger Ressmeyer/Corbis; A-30 Andrew Lambert Photography/Photo Researchers, Inc.; A-32 Lisa Preuss/Shutterstock; A-39 Aaron Haupt/Photo Researchers, Inc.; A-41 Martin Shields/Photo Researchers, Inc.; A-45 Larry Mulvehill/Corbis; A-46 AJPhoto/Photo Researchers, Inc.

UNIT B

Unit title (B-1): ©Wolfgang Kaehler/Corbis; Unit Opener (B-2, B-3): tl: Bob Krist/Corbis; tr: Peter Bowater/Photo Researchers, Inc.; cl: John-Francis Bourke/Getty Images; bl: ©Amet Jean Pierre/Corbis Sygma; br: ©Free Agents Limited /Corbis; B-7 John-Francis Bourke/Getty Images; B-8 © DK Limited/Corbis; B-9 Chris Knapton/Photo Researchers, Inc.; B-10 l: Beh Johnson/Photo Researchers, Inc.; r: Juan Silva/Getty Images; B11 l: ©Bob Krist/Corbis; r: ©Amet Jean Pierre/Corbis Sygma; B-12 David Nunuk/Photo Researchers, Inc.; B-14 l: © image100/Corbis; r: PhotoDisc; B-19 Andrew Lambert Photograph/Photo Researchers, Inc.; B-22 Tom Morrison/Getty Images; B-23 SPL/Photo Researchers, Inc.; B-24 l: Hulton Archive/Getty Images; r: Wikipedia; B-29 t: ©Tom Grill/Corbis; b: Photodisc; B-31 © Free Agents Limited/Corbis; B-34 ©Wolfgang Kaehler/Corbis; B-39 l: Mauro Fermariello/Photo Researchers, Inc.; r: Volker Steger/Photo Researchers, Inc.; B-41 Lab-Aids©, Inc.; B-42 Spencer Grant/Photo Researchers, Inc.; B-43 Lab-Aids©; B-44 t, b: Lab-Aids©, Inc.; B-46 l: © Underwood & Underwood/Corbis; r: ©Alen MacWeeney/Corbis; B-48 l: Keystone/Getty Images; r: Lab-Aids©, Inc.; B-49 Doug Menuez/Getty Images; B-51 l: © Comstock/Corbis; r: © Bisson Bernard/Corbis Sygma; B-54 l: Maximiliam Stock/Photo Researchers, Inc.; r: Maximiliam Stock/Photo Researchers, Inc.; B-57: tl: Per-Anders Pettersson/Getty Images; tr: Peter Bowater/Photo Researchers, Inc.; bl: © Farrell Grehan/Corbis; B-58 l: © Ed Young/Corbis; r: © Lowell Georgia/Corbis; B-64 Lawrence Migdale/Photo Researchers, Inc.; B-68 ©Vince Streano/Corbis; B-71 l: David Taylor/Photo Researchers, Inc.; r: Andrew Lambert Photography/Photo Researchers, Inc.; B-75 © Philippe Eranian/Corbis; B-80 Paul J. Richards/AFP/Getty Images; B-83 tl: © Karen Kasmauski/Corbis; br: © SW Productions/Brand X/Corbis; B-84 tl © Tom Grill/Corbis, br: © Colorblind/Corbis.

Kit item: Element Card Photos: © 2007 Theodore Gray/www.periodictable.com

UNIT C

Unit title (C-1): Ted Mead/Getty Images; Unit Opener (C-2, C-3): tl: John Lund/Getty Images; tr: Chris Knapton/Photo Researchers, Inc.; cl: Karl Weatherly/Getty Images; bl: Russell Illig/ Getty Images; br: Mike Kemp/Getty Images; C-4 l: Louis Fox/The Image Bank/Getty Images; r: Lawrence Migdale/Photo Researchers, Inc.; C-11 RM/©Bettman/Corbis; C-15 Herbert D. Thier; C-16 Wellcome Library, London; C-17 courtesy Mary Evans Picture Library; C-21 Ted Mead/Getty Images; C-22 Fotosearch; C-23 t: CNRI/Science Photo Library/Photo Researchers, Inc.; b: Altrendo Images/Getty Images; C-25 Ernst Haas/Getty Images; C-26 © Patrick Barta/ Corbis; C-34 Roine Magnusson/Getty Images; C-38 Phanie/Photo Researchers, Inc.; C-42 Mike Kemp/Getty Images; C-48 Russell Illig/Getty Images; C-49 Mary Hollinger/NOAA; C-51 © Florida Department of Citrus; C-56 Colin Cuthbert/Newcastle University/Photo Researchers, Inc; C-62 ©Raymond Gehman/Corbis; C-65 Chris Knapton/Photo Reseachers, Inc; C-76 Lawrence Migdale/Photo Researchers, Inc.; C-80 l: Andrew Lambert Photography/Photo Researchers, Inc.; r: Andrew Lambert Photography/Photo Researchers, Inc.; C-84 Karl Weatherly/Getty Images; C-86 l: © Envision/Corbis, r: Susan Spann; C-92 Bob Handelman/Getty Images; C-96 Andrew Lambert Photography/Photo Researchers, Inc.; C-105 Michael St Maur Sheil/Getty Images.

UNIT D

Unit title (D-1): © John Nakata/Corbis; Unit Opener (D-2, D-3): tl: Stockbyte/Getty Images; tr: © Mick Roessler/Corbis; cl: Purestock/Getty Images; bl: John A Rizzo/Getty Images; br: Don Farrall/Getty Images; D-6 l, r: ©Brad Simmons/Beateworks/Corbis; D-12 Purestock/ Getty Images; D-15 © Noah K. Murray/Star Ledger/Corbis; D-16 © Richard Cummins/Corbis; D-20 Lab-Aids©; D-22 l: Copyright © 2003-06 California Cars Initiative, an activity of the International Humanities Center, http://www.calcars.org/; r: © Issei Kato/Reuters/Corbis; D-26 © John Nakata/Corbis; D-27: Martin Shields/Photo Researchers, Inc.; D-29 t: Andrew Lambert Photography/Photo Researchers, Inc.; c: Porterfield–Chickering/Photo Researchers, Inc.; b: Philippe Psaila/Photo Researchers, Inc.; D-30 William Thomas Cain/Stringer/Getty Images; D-32 NASA; D39 © Jonathan Feinstein/Shutterstock; D-41 tl: © Margot Granitsas/ The Image Works; tr: © Alan Weintraub/Arcaid/Corbis; bl: Taylor S. Kennedy/Getty Images; br: George Hunter/Getty Images; D-42 Bernard Hoffman/Time Life Pictures/Getty Images; D-43 © Underwood & Underwood/Corbis; D-46 © Comstock Select/Corbis; D-50 John A Rizzo/ Getty Images; D-55 Lab-Aids, Inc.; D-57 Russell Illig/ Getty Images; D-60 t: Kevin Phillips/ Getty Images; b: © Larry Lee Photography/Corbis; D61: t: Stephen Simpson/Getty Images; b: Pete Turner/Getty Images; D-62 © Larry Lee Photography/Corbis; D-63 © t: Mick Roessler/ Corbis; b: Martin Bond/Photo Researchers, Inc.; D-64 John R. Foster/Photo Researchers, Inc.; D-66 Stockbyte/Getty Images; D-74 Mike Agliolo/Photo Researchers, Inc.; D-75 tl: André Karwath; br: Spencer Grant/Photo Researchers, Inc.; D-76 Paul Katz/Getty Images; D-80 Yamada Taro/Getty Images; D-84 © Annebicque Bernard/Corbis Sygma; D-85 © Lawrence Manning/ Corbis; D-86 GIPhotoStock/Photo Researchers, Inc.; D-89 Dennis O'Clair/Getty Images; D-93 Frederic J. Brown /AFP/Getty Images; D-94 Sam Diephuis/Getty Images; D-96 Don Farrall/ Getty Images; D-100 Tek Image/Photo Researchers, Inc.; D-101 © Morley Von Sternberg/Arcaid/ Corbis; D-103 Melanie Conner/Getty Images.

UNIT E

Unit title (E-1) David Madison/Photodisc/Getty Images; Unit Opener (E-2, E-3) tl: Photodisc/ Getty Images, tr: ©Jason Horowitz/zefa/Corbis; cl: © Royalty-Free/ Corbis; bl: Steve Smith/ Taxi/Getty Images; br: Jess Alford/Photodisc/Getty Images; E-7 Stockdisc Classic/Getty Images; E-8 © Duomo/Corbis; E10 Image Source/Getty Images; E-11: © Joseph Sohm, ChromoSohm Inc./Corbis; E-12 Sarah Leen/National Geographic/Getty Images; E-13 © Thinkstock/Corbis; E-16 TRL Ltd./Photo Researchers, Inc.; E19 Photodisc/Getty Images; E-21 l: © Chris Trotman/ NewSport/Corbis, r: © Chris Trotman/NewSport/Corbis; E-23 © Thinkstock/Corbis: E-25 Lutz Bongarts/Getty Images News/Getty Images; E-27 ©Jason Horowitz/zefa/Corbis; E-29 l, r: Rare Book and Special Collections/Library of Congress; E-31 l: © Royalty-Free/Corbis,br: © Royalty-Free/Corbis; E-32 l: David Madison/Photodisc/Getty Images, r: Steve Smith/Taxi/Getty Images; E-33 Jess Alford/Photodisc/Getty Images; E-34 Matt Campbell/AFP/Getty Images; E-35 Indian Space Research Organisation/Photo Researchers, Inc.; E41 NASA/Photo Researchers, Inc.; E-45 Patrick Molnar/Taxi/Getty Images; E-47 Jim Reed/ Photo Researchers, Inc.; E-49 © Royalty-Free/Corbis; E-50 Courtesy of U.S. Representative Frank R. Wolf (Va.); E-51 l: Martyn F. Chillmaid/ Photo Researchers, Inc.; r: David R. Frazier/Photo Researchers, Inc.; E-53 Patti Conville/Getty Images; E-54 Ryan McVay/Photodisc/Getty Images; E-55 TRL Ltd./Photo Researchers, Inc.; E-56 Maximilian Stock Ltd/Photo Researchers, Inc.; E-62 Chad Slattery/Stone/Getty Images

UNIT F

Unit title (F-1): ©Pete Ginter/Getty Images; Unit Opener (F-2, F-3): tl: ©Philippe Henry/Getty Images; tr: ©Ken Straiton/Corbis; cl: © Charles Dharapak/AP/Corbis; bl: © Leonard Lessin/ Photo Researchers, Inc.; br: ©Eric & David Hosking/Photo Researchers, Inc.; F-6 ©Gary Braasch/ Stone/Getty Images; F-14 ©Leonard Lessin/Photo Researchers, Inc.; F-19 ©Ken Straiton/Corbis; F-23 l: ©Eric & David Hosking/Photo Researchers, Inc.; r: F. Stuart Westmorland/Photo Researchers, Inc.; F-28: l: ©Anthony Cooper/Ecoscene/Corbis; r: ©Charles Dharapak/AP/Corbis; F-32 ©Philippe Henry/Getty Images; F-34 ©Maziar Nikkholgh/Document Iran/Corbis; F-41 ©Peter Ginter/Getty Images; F-42 l: Steven Kazlowski/Science Faction/Corbis; r: ©Pete Turner/Getty Images; F-46 ©Steve Horrell/Photo Researchers, Inc.